Writing Home

Representations of the Native Place in
Modern Japanese Literature

Harvard East Asian Monographs 240

Writing Home

Representations of the Native Place in Modern Japanese Literature

Stephen Dodd

Published by the Harvard University Asia Center
Distributed by Harvard University Press
Cambridge (Massachusetts) and London, 2004

Printed in the United States of America

The Harvard University Asia Center publishes a monograph series and, in coordination with the Fairbank Center for East Asian Research, the Korea Institute, the Reischauer Institute of Japanese Studies, and other faculties and institutes, administers research projects designed to further scholarly understanding of China, Japan, Vietnam, Korea, and other Asian countries. The Center also sponsors projects addressing multidisciplinary and regional issues in Asia.

Library of Congress Cataloging-in-Publication Data

Dodd, Stephen, 1955-
  Writing home : representations of the native place in modern Japanese literature / Stephen Dodd.
    p. cm. -- (Harvard East Asian monographs ; 240)
  Includes bibliographical references and index.
  ISBN 0-674-01652-1 (cloth : alk. paper)
    1. Japanese literature--Meiji period, 1868-1912--History and criticism. 2. Japanese literature--Taishō period, 1912-1926--History and criticism. 3. Birthplaces in literature. I. Title. II. Series.
  PL726.57.B59D63 2004
  895.6'4093552--dc22

                                                            2004019446

Index by Duncan Adam

⊗ Printed on acid-free paper

Last figure below indicates year of this printing
14 13 12 11 10 09 08 07 06 05 04

This book is dedicated to
Roma and Arnold Dodd

旅人と
我名よばれん
初しぐれ

first winter shower;
traveler
shall be my name

—Matsuo Bashō

Acknowledgments

Since this book has evolved over a number of years, it is impossible for me to name all those who have encouraged, stimulated, advised, prodded, corrected, and inspired me to transform what began as a Ph.D. dissertation into the present work. Those I do not mention by name may be certain of my heartfelt gratitude.

To my advisor at Columbia University, Paul Anderer, I owe my deepest debt for the way he never stopped encouraging me to find my own voice, and there could be no better advice than that. Donald Keene, I must thank for his kind attention throughout my graduate years, and for producing works on Japanese literature with such evident love that he drew me to it as well. During my research stay in Tokyo in 1990–91, I received invaluable insights from Karatani Kōjin, and Kawamura Minato suggested many approaches that proved to be immensely beneficial to my research.

It was during a short teaching spell in 1993 at University of California, Santa Barbara, that I first learned the thrill of sharing ideas with students. And I will never forget the warmth and intellectual encouragement of my colleagues at Duke University, North Carolina, in 1993–94. Their enthusiasm for learning remains a source of great inspiration. At SOAS, I have benefited more than I can say from the help, encouragement, and daily chats of my colleagues. I should not fail to mention my students at SOAS, both undergraduate and graduate, who never cease to offer new insights and remind me of the significance and excitement of the work we do.

The fact that I have found the time to carry out research and devote myself to writing is due in large measure to my good fortune as the recipient of various awards. I make particular mention of a Japan Foundation Research Fellowship I received in 1990–91, a Japan Foundation Endowment Committee Research Grant in 1995, and an award from the Japanese Society for the Promotion of Science in 1997.

On a more personal note, I recall the openhearted kindness I received from Norihiko and Akiko Date, my surrogate "parents" during my first stay in Japan in 1977–79. Deep thanks are also owed to Yō and Minoru Nomura for taking good care of me in Roppongi during 1990–91.

I have received endless advice and encouragement from many friends and colleagues in various countries. To name but a few, James McMullen gave me the initial confidence to pursue my studies. Komori Yōichi, Chiba Shunji, Haruo Shirane, Usami Takeshi, and Kawasaki Kenko pushed me to go further with my ideas. Marion Yass, Betty Williams, Tim Stanley, Sarah Bennet, John Breen, Gus Heldt, and Tim Screech offered words of encouragement just when I needed them. I thank Izawa Kōzō for permission to use his painting on the book cover. Fukiko Kitagawa went out of her way to help me obtain the artist's consent. Duncan Adam produced the index for this book. I greatly benefited from the advice of my two anonymous readers in the initial stages of publication. I offer special thanks to Mark Morris, who very kindly read the whole of my manuscript and provided a wealth of concise and perceptive comments.

Earlier versions of parts of this book have appeared in other publications: "Different Feelings: The Intellectual Shift between Meiji and Taishō," *Currents in Japanese Culture: Translations and Transformations* (Columbia University Press, 1997); "Fantasies, Fairies, and Electric Dreams: Satō Haruo's Critique of Taishō," *Monumenta Nipponica* (1994); "The Railway as Rupture: The Writings of Shimazaki Tōson," *Disrupted Borders: An Intervention in Definitions of Boundaries* (Rivers Oram Press, 1993); and "Shimazaki Tōson: The Language of Home," *Waseda Journal of Asian Studies* (March 2001).

Finally, I thank Sunil Gupta for the years we shared together, and I thank my parents who gave me everything.

—S.D.

Contents

Writing Home

Representations of the Native Place in Modern Japanese Literature

INTRODUCTION

A Time and a Place

Approaches

This book examines how Japanese literature depicting the native place (*furusato*) developed from its emergence in mid-Meiji (1868–1912) through Taishō (1912–26) to the early years of Shōwa (1926–89), specifically the late 1930s, as a way of articulating a sense of uprootedness and loss experienced by many writers during Japan's period of modernity. In the 1890s, fictional works began to describe a protagonist, usually based in a city, who returns briefly to his native place. There he reflects on the evils of city life compared with an idyllic past associated with the childhood home. The book concentrates on the literary works of four authors who typify this trend: Kunikida Doppo (1871–1908), Shimazaki Tōson (1872–1943), Satō Haruo (1892–1964), and Shiga Naoya (1883–1971).

Chapter 1 discusses Doppo's writing as part of the first wave of this literature during Meiji. In fact, the furusato he described is not related to his actual place of birth; rather, it stands for a metaphorical "other" articulating both his criticism of society and an idealized alternative. Doppo's own experience of growing up—he moved around constantly as a child and later flirted with various aspects of religion and politics—pushed him to seek a more settled literary native place to compensate for the furusato he never experienced in reality. Such a site is the product of native influences as well as new ways of perception drawn from the West.

Chapters 2 and 3 look at works by Tōson. This author differs
from Doppo in the sense that he often wrote about his actual
birthplace, but even here the link between place and the literature
describing it is less straightforward than might at first appear. Tōson left his native place for Tokyo when he was eight, and consequently his urban experience profoundly shaped the way he later
depicted his original home. Urban intellectual currents are especially influential in his interpretation of the furusato's significance
and attempts to recapture it in his writings. Ironically, the very
knowledge he gained through his urban experiences and used as the
tool to give literary expression to the furusato also ensures that it
remains forever beyond full articulation.

In Chapter 4, I examine Satō Haruo as exemplary of a later generation of writers that emerged in Taishō. He was forced to seek a
sense of home less through representations of any real native place
than through a series of fantastic "landscapes of belonging" in order to overcome his exclusion from mainstream Japanese culture. I
look at his use of three aspects of the fantastic—the miniature, theatrical spectacle, and electric lighting—that enabled him to create a
very personal and imaginary "native place" in keeping with the introverted mood of the period.

Chapters 5 and 6 relate to Shiga Naoya, another writer who
came of age during Taishō. Unlike the other three writers, Shiga
was brought up from infancy in Tokyo and lacked any real furusato consciousness; yet, he has been described as the "furusato of
literature." This may be explained in part by his customary association with "authenticity," a quality that I examine further in conjunction with the general concept of "Japanese-ness." Shiga's work
may be usefully read against the background of other writers addressing similar themes active around the 1930s such as Kobayashi
Hideo (1902–1983), Sakaguchi Ango (1906–1955), and Hagiwara Sakutarō (1886–1942). My principal aim in Chapter 5 is to deconstruct
Shiga's reproduction of what appears to be a seamlessly authentic
furusato; Chapter 6, however, concentrates more on his skill in
fleshing out the concept, particularly as an effective means to silence alternative, more confrontational literary interpretations of
what it meant to be Japanese. Shiga's apparently ahistorical sites

are actually tightly connected to the conditions of his time, and his "empty" mythologized literary landscapes should be seen in the context of a nation increasingly militarized and involved in overseas ventures.

Since Tōson is the only one of these writers who described the place where he was born, my understanding of the term "furusato" requires further explanation. Each writer may be identified with the furusato in a manner unique to himself—all of them arguably in ways more metaphorical than real—but each draws on the term's literary associations in an attempt to map out what it meant to be Japanese in the landscape of modern Japanese fiction. Even in the 1890s, some critics rejected the interpretation of such works as simple reminiscences of a lost childhood locality and argued that they needed to be seen instead as part of a larger endeavor to locate compensatory sites, a chance for writers to reintegrate themselves imaginatively into their environment. In other words, the furusato corresponds less to an external locality that may (or may not) exist in reality than to an amorphous phenomenon subject to shifting developments over time. Although it sometimes overlaps with a specific physical location, its broader significance in modern Japanese literature is as a mythical construction through and against which radical alternatives to prevalent ideas about what constitutes modern Japan have been played out.

To a certain extent, all four writers may be understood as trying to make sense of the world in which they found themselves. However, individuals also belong to larger communities and cultures. In the Japanese context, each writer's articulation of the native place reflects an engagement with a wider range of social, intellectual, economic, and technological discourses that create a network of shared experience among people of a similar age and also allow more general observations about transformations between one period and the next. As appropriate, this book refers to these discourses through specific readings of the literary works. Yet it would be remiss to leave the authors floating in their separate universes without attempting to draw together the threads and construct a more coherent picture. I cannot repress a certain hesitation here, since viewing the details through a monolithic lens threatens to oversimplify a complex set of realities defying easy interpretation. With this caveat, I still think it worthwhile to consider them as important contributors to the general debate over an emerging Japanese national identity that took place between Meiji and early Shōwa. To clarify how I intend to proceed, I begin with some general observations on nation and nationalism.

Opinions vary widely among historians on the nation's significance, when it appeared as a recognizable phenomenon, and even whether it benefited the world. Nevertheless, Anthony Smith defines the nation emerging in late eighteenth-, early nineteenth-century Europe, in a way that most would recognize, as "a named human population sharing an historic territory, common myths and historical memories, a mass, public culture, a common economy and common legal rights and duties for all members."[1] Of course, the nation was preceded by a wide variety of other pluralistic societies, but reference to a commonality of interests hints at certain characteristics that set the nation apart. For one thing, a sense of national unity was often consolidated by a common language, as in the case of England and France, and for some emerging nations like Italy and Germany, a shared language provided the single, central argument for a unified state.[2] Another characteristic was a greater degree of political involvement by its people. Although full popular participation in politics may have remained nominal for most nations until the twentieth century, by the second half of the nineteenth century states needed the loyalty of their citizens to an unparalleled extent compared to earlier times. The case of modern warfare illustrates this point: "Whether the armies were composed of conscripts or volunteers, the willingness of men to serve was now an essential variable in government calculations; and so indeed was their actual physical and mental capacity to do so."[3] It was the production of "common myths and historical memories," as well as greater attention to the physical and mental well-being of citizens, that led a considerable number of a nation's people to feel willing, or at least obliged, to defend it with their lives.

An important related question—and one that has taxed many a historian—is why the nation emerged at this particular point in history. The word "nationalism" was coined only in the late nine-teenth century, but Ernest Gellner argues against the idea of defin-ing it in terms of the age of the nation:

It is not the case that the 'age of nationalism' is a mere summation of the awakening and political self-assertion of this, that, or the other nation. Rather, when general social conditions make for standardized, homoge-neous, centrally sustained high cultures, pervading entire populations and not just elite minorities, a situation arises in which well-defined educa-tionally sanctioned and unified cultures constitute very nearly the only kind of unit with which men willingly and often ardently identify.[4]

In other words, far from being created simply by the conscious will of the people, the nation evolved out of a pre-existing nation-alist sentiment that took shape over an extended period of time, drawing on a variety of impulses toward self-definition. These ranged from interventions in the cultural, literary, and folkloric fields to more obviously political arguments on behalf of the na-tional idea. Moreover, although it is possible to interpret national-ism from a variety of angles, Smith emphasizes that at its broadest level it is

a form of historicist culture and civic education, one that overlays or re-places the older modes of religious culture and familial education. More than a style and doctrine of politics, nationalism is *a form of culture*—an ideology, a language, mythology, symbolism and consciousness—that has achieved global resonance, and the nation is a type of identity whose meaning and priority is presupposed by this form of culture.[5]

As a literary critic and not a historian, I am concerned less with offering a novel interpretation of nation and nationalism than with locating a set of working definitions that allow me to explore links between furusato literature and the theme of national identity in a fruitful manner. Certainly, these general observations help place my own study in a clearer context. For instance, historians of Ja-pan commonly point to intellectual currents of the earlier Toku-gawa period (1603–1868)—especially Dutch studies (*rangaku*) and what came to be called the school of National Learning (*koku-gaku*)—as important factors contributing to the further growth of Japanese nationalism in Meiji. More specifically with regard to the furusato, a wide-ranging debate during Meiji over a common language that might "transparently" express the modern experience helped shape a variety of literary forms used to present the native place as a distinctly Japanese experience in the global environment. Moreover, the furusato proved to constitute a powerful myth capable of firing the imagination of a broad range of people, including both producers and consumers of literature. But of particular interest for a general understanding of the furusato is the way nationalism can be interpreted as a "form of culture."

On this point, Eric Hobsbawm notes that nationalism began in Europe as a cluster of ideas often associated with the left and liberalism but developed increasingly into "a chauvinist, imperialist and xenophobic movement of the right," particularly after 1870.[6] This movement contributed to the harsh international environment in which modern Japan was forced to carve out its own national identity. Not surprisingly, Japanese leaders felt it necessary to engineer structural shifts in society to ensure survival; one example is the transfer of military loyalty from the local domain (*han*) to the emperor as symbol of a more centralized modern nation. Other symbols, for example, the national flag and anthem, were designed to promote a mood of national unity among the general population. Kenneth Pyle has identified this "structuralist approach" as one of several available to scholars to discuss Japanese nationalism as a major organizing theme of modern Japanese history. Another method he highlights is the "cultural approach," which he describes as an analysis of "Japanese cultural patterns and symbols as the shaping force in the formation of nationalist ideology." Even this single field can be approached through a variety of angles—from attention to clearly articulated ideas to less easily defined symbols and myths—but it resonates with my own understanding of furusato literature. Pyle points out an underlying assumption among theorists using the cultural approach that nationalism emerged to compensate for disruption and dislocation engendered by rapid social change. According to this view,

modern nationalism rises in response to a cultural crisis that occurs when a more highly differentiated polity (the modern nation-state) is developing and when the former central organizing principles of political life become discredited and outmoded. In the face of radically new problems, received images of the political process seem no longer adequate. This cultural confusion sets off an intense search for "a new symbolic framework in terms of which to formulate, think about, and react to political problems." To be successful, such a framework must be constructed from symbols and images that have meaning in the nation's cultural heritage, but that have been remolded to fit a new political environment.[7]

Pyle is concerned mainly with cultural reformulation at the political level, but his words also apply to literary writers who were equally engaged in reinterpreting "symbols and images" that spoke to the needs of their time. In this light, the furusato emerged in Meiji as a newly invigorated symbol of desire and discontent, and it continued to evolve under the pressure of changing social and historical conditions through Shōwa.

Although it seems to me that a narrative linking literary writers to nation and nationalism is worth exploring, it is important to guard against the possibility of oversimplification by too closely equating one with the other. Hobsbawm's warning against an excessively restrictive definition of the nation is pertinent here, since "we cannot assume that for most people national identification—when it exists—excludes or is always or ever superior to, the remainder of the set of identifications which constitute the social being. In fact, it is always combined with identifications of another kind, even when it is felt to be superior to them."[8] In the following pages, I hope to show that each writer's work is informed by a series of multiple identifications; to imply that the authors merely reproduced some official viewpoint would be naïve and simplistic and would do an injustice to the complexity of their engagement with the theme of national identity. Writers of state propaganda may be an interesting topic, but they are not the object of my investigation.

In fact, the problem of trying to articulate the relationship between individual writers and contemporaneous sociopolitical conditions has been raised by Alan Tansman in a recent essay on possible connections between Shiga and fascism in the 1930s. Although a writer's work is "worldly" in the sense of being enmeshed in the ideological language of the time, any link between them should be approached with caution:

That the language of ideology might be taken up and written down in a more abstract and troped way by writers of fiction and *belles lettres* should come as no surprise, as the material of their work is language itself and the tools of their art include the fresh play with words, the elegant turn of phrase, the suggestive evocation of moods and feelings, the nontendentious exposition of states of mind and conditions of living. Such writers were not raising questions to answer them, but were casting spells and creating atmospheres.[9]

I will explore the details of Tansman's ideas further in my reading of Shiga, but there are a few points I will elaborate here. Literary writers (at least, the best of them) tend to be exceptionally sensitive to the linguistic world they inhabit, and this sensitivity precludes the facile interpretation of lived reality. A particular writer may well be largely in accord with the dominant ideological norms of the day, but writers are not politicians, and their critical distance inevitably produces more questions than answers. This is not to deny their complicity in the production of ideological formulations; access to readers gives them a privileged position to contribute to the general environment of ideas. Indeed, my contention is that the literary figures I examine were significant participants in the broad debate on national identity. But the manner of their contribution sets them apart as particularly hard to pin down—nuanced, amorphous, in Tansman's apt phrase, "casting spells."

The issue of ideology can help us locate the furusato in its broader social context. Like "nation," ideology is notoriously difficult to define, but Carol Gluck's outline of the term in *Japan's Modern Myths* is helpful. She insists that its common interpretation as "a systematic and manipulative political program" is too restrictive; instead, she prefers to consider it as "less thing than process." Endorsing Clifford Geertz's view that ideologies provide "maps of problematic social reality," she suggests that they "not only reflect and interpret the social realities that sustain them; they also, in Berger and Luckmann's term, construct those realities and remain in constant dialectical relationship with them." Moreover, any society consists of diverse viewpoints, with the result that a variety of ideological formations are continuously locked in struggle:

The question then arises, which—or whose—set of values and meanings become dominant and by what means. Gramsci's conception of hegemony recognizes that when a social group is successful in persuading others of the validity of its own world view, force does not greatly exceed consent. The consent, moreover, so permeates the society that to many it seems commonsensical, natural, and at times invisible.[10]

As a manifestation of ideology, furusato literature represents the efforts of literary producers who are not only seeking a stable map with which to anchor themselves in a disruptive modern society but also dialectically engaged in the further construction of their own realities. Furthermore, this process of furusato formation underwent constant change: from Meiji attempts to piece together uncomfortably fragmented realities to Shiga's early Shōwa texts in which conflict appears to have been so effectively ironed out that their landscapes seem "commonsensical, natural." This later development was possible, however, only against the background of an increasingly repressive political environment that forcibly excluded other ideological viewpoints.

A consideration of the furusato in terms of an ideological *process* helps avoid the pitfall of viewing it merely as a spatial configuration existing outside time. Although my book is concerned primarily with the literary representation of space, this does not mean that temporality—the historical specificity of each writer and his works—can be overlooked. Harry Harootunian's comments on Tōson's *Before the Dawn* (*Yoake mae*, 1929–35) serve to elaborate this point. Often read as a fascinating record of the turbulent years of Meiji, it gains its power as an epic novel because of incisive insights into how historical forces affect one young man (based on the author's real father) experiencing the vicissitudes of daily life in what is now Nagano prefecture. Written in the 1930s, Tōson's book aims to reclaim an age already long passed; in that sense, the work confirms an interaction between time and space in which isolated place-specific memories are finally reintegrated into the aging author's experience of passing time. But as Harootunian notes, the book goes further by raising the possibility of an "imaginary culture and community" that challenges the "metropolitan interpretation of its own experience as universal." If much of Japan had already experienced large-scale urbanization when the book was written, countryside areas still offered "reminders of other modes of existence" that promised the "recovery of a lost unity and coherence out of time." Any such recovery became increasingly problematic during the interwar years because social change meant that the specificity of place, as Harootunian defines it, was gradually overwhelmed by a more generalized concept of space:

Modern capitalism especially insists on separating space from place—locale—because it is driven by relations and operations that are not immediately present, such as the market or exchange. In this regard, the locale becomes subject to the movements of abstract space, distant forces, and faceless and nameless others. The effort to circumvent this problem of a concrete, immediate place and abstract space required . . . an almost heroic attempt to reconnect space to place and localize the pace of temporality, subordinating it to the spatio-place and the world of the immediate and always present localized activities.[11]

Although this is a summary of specific developments during mid-Taishō, it hints at an underlying dynamic at work in all writers of furusato literature from the 1890s. Even if the genre sought to recapture an experience "out of time," the temporal factor intervened to create a distance, especially through the linear quality of language as a medium and the particular needs of a contemporary literary market. Conversely, it is the ever-present potential of language to deliver and the desire to satisfy the market that pushed writers into their "heroic attempt" to re-create the native place.

   In fact, the correlation between time and space is a concern shared by a wide range of scholars. W. J. T. Mitchell's study on ways to interpret landscape painting offers good advice on how these apparently separate categories might be seen to inform each other. One should ask "not just what landscape 'is' or 'means' but what it *does*, how it works as a cultural practice."[12] Spatial configurations—whether in pictorial or literary form—are not sites that exist outside time; they are themselves part and parcel of a series of constantly evolving human interventions through time. In this connection, some comments by Edward Soja, who has attempted to reconstruct a spatial hermeneutic for the study of what he calls "postmodern geographies," are useful. Soja is keen to point out that "space, time, and matter," which "delineate and encompass the essential qualities of the physical world," should not be perceived as discrete elements but as part of a more general material process in which all three are integral to each other: "Spatiality, temporality, and social being can be seen as the abstract dimensions which together comprise all facets of human existence. More concretely specified, each of these abstract existential dimensions comes to life as a social construct which shapes empirical reality and is simultaneously shaped by it."[13] In this sense, far from constituting a passive arena in which historical events simply "take place," the furusato is the trace of each writer's distinctive and dynamic contribution to the complex cultural discourses of his time.

Soja was writing in the late 1980s, and his work was itself a product of its age. It attempted to reinvigorate spatiality as a tool for social critique in the context of an often Marxist-inspired historicism that had driven the western intellectual tradition for over a century and was now perceived to be in crisis, as well as to challenge potentially antihistorical and neo-conservative tendencies in postmodern thought. He was not, however, the first to describe a shift toward more space-centered analyses. If the nineteenth century was dominated by history, notes Michel Foucault, then "the present epoch will perhaps be above all the epoch of space."[14] And Benedict Anderson outlines centers of power in terms of spatial configurations: Premodern concepts of kingship in Europe—the idea that a king derived his legitimacy from divinity—led to the development of kingdoms with porous boundaries and rule over heterogeneous populations, whereas more modern systems of state sovereignty tended to operate within more clearly demarcated geographical territories.[15] Other approaches include those of Henri Lefebvre, who attempted to broaden the traditional Marxist approach through a detailed and systematic consideration of a unitary theory of space,[16] and of Doreen Massey, who has adopted a feminist approach by seeking connections between "space, place and gender" in her book of the same name.[17] More recent works such as *Land-*

scape and Memory by Simon Schama and David Matless's *Landscape and Englishness* are witness to its continuing usefulness as a methodological approach.

In the field of Japanese studies, considerable attention has been paid to what Thomas Keirstead describes as "the spatial turn of the age" in various academic disciplines.[18] Keirstead's study of medieval gardens and estates begins with a discussion of the present "crisis" of time and narrative, and his own work draws from the emerging language of contemporary theory "with its mappings, its re- and deterritorializations, its refrains of displacement and dispersal, discursive fields and subject positions."[19] From a historical perspective, Henry Smith has examined Tokyo's significance as a new imperial capital during Meiji in terms of its geographical relation to the rest of Japan, and he has also outlined a variety of nonurban environments, including the furusato, during the Tokugawa period.[20] In anthropology, Marilyn Ivy touches specifically on the importance of the furusato in everyday Japanese life, and Jennifer Robertson has frequently made it the subject of her research.[21] A concern with traditions in the modern period, including nostalgic rural and furusato myths from both anthropological and historical viewpoints, is the subject of a recent book edited by Stephen Vlastos.[22]

As far as literary studies are concerned, it was Raymond Williams's *The Country and the City*, a groundbreaking work on the social and historical context for English literary perceptions of rural life, that first introduced me to the possibilities of a space-centered approach, although it soon became clear that the particular English concept of the "countryside" had no direct equivalent in the Japanese context. But even here, Williams's book helped by pushing me to identify the furusato as a more fruitful and appropriate area of research. Other books directly concerned with Japanese literature include Paul Anderer's examination of Arishima Takeo (1877–1923) particularly the way that author may be seen to have written against "the prevailingly grounded, place-haunted nature of Japanese fiction,"[23] and James Fujii's *Complicit Fictions* contains some interesting observations on Meiji fictional writers who reveal a rural/urban dichotomy in their novels. Among Japanese critics, works on a similar theme include Okuno Takeo's discussion of the furusato,[24] and Karatani Kōjin has discussed the possibility that the very concept of landscape was "discovered" during the Meiji period.[25] Maeda Ai's writings remain the most sustained and outstanding investigation of literature in terms of landscape.[26]

As this survey suggests, relatively little has been written on the subject of the native place in modern Japanese literature, especially in English. The present book aims to address that lack.

The Furusato in Context

"Nostalgia," remarks Raymond Williams at the beginning of *The Country and the City*, "is universal and persistent; only other men's nostalgias offend." He came to this conclusion after considering the frequent laments of English writers about what they see as the recent demise of decent, wholesome country life. Beginning with works of his own day, he traces what he calls an "escalator" of sentimentality vis-à-vis the countryside whereby each supposedly golden age turns out to have produced its own literary lament for a slightly earlier period.[27] Williams's book investigates how this generalized sentimentality tends to obscure the specific conditions of lived experience that engendered this response in the first place, and he succeeds brilliantly in throwing light on those conditions. It may be that other people's nostalgias "offend" because any particular nostalgic mood is intimately tied to temporal as well as more personal circumstances, with the result that it remains fundamentally contained and inaccessible to others of another age and experience. The only way it might be explained is through examining its historical context.

Indeed, nostalgia itself has its own history. The term comes from the Greek *nostos* (to return home) and *algia* (a painful condition), and was coined by the Swiss physician Johannes Hofer in the late seventeenth century to describe the mood of despondency and melancholia frequently encountered among Swiss mercenaries fighting far from their native land. It was only around the beginning of the twentieth century that the term came to be used outside the fields of medicine and military life and only after the 1950s that it escaped the specialized world of psychiatry to enter more popular English usage.[28] However, as Williams implies in his own study, some of nostalgia's characteristics—in particular the tendency to evoke a pleasurable and positive past in order to express dissatisfaction with the present—preceded the term itself.

In the Japanese context, nostalgia has been frequently linked to the furusato. Robertson, for instance, suggests that the word literally means "old village" but is used

> most often in an affective capacity to signify not a particular place—that is, an actual old village—but rather the generalized nature of such a place and the nostalgic feelings aroused by its mention. "Furusato Japan" thus imbues the state with a warm, fuzzy, familial, and ultimately maternal aura. Native place-making is the process by which *furusato* is evoked into existence as a political project through which experiences and memories are shaped and socially reproduced.[29]

Robertson's specific concern is with the implications of a furusato mood constructed since 1945 but, as in the English case, such a mood was by no means new. Its long genealogy has been traced by Katagiri Yōichi at least to the eighth-century anthology of Japanese poetry, *Man'yōshū*. Although originally indicating "the village/ home (*sato*) where one has lived for ages past," its meaning subtly changed to "the village/home one has been connected with for ages past," and even further to "the place where the capital (*miyako*) was in ages past." All three definitions share the common root of "a village/home that one has been connected with for ages past, but which has now become a thing of the past."[30] In other words, the furusato came to stand for an object of desire that is always already lost; its meaning emerges precisely through experience of this loss and the desire to reclaim it. "Desire" might be usefully understood here as implying not so much a simple negative sense of lack than Elizabeth Grosz's affirmative reading of it as "an actualization, a series of practices, bringing things together or separating them, . . . making reality."[31] In short, the furusato as lack initiates the impulse to articulate or reproduce it in literary terms.

Edwin Cranston also alludes to the furusato's link with the old imperial capitals when he locates a mood of loss and nostalgia among *Man'yōshū* poets directed at Nara as the abandoned capital during the eighth century. In particular, a "long poem" (*chōka*) by

Tanabe no Sakimarō identifies the capital of Nara with the "ancestral god" (i.e., the First Emperor, Jimmu) of the imperial clan, thus confirming the legitimacy of the urban aristocracy's ancestral clan holdings and their sense of home.[32] Ivy underlines this connection between furusato and ancestors when she notes that some Japanese folklorists have been inclined to identify the term less with a particular village than with the neighboring mountains:

In much of Japan, the spirits of one's ancestors were thought to return to the nearby mountains; these ancestral spirits then were transformed into *yama no kami,* or the "mountain deity," who seasonally descended to the village to become *ta no kami,* or "deity of the rice fields." The mountain is a prototypical furusato, a place of return and security after death. Yet mountains are also sites of the terrifying and mysterious, of violent abductions and ghastly crimes. Thus mountains are at once familiar homes and strange territories, sites of death: sites of the ancestors' graves, sites of possible death for the living who venture into their recesses.[33]

As Ivy makes clear, a mountain space with its furusato connotations provides the link between past and present, and between life and death in a way that may satisfy the need to locate a sense of generational continuity. On the other hand, it also offers the disquieting prospect of a breakdown between what are perceived to be properly separated states and the threat of being absorbed into an undifferentiated flow; the danger, as it were, of being consumed by the object of desire. In any case, she confirms that demarcations of space have been important in sketching out a fragile balance between the need to belong and the need to maintain a discrete identity.

Haruo Shirane, in his study of the seventeen-syllable *haikai* tradition of the Tokugawa period, has examined one literary example of this delicate negotiation through spatial configurations. Matsuo Bashō (1644–94) saw the poetic canon not so much in terms of texts as "a highly encoded body of poetic topics (*dai*) and their poetic essences, which the *haikai* poet inherited, worked against, and transformed."[34] Ties to the earlier tradition were maintained through continued use of seasonal words (*kigo*) such as "lingering snow" (*zansetsu*) to indicate spring, but a more contemporary element was added by the poet's introduction of humor and parody, with the result that classical associations were transformed into a common or vulgar form more accessible to the readers of the age. The play between tradition and novelty is particularly apparent in the *haikai* poet's continued use of *utamakura*: "poetic toponyms or places associated with classical poetry" that served as "the spatial or topographical equivalent of seasonal topics (*kidai*)." *Utamakura* indicated both a specific geographical location and "a matrix of poetical associations based on classical precedent."[35] It was rare for medieval poets to visit these places physically but, in part because of improved traveling conditions, Bashō stands out because he undertook actual journeys. His purpose, however, was double-edged: not only to experience the real locality but also to share a "collective memory" with his literary predecessors. The result was that poetry emerged

from the interaction between the immediate experience based on direct observation, which provided new perspectives and approaches but which alone was insufficient to create lasting poetry, and the broader experience embodied in the *utamakura*, in the associations of the poetic place, which bore the collective memory. . . . These two fundamental experiences, one rooted in the present and the other in the past, interacted in *haikai* fashion in Bashō's poetry and prose, defamiliarizing and refamiliarizing the cultural landscape.[36]

In short, one of Bashō's outstanding skills was his ability to evoke both continuity and separation, to transgress boundaries at the same time as he confirmed them.

A major literary shift during the Meiji period was the rupture of this intertextual engagement, as writers became more attracted to western concepts of realism and individualism. This does not mean, however, that what Shirane calls the "interpersonal, communal [and] performative dimension"[37] associated with *haikai* became suddenly defunct. Rather, links between people and place were realigned in a manner that better suited the newly western-oriented needs of the age. In the broader arena, the process by which Japan became integrated into a hierarchy of other "modern" nations was intimately related to a discourse in which the very geography of the land was seen to have an important role to play in redefining a sense of belonging. In other words, new perceptions of space were an important factor in giving shape to an emerging national identity.

One example of this tendency to equate space with identity, and a highly influential book at the time, is *Japanese Landscape* (*Nihon fūkeiron*, 1894) by Shiga Shigetaka (1863–1927). Shiga studied western sciences such as botany, geology, and meteorology at the Sapporo Agricultural School (Sapporo nōgakkō). After his graduation in 1884, he traveled widely; for instance, in 1886 he took a ten-month cruise to Australia, New Zealand, Samoa, Fiji, and Hawai'i.[38] Against the background of his country's humiliating signing of the unequal treaties, his book countered what he believed to be a spineless stance toward the West by asserting that Japan's natural landscape was exceptionally beautiful and equal to anything the West could offer. A man of his times, Shiga attempted to mythologize Japan's flora and fauna as a site imbued with elegance (*shōsa*), beauty (*bi*) and power (*tettō*)—qualities, it was implied, that characterized the Japanese people themselves—through a detailed knowledge of western science. Although critics have quite rightly identified him as a leading conservative advocate of Japanese essentialism—he is frequently mentioned in conjunction with the amorphous term "national essence" (*kokusui*)—the effect of his book went beyond the assertion that the Japanese had a "uniquely" close relationship with nature. By claiming the very earth as the pride and inspiration of the whole Japanese people, he expanded a sense of propriety vis-à-vis nature by prying it from the hands of elite writers and artists who had claimed it as their own until that time. The book's popularity—it was reprinted fifteen times in eight years—attests to its inspirational effect.[39] Moreover, by reinterpreting links with past and present for the modern age, by defining a newly expanded understanding of what it meant to be a Japanese (as opposed to a foreigner) in a worldwide order, Shiga was also contributing to a concept of national difference—a native place writ large—that would prove vital in the growing impulse toward colonial expansion over others.

An analogous redefinition of the relationship between people and place went on at the more local (*naichi*) level in a way that had a more immediate effect on modern literary representations of the furusato. Ivy notes that in the first two decades of Meiji the government was keen to promote the countryside as a site of mod-

ernization and innovation. However, since many who had moved
to cities felt an increasing sense of alienation, "the government began to revalorize rural customs as a means of stabilizing the nation.
A preoccupation with custom developed as the pretext for defini-
tively locating the traditional."[40] And this search for newfound tradition in reaction to negative aspects of urban life extended beyond
the exigencies of government policy. The first influential literary
work to eulogize the native place, setting the standard for later
novels on a similar theme, was *Returning Home* (*Kisei*, 1890) by
Miyazaki Koshoshi (1859–1919). Divided into nine sections, each
beginning with quotations from poetry of the Tang dynasty Li Bo
(701–62) and the Six Dynasties Tao Yuan-ming (365–427), it tells of
a youth who had gone to study in Tokyo six years earlier but had
now returned to his native place in order to commemorate the first
anniversary of his father's death. During his half-month stay, he
reacquaints himself with family and old friends and becomes aware
of the futility of city life compared to the beautiful simplicity of
his furusato. The youth's ulterior motive, meanwhile, is to renew
contact with a former sweetheart, whom he still loves. Koshoshi
depicts a rather naïve and simplistic urban/rural dichotomy, but
the work was so popular that it went through 25 editions by the
end of Meiji.[41] Its appeal, according to Yanagita Kunio (1875–1962),
who is usually considered the founder of modern folklore studies
in Japan, lay in its unparalleled ability to capture the feelings of
young people at the time.[42]

The reason the furusato began to attract literary interest during
Meiji may be further clarified through a comparison with two related and, to a certain extent, overlapping concepts, countryside
and nature. The word commonly used for countryside (*inaka*) has
carried associations of crudity and country bumpkins throughout
most of Japan's literary history, often eliciting a lack of interest or
even scorn in the majority of writers. To outline its genealogy
briefly, it may be traced at least to the Heian period, when court
life in Kyoto, the imperial capital, constituted the main arena for
literary activities. For diarists and writers of tales (*monogatari*), the
life of those outside the court usually remained an alien and threatening presence. Sei Shōnagon's tenth-century *Pillow Book* (*Makura*

no sōshi) offers an example of how a particularly haughty court woman creates a safe distance for herself from the lives of the uncultured poor, even when they lived in relative physical proximity. After attending a Buddhist service, she returns home through the snowy landscape late at night. The surrounding roofs are completely white, and "even the wretched huts of the poor people were very pretty under their covering of snow, evenly lit by a pale moon as though they were thatched with silver."[43] The impoverished dwellings of those excluded from the cultural center are credited with value only to the extent that they can be aestheticized, that is, removed from the daily experience of their inhabitants.

Even seven hundred years later, when Bashō journeyed through large tracts of the countryside, his intention was primarily to visit pre-existing sites of cultural interest; most of the land he traversed remained unremarkable *inaka*, which therefore went largely unreported. And the countryside as a site of uncultured brutality continued to find echoes in Meiji. Tayama Katai's (1872–1930) *Country Teacher* (*Inaka no kyōshi*, 1909) presents a far from ideal set of relationships, and Nagatsuka Takashi's (1879–1915) *The Soil* (*Tsuchi*, 1910) depicted peasant life so harshly that Natsume Sōseki's (1867–1916) review of the book expressed surprise that anyone would want to read of such things.[44] These impressions stand in strong contrast to the furusato and its "fuzzy" associations of warmth and belonging.

In the following chapters, I note that romanticized eulogies to country living certainly featured in the Meiji imagination, but it was not until early Shōwa that the *inaka* had become more comfortably interwoven with the furusato into a generalized myth of the Japanese heartland. An important early contributor to this more positive evaluation of the countryside was Yanagita Kunio with his *Tales of Tōno* (*Tōno monogatari*, 1909–10):

Presented as an unmediated transcription of oral tales and lore told to its "author" (the father-to-be of the nascent discipline of folklore studies, Yanagita Kunio) by a local storyteller, the *Tales* enscripted the uncanny remainder of capitalist modernity, that which could not be contained within the nationalist, rationalist discourse of the maturing state system. The *Tales* took its place among numerous texts signifying the rediscovery of the rural countryside; in time, it would come to be one of the most famous of these late Meiji texts.[45]

Yanagita was concerned primarily with drawing on *inaka* experience to confirm and broaden a sense of Japanese identity, but there are other clear parallels with the furusato ideal. The *Tales* speak of origins, or more correctly of the need to locate origins, and in that sense they embody a search for sites of continuity within the traditions of the ancestors in the face of the ever-expanding western-style capitalism emanating from the cities. On the other hand, as with most major intellectual figures, it was the very fact that Yanagita lived in a city and was western-educated that drove him to seek sites of supposedly more "authentic" Japanese experience; in this, he replicated the endeavors of the first writers of furusato literature. Yanagita's book also reveals that the nationalist discourse (like the furusato discourse) was not a singular one; writers and intellectuals contributed to its shape from a variety of angles. Literary attention to both furusato and countryside represented a re-evaluation of space that constituted one element by which a new national identity was being forged. The four writers under discussion in this book may be seen to have helped that process along.

The other concept related to the furusato is that of nature. Tessa Morris-Suzuki notes that in the Sino-Japanese tradition, it was conceived in two contrasting ways. One view, influenced by Daoist philosophy (and compounded by native animist traditions in the Japanese case), considered human beings to be part of a "single, vast and dimly comprehended natural unity."[46] On the other hand, Confucianism tended to emphasize a more anthropocentric universe in which greater value was given to virtuous relations between people, a view that promoted channeling the natural world for the benefit of humans. During the Tokugawa period, Japanese Neo-Confucianists attempted to conflate the two strands through a philosophy that addressed both the matter from which the universe was thought to be formed (*ki*) and its organizing principle (*ri*), although greater emphasis was placed on social order. They considered humans to have a special role in preserving the natural order, and interest shifted increasingly to a sense of human uniqueness. As a sign of this, from the late seventeenth century a key word in the discourse on nature, *kaibutsu*—meaning to reveal the nature of things or to develop the natural world—found practical application through the classification of phenomena in the natural world, and this gradually developed into an examination of ways in which nature might properly be exploited for human needs.

At the same time, Motoori Norinaga (1730–1801) promoted a view of nature connected to human emotions that was closer to the Daoist model. Although humans were part of nature's great pattern, they were additionally "endowed with an innately pure heart (*magokoro*), which they must recover by (as it were) wiping away the cobwebs of imposed ideas and conventions."[47] It was through an appreciation of the "pathos of things" (*mono no aware*), sparked by natural emotions of joy and sadness, that humans gained access to this pure heart. Motoori famously reinterpreted the *Tale of Genji* (*Genji monogatari*), previously seen as excessively crude and sensual, as the literary embodiment of a distinctly Japanese sensitivity to spontaneous and sincere feelings. Against this background, Meiji began with two understandings of nature that contributed to the development of a modern nation and its sense of identity: "At one end of the spectrum, the practical concept of *kaibutsu*—the opening up of nature—offered a philosophy which could readily be related to imported notions of industrial development. At the other, Motoori Norinaga's association of personal morality with a distinctively 'Japanese' sensitivity to nature provided inspiration for emerging nationalist imagery."[48]

Writers of furusato literature reflected both views of nature in their work as they skillfully wove some of its traditional attributes—spontaneity and sincerity, for example—into the modern furusato myth. Yet especially in Meiji, nature also engendered antagonistic feelings. Doppo and Tōson were certainly not alone in their keenness to strip nature of earlier associations—particularly the "famous places" (*meisho*) of the literary tradition—and revel in its novelty. By contrast, their attraction to the furusato indicated a deep anxiety about the modern condition as they sought to relocate an established history and sense of origin. Only gradually were writers like Satō and Shiga able to employ more imaginative and emotional strategies in order to reintegrate nature into their sense of belonging. Such conflicts reveal the contradictory impulses at work in their articulation of a national identity, as they struggled to reinvent themselves while seeking to embrace a supposedly unchanging essence.

Indeed, Narita Ryūichi argues that in Japan's modern period, the furusato has featured particularly strongly as a subject of concern at moments of greatest change, when anxiety about national identity has been at its highest—in his view, the 1880s, the 1930s, and the 1960–70s.[49] Leaving aside the third period, which lies outside the ambit of the present book, we can characterized the 1880s as an age of disappointment following the defeat of political activities centered on the Movement for Freedom and Popular Rights (Jiyū minken undō) and the corresponding search for sites of consolation: it was around this time that examples of furusato literature first emerged. By the 1930s, huge numbers of people had migrated to the cities; they carried not only expectations of a better life but also nostalgic memories of the places they had left behind. A revival of traditional folk songs, as well as numerous records and magazines that took the furusato as their central theme, attests to an emerging urban-based mass media's ability to respond to these emotional needs.[50] To borrow Hobsbawm's well-known phrase, the furusato functions as an "invented tradition," characterized by "the contrast between the constant change and innovation of the modern world and the attempt to structure at least some parts of social life within it as unchanging and invariant."[51]

Mention of cities leads to my final introductory point. Although the furusato is the primary concern of this book, it must always be understood as part of a binary: the city and the furusato exist in conjunction. Again, Narita provides some informative comments on how this symbiosis evolved. From the late 1880s, "provincial associations" (*dōkyōkai*) were formed to create a communal feeling among men from the same regions—women were seldom allowed to participate—who were now scattered in Tokyo and other cities. Magazines devoted to local issues as well as literary contributions reveal that the main purpose of such groups was not so much to forge mutual financial links as to foster an affectionate regard for the old native place. In other words, the disorienting experience of urban life was to be countered by common emotional bonds created through a shared local history, geography, and dialect.[52] Needless to say, nostalgia played a major role, since these experiences belonged to the past. However, to claim that these displaced people "belonged" to one particular camp or another ignores the complexity of their lived experience: any sense of belonging emerged from a conjunction of daily urban life and persistent memories of the native place. Their sense of loss and the desire to reclaim a degree of integrity may be a mood shared even by the displaced emperors of Nara, but the defining characteristics of their sense of home—their furusato consciousness and its distinctive representation in literature—makes sense only in terms of their particular social and historical context.

Since many of the points sketched above are discussed in further detail in the following pages, I conclude by simply noting that the furusato continues to evoke a powerful response among many Japanese. However, although many people obviously retain a sentimental attachment to their place of birth—witness the enduring appeal of numerous emotional popular ballads (*enka*) at any karaoke bar in Japan—the ambivalent relation between physical locality and the furusato mood has been effectively reformulated to suit the needs of late capitalist society better. During the course of my research in Japan, I would ask people now resident in larger cities whether they felt strong ties to their native places. Although many confirmed this to be the case, they also admitted they return "home" only during the summer O-bon festival, if at all. It would be entirely wrong to deny the continuing importance of these perceived links in the minds of many, but I would suggest that it is through the media, such as advertisements for housing developments promising "the heart of the furusato," that the native place now lives most vividly in people's daily experience. At its barest, the furusato is a figment of the imagination, although no less important for that. This book traces the shape of that imaginary process.

ONE

Kunikida Doppo:
Another Place Called Home

The Power of Rootlessness

Anthony Smith suggests that although the nation is primarily spatial, it cannot occupy just any land. The space must be the historical cradle of the people:

A 'historic land' is one where terrain and people have exerted mutual, and beneficial, influence over several generations. The homeland becomes a repository of historic memories and associations, the place where 'our' sages, saints and heroes lived, worked, prayed and fought. All this makes the homeland unique. Its rivers, coasts, lakes, mountains and cities become 'sacred'—places of veneration and exaltation whose inner meanings can be fathomed only by the initiated, that is, the self-aware members of the nation.[1]

Speaking from a western perspective, Smith uses a vocabulary tinged with Christianity, but strong parallels can be found in the Japanese case. Native Shintoism has been especially adept at marking outstanding natural sites as centers of veneration, and a literary tradition privileged certain geographical areas precisely through extended links with the past. The problem for Kunikida Doppo's generation was how to dispense with what they felt to be stifling traditions and find "heroes" more suitable for a new age, even as they attempted to define a coherent identity. Inevitably, given the contemporary international order, that identity would be a national one and necessarily shaped in part by the very traditions they wished to abandon. Ironically, it was the fragmented nature of their daily experience that provided the potential for reconciliation of this conflict.

In a letter written in 1891 from his parents' house in Yamaguchi prefecture to a friend in Tokyo, Doppo praised the countryside (*inaka*) as having been shaped "by the hand of God," in contrast to the inferior, man-made environment of the city.[2] His words demonstrate an interest in Christianity, but also link him with other writers of the third decade of Meiji (roughly the 1890s) who were beginning to question an earlier generation's enthusiasm for city life as the means to self-improvement and social success. It is around this time that the furusato emerges as a major theme in modern Japanese writing. Indeed, Maeda Ai specifically identifies *Returning Home*, Miyazaki Koshoshi's (1859–1919) furusato-inspired novel of 1890, as the endpoint of a cycle of novels aimed at youths driven by the ideal of "establishing oneself and making it in the world" (*risshin shusse*).[3]

What might be called the new furusato literature[4] was produced largely by writers who had moved to the city but found themselves unable to fulfill their potential in the way promised in earlier writings such as Samuel Smiles's *Self Help* (translated by Nakamura Keiu in 1870) and Fukuzawa Yukichi's (1835–1901) *Encouragement to Learning* (*Gakumon no susume*, 1872). It may be read both as a critique of the prevailing self-help ideology and as the articulation of a need to locate an idealized "other place" to compensate for the daily experience of urban life. Of course, criticisms of urban reality as a betrayal of youthful expectations were not limited to this literary form: Bunzō's wretched realization in Futabatei Shimei's (1864–1909) *Floating Clouds* (*Ukigumo*, 1886–89) that a graduation certificate alone no longer guarantees official or personal success takes place entirely in Tokyo, even if the presence of his devoted mother in the Shizuoka countryside compounds his sense of failure. Nevertheless, the emergence of furusato literature was noteworthy in that it generated a highly productive literary dynamic between representations of city and native place that was subsequently played out in numerous works of Meiji and Taishō fiction.

Although Doppo's works also address other themes, he is significant for any consideration of what has been called the "furusato consciousness"[5] because his writing demonstrates a particularly restless quality that leads him to problematize the very nature of the native place. Already in a letter of 1894, he speaks of being caught between two extreme poles: "When I am in the city, I miss the countryside, and when I return to the countryside, I yearn for the city."[6] It is not surprising, then, that the localities in his later writings not only include Tokyo but range to the extremes of the Japanese archipelago, Kyushu and Hokkaido.

This pattern of shifting attention in his work reflects his own life. Compared with that of other Meiji writers, his experience was remarkably fragmented. Yanagita once described him as "already a stray child when he was born."[7] His place of birth was Chōshi, Chiba prefecture, but his father's work on the Yamaguchi court circuit meant that the years 1875–78 were spent moving from town to town in Yamaguchi and Hiroshima prefectures. The family settled in the Yamaguchi district of Iwakuni until 1883, when they moved back to Yamaguchi town. Doppo went to study in Tokyo in 1887 but returned to his parents' home in May 1891 for a year's stay. Back in Tokyo from June 1892, the need for employment led him to take a teaching appointment in Saeki, Kyushu, from October 1893 until his return to Tokyo the following July. He was soon off again, this time as a reporter based on a battleship during the Sino-Japanese war. He was in Tokyo from March 1895, but made a one-week trip to Hokkaido in September of that year. In 1896, following the failure of his marriage with Sasaki Nobuko, he spent the summer in Kyoto, and the next year found him in Nikkō between April and June with the writer Tayama Katai. Until his untimely death from tuberculosis in 1908, he was based mostly in Tokyo, although he made various trips to hot springs during his last three years for health reasons.

The experience of traveling around the country was not a new phenomenon; there is a long tradition of premodern travel literature in Japan. In the Tokugawa period, for instance, the pilgrimage became a pretext for considerable numbers of people from all social ranks to leave home for a period of time, despite laws aimed at restricting movement. The result was that travel became "a form of recreation, or *yusan tabi* ('pleasure seeking travel'), an escape from the rigid pattern governing day-to-day living."[8] With the breakdown of older social hierarchies and the arrival of technological innovations like the railway during Meiji, such mobility was available on a greater scale and for larger numbers than ever before. Doppo may be seen as an extreme example of this tendency.

Like other writers of furusato literature, Doppo was led by the very fact of uprootedness to try and recapture some moment of belonging in his writing, yet the disrupted nature of his upbringing complicated his ability to locate a native place in which to anchor himself. Indeed, the area that serves as a background to his furusato stories, two of which—"River Mist" ("Kawagiri," 1898) and "Let Me Return" ("Kikyorai," 1901)—are discussed in this chapter, is not his actual birthplace but Iwakuni, where he lived an almost idyllic life during the formative years between age 7 and 12.

In addition, personal complications surrounding his relationship with his father suggest why he felt little literary interest in Chōshi and why his understanding of the native place should depart from the more conventional attachment to the family home. There has been considerable scholarly debate whether Doppo was the son of Senpachi, the man who raised him, or of Masajirō, his mother's first husband.[9] His story "The Fatalist" ("Unmeironsha," March 1903), which concerns a man whose uncertain parentage has tragic effects on his own love life, shows the writer's concern about family origins. In fact, Senpachi's marriage to Doppo's mother was his second; the failure of an earlier union forced him to give up contact with three children from the first marriage, his patrimony, and free access to his own furusato of Tatsuno in Hyōgo prefecture. In 1890, Tokutomi Sōhō wrote an enthusiastic review of *Returning Home* in his journal, *The Nation's Friend* (*Kokumin no tomo*), in which he praised Koshoshi's evocative re-creation of his real native place and suggested that the furusato might best be perceived not as an actual locality but as a site embodying one's earliest unforgettable sensations.[10] However, Doppo's life precluded the possibility of conceiving of home as a site of generational continuity. In that sense, his personal experience prefigured Tokutomi's later imaginative reinterpretation.

His inability to settle attention on one area for long is also shown in his tenuous relationship with contemporary intellectual currents, particularly politics and Christianity. His involvement with these two aspects of Meiji society is worth examination, since his problems clarify his unease vis-à-vis society and consequently gave shape to the furusato that emerged in his literature.

It was very much in the spirit of *risshin shusse* that Doppo first arrived in Tokyo. The content of the courses he chose to study— he began with a private law school in Kanda, moved in 1888 to the English Department of Tokyo senmon gakkō (present-day Waseda University), then transferred in 1889 to the Department of English and Politics—demonstrates his eagerness to be fully engaged with the Meiji enlightenment project. However, the promulgation of the Constitution in 1889, followed the next year by the opening of the first session of the Diet, signaled the end of many of the possibilities for creating a new society excitedly raised by the Movement for Freedom and Popular Rights. In 1907 Doppo recounted his boyhood dream of making a name for himself as a great general like Napoleon, but the times demanded that, like others of his generation, he somehow rechannel his energies. He left college without graduating to return to Yamaguchi in 1891, but the ideal of ambition—the English term is transcribed in *katakana*—remained problematic and had been the subject of an earlier article in 1889.[11] This is not to say he was entirely removed from practical political involvement; he worked for the Liberal Party newspaper *Jiyū shinbun* for a few months in 1893, and he was linked for several years with Sōhō's Friends of the Nation society (Min'yūsha) and its publications *Kokumin shinbun* and *Kokumin no tomo*, both initially progressive publications.

Doppo's interest in Christianity was not unrelated to the political sphere. His post on the Liberal Party paper came about through an invitation from Kanamori Tsūrin (1857-1945), head of the company that produced the newspaper, who had been a preacher at the church in Kōjimachi that Doppo attended. His interest in Christianity was not unrelated to his admiration for "men of action" (*shishi*) like Yoshida Shōin (1830–59), who had engaged in political struggles around the end of the Tokugawa period. The word he used to sum up their admirable qualities was sincerity (*makoto*), a term that first became familiar to Doppo from reading Thomas Carlyle's *On Heroes* (1841). This book is a record of lectures on the lives of various religious, political, and literary figures singled out for heroic status because of the depth of their sincerity. As Takitō Mitsuyoshi has pointed out, Doppo was prompted to seek similar values in Christianity.[12]

In the process of exploring politics and Christianity for adequate answers to fundamental questions of life and becoming disillusioned with them, Doppo began to give shape to the landscapes that would inform his texts. A useful comparison can be made here with Kitamura Tōkoku (1868–94), a passionate young contemporary whose suicide at the age of 26 shocked the literary and intellectual worlds. Both men were impressed by the democratic implications of the Christian belief that all were born equal but soon shifted from an early political engagement to a more private goal of spiritual development; both ultimately found it impossible to accept the concept of Christ as a human manifestation of God and instead attempted to find a less personalized religion related to the natural world.[13] But whereas Kitamura ended his own life in exasperation, Doppo made a momentous decision in 1897 to abandon orthodox Christianity in favor of literature as the best means of continuing that spiritual search. His self-deprecatory comment that, compared with the certainties of religious belief, literature is "merely the hiding place of the doubter"[14] simply confirms a self-questioning dynamic that would drive the production of his landscapes.

This spatial dimension was determined through the process of identifying literary sites that could best articulate the contours of his inner doubts. More precisely, the very landscapes he came to depict were both a response to and an integral part of the attempt to answer those difficult questions. Describing his spiritual crisis of 1892, Doppo recounted:

I arrived at questions such as "Where did I come from?," "Where am I going?," "What am I?" . . . The result, then, was that I underwent a fundamental spiritual revolution, and the great hopes I had harbored until then faded away. Napoleon and Hideyoshi completely lost any sense of grandeur for me. . . . Thus, I inevitably became drawn to matters of philosophy and religion.[15]

The writer's immediate concern was to show how he became drawn to Christianity. More generally, he is voicing concerns shared by his contemporaries about how, figuratively speaking, they could identify a place for themselves in the new society. For Doppo, however, a more literal reading is also possible. Although his engagement with practical politics and religion—encapsulated in his personality clash with Kanamori while working on the Liberal Party newspaper—ended in disillusionment, the experience allowed him to focus more clearly on self-realization as an ideal. The need for a literary medium to express this ideal and work out where he was "going" led him toward the Romanticism of Wordsworth and, in spatial terms, its representation through a revised interpretation of the world of nature.

It is possible, then, to see Doppo's literary work as driven by a powerful impulse to locate a settled space in the intellectual landscape of the time and, more specifically, through the spatial configurations set out in the texts. Such a reading, I suggest, is a productive one since it generates an important set of questions, ones that will run throughout this book; namely, how to link a writer's personal hopes and aspirations and ideals with the social environment into which he is born, and how to identify such experiences and ideals in the physical landscapes produced in his literature. In the Introduction, I noted Soja's concern with the general concept of a spatial hermeneutic and, in particular, his assertion that the physical world consists of a complex interaction among the equally essential elements of "space, time, and matter." These ideas cast an interesting light on Doppo's work.

At one level, Doppo's disenchantment and shift to literature may be seen as an abandonment of the "real" world to concentrate on more personal concerns. But the sites that Doppo chose to depict are not pre-existing empty arenas in which actions simply take place. Rather, the sites themselves constitute part of that transformative process by which each of these three elements—spatiality (landscape/furusato), temporality (history), and social being (writer)—inform and reproduce each other. If Kitamura's narrative poem *Tale of Mount Hōrai* (*Hōrai kyoku*, 1891) has sometimes been read as a critique of the brash materialism of capitalism, Doppo's concern with nature may be seen as his stand against the dominant version of modernity, whose symbol is Tokyo and in which only fame and fortune matter. Togawa Shinsuke even suggests that his furusato literature is an act of rebellion against a society that refused to implement the ideals of the Freedom and Popular Rights movement.[16] In that sense, temporality as an axis of political progress and spatiality as a praxis of liberation remain intimately connected, but the emphasis has shifted from emancipatory politics to the politics of emancipatory space.

The writer's engagement with spatiality at a particular historical juncture can be seen at work in "Unforgettable People" ("Wasure-enu hitobito," April 1898), identified by Karatani Kōjin as seminal in Meiji fiction for its new understanding of landscape.[17] It is the story of Otsu, a young writer who arrives unannounced at the Kameya inn on a bleak March night. Although the innkeeper eyes him suspiciously, Otsu is allowed to stay. To wile away the time, he gets into an intimate conversation with Akiyama, a young painter and the only other guest. As the night advances, Otsu launches into a discussion of "unforgettable people" from his past, three people in particular. The first was observed on an island as Otsu made his way home from Tokyo on a boat traveling through the Inland Sea:

As I watched, I noticed a man standing on part of the beach, where the tide had receded, that was gleaming in the sunlight. I was sure it was a man and not a child. He appeared to keep picking things up and putting them in a basket or bucket. He would walk two or three paces, then squat down to pick something up. I stared at this man scouring the small beach under the shadow of this lonely island. As the boat went on, the man became nothing more than a black dot. Before long the beach, the hills, and the whole island disappeared into the mist. In the almost ten years that have passed since that day, how many times have I recalled this man, his face unknown to me, standing in the shadow of the island. For me, he is one of those "unforgettable people."[18]

The second encounter takes place during a trip to his parent's home at New Year's. After he and his brother visit the awesome crater of Mount Aso in Kyushu, they reach a lively village in the foothills at dusk and set out for the place where they will stay the night. On the way, as they pause at a bridge and turn back to watch the distant volcanic smoke tinged with the setting sun, he hears someone singing and "still gazing at the volcano's smoke, I strained my ears and without any particular effort waited for this sound to come closer." It turns out to be a local youth passing by on a horse-drawn carriage. Otsu is touched by the song's sadness as he "stared at the disappearing form of the sturdy young man, and looked up at the smoke of Mount Aso."[19] The third unforgettable person is a monk playing the lute (*biwa*), his sad face matching the tone of the tune, in a quiet street of an animated fish-market town in Shikoku. As Otsu listened intently, "none of the harbor people seemed to notice [the monk], and people in surrounding houses showed no interest in listening to his lute."[20]

Karatani focuses on "landscape" primarily as an epistemological system, a new way of seeing the world, which he says began to appear in conjunction with the literary trend of realism in the 1890s, especially through Doppo's works. Karatani alleges that it caused a fundamental break with the past. In painting, for instance, he notes that the traditional Japanese nature artist resembled his medieval European counterpart in being drawn less to look at a particular object than to envision the transcendental: "When a brush painter depicted a pine grove, he depicted the concept [signified as] 'pine-grove' rather than an actual one. In order for an actual pine grove to appear as a subject, this transcendental 'site' had to be overturned. This is the point at which perspective appears."[21] Such a "modern perspective" emerges in the literary text of "Unforgettable People" when Otsu describes the kind of moments at which he recalls figures from the past:

I sense my isolation in this world, and an unbearable sadness visits me. At such times, I become disoriented within myself and yearn for the company of others. I begin to think of friends and various things from the past. It is then that these people float freely up into my mind or, rather, these people as they stand framed by the surrounding landscape in which I first saw them.[22]

By associating unforgettable figures with a landscape—"people as landscapes," in Karatani's words[23]—especially in combination with a "sense of isolation," Doppo is presenting a new perspective between viewer and viewed. For the landscapes and "ordinary people" represented by this new realistic mode "did not exist in the external world from the beginning but had to be discovered as landscapes from which people were alienated."[24] Once discovered, the landscape and the people become visible to the eye and seem to have been there, external to us, from the very beginning. This irreversible transformation of perception is essentially different from earlier Japanese literary constructions of nature based around "famous places" (*meisho*).

Although much of what Karatani says is compelling, some questions remain. For one thing, his strong emphasis on Doppo's work as the point of the "*discovery* of landscape" seems to downplay a particularly rich vocabulary for the natural landscape found in premodern Japanese literature, even if the separation of the viewing self and the "out there" remained undeveloped. I also wonder if a concern with "realistic" representations of place did not begin earlier. For instance, although Matsuo Bashō's *Journey to the Deep North* (*Oku no hosomichi*, 1689) was definitely constructed around *meisho*, the record of the trip kept by his traveling companion Sora offers a different, albeit more prosaic, version of the actual itinerary. In other words, whereas Bashō's work confirms the lack of interest in "real" landscape characteristic of premodern literature (even if he took the rare step of actually visiting places mentioned in earlier literature), Sora's document offers a more realistic account. Of course, Sora's comments are considered significant only as an addendum to a masterpiece, but they had the effect of mapping an alternative, "real" landscape that allowed subsequent scholars to read Bashō's relationship with the places detailed in his text from a different perspective.

It seems more likely to me that Doppo's vital contribution was to clarify and build on a potential relationship with landscape that had lain dormant in the literary tradition at least since Bashō's time. On the other hand, the way he problematized the integration of human feeling into literary representations of place is worthy of note. In large part, the three unforgettable figures are completely rooted in their own isolated landscapes, cut off from the company of others and oblivious to Otsu's attention. Their activities— foraging aimlessly on a beach, voicing some snatch of a song against the backdrop of a massive volcano, playing an instrument that no one hears—seem insignificant and pathetic. What makes them unforgettable is the narrator's highly personal and emotional involvement in the scenes. Otsu details his feelings of deep longing for people like these three:

I never feel such tranquility in my heart as I do at such a time. I never feel such freedom. I am never able to erase worldly thoughts of the struggle for wealth and fame and feel deep sympathy (*dōjō*) for all things so much as I do then. I feel that somehow I must get these thoughts written down. For I believe there must be other people in the world who feel the same.[25]

The key word here is "sympathy," since his earlier acknowledgment of isolation from others—that is, the alienating perspective discussed by Karatani—is also the very point at which at least some form of human contact can arise. For this reason, it is the inn- keeper and not Akiyama who ends up recorded in Otsu's subse- quent version of "Unforgettable People"; the very coolness with which the young traveler is treated both confirms an unbridgeable gap between people and fuels Otsu's corresponding need to over- come it through a sympathetic contemplation of the human condi- tion.[26] On the other hand, Otsu's spontaneous reaction to the pa- thos (*mono no aware*) of seemingly inconsequential events evokes the more traditional concept of a pure heart (*magokoro*). The exis- tence of what Motoori would have defined as a quintessentially Japanese characteristic in this typically modern man suggests that Doppo's portrayal of his own generation's struggle for self- identity—embodied in Otsu's appeal to others who "feel the same"—is more complex than a simple rejection of the old.

This leaves the question of why Akiyama does not become an unforgettable person in the later version of the story and, indeed, why he appears at all. Takitō may be right in suggesting that the

writer is putting into practice Wordsworth's underlying belief that
the poet "is someone who tells stories to people" by assigning Akiyama the role of listener.[27] But another reason is the young
painter's personality. He is amiable (*aikyō*), in contrast to the
unamiable (*buaikyō*) innkeeper.[28] A cursory reading might suggest
this quality to be more amenable for the sympathetic ideal articulated by Otsu. But Doppo is concerned with something more than
easy intimacy and, in terms of confirming the near-impossibility of
human interaction, the innkeeper is the more significant character.
In a sense, however, Akiyama is included after all. He may not be
on Otsu's list, but this very exclusion underlines a more general
point about human alienation. In other words, his isolation guarantees him a place in Doppo's "Unforgettable People."

Nature Repatterned

By the time Doppo began to write fiction, he had experienced
various forms of rural life that he would later use to articulate a
compensatory site beyond the constrictions of urban reality: the
furusato (centered on Yamaguchi), the countryside (*inaka*, experienced during his stay in Saeki), and largely uninhabited forested areas (sometimes described as *sanrin*, or "mountains and forests,"
found in Hokkaido). To a certain extent, these terms overlap in
meaning and fall under the general rubric of Doppo's interest in
nature. This broader theme complicates any simple notion of a
rural-urban dichotomy and puts his specific concern with the furusato into a wider context.

"The Musashi Plain" ("Musashino," January and February 1898)
was one of his first texts to present elements from different "natural" landscapes. One of Doppo's motives in writing it was to recover from his relationship with Sakaki Nobuko, from whom he
became estranged after less than a year of marriage. Ironically, the
plain featured in the early days of their romance; after meeting in
June 1895, they defied the wishes of Nobuko's parents and eloped
there during the month of August. Hokkaido, too, figured in their
relationship: it was the place they chose to set up a farm together
and live the "natural" life. The writer's trip there in September was
to purchase land next to the Sorachi River. In fact, the farm never

materialized, and, in August 1896, after considerable heartbreak following their separation in April, Doppo settled for almost a year with his brother in what was then the village of Shibuya on the Musashino outskirts of Tokyo. His contemplative strolls round the area became the subject of the literary piece. These walks may have been an attempt to lose himself totally in an imaginative engagement with the natural environment, but it has also been suggested that the casual style of his rambles gave him a "traveler's" role, reminiscent of Otsu in "Unforgettable People," and helped maintain a self-protective distance from painful associations with the place.[29]

Beyond this personal element, however, the way in which he represents the Musashi Plain as a "natural" landscape exhibits a separation that confirms Karatani's notion of Doppo's use of landscape as a distancing perspective. The text is structured like a collage: the area is described, among other means, through extracts from the narrator's diary, letters from friends, the narrator's own impressionistic passages, a *waka* by an Edo poet, and translations of passages by Turgenev. In other words, the Musashi Plain is "known" from a wide range of different times and cultural perspectives that complicates any single appreciation of this "natural" world. The work might best be described as an amalgam of diverse points of view that do not quite come together, rather like the fragmented image seen in a broken mirror. In any case, it is a highly self-conscious construction of nature observed at a distance.

When first published in *Kokumin no tomo*, the text's title was "The Present-Day Musashi Plain" ("Ima no Musashino"). This initial temporal restriction seems to indicate Doppo's awareness of a considerable gulf of perception between his work and earlier Japanese literary representations of the place. The excision of "present-day" when the piece was published in Doppo's 1901 short-story collection, also entitled *The Musashino Plain*, may indicate a wish to draw attention to the more general historical context, but this cannot obviate the fact that a fundamental perceptual change had occurred.[30] The narrator acknowledges as much when, noting that this may be the site of skirmishes between the Taira and Minamoto clans in the fourteenth century, he decides to take a look for

himself. Driven by the desire to find out "how much of the old
Musashi Plain remained," he wonders if

this desire can in fact be satisfied by one's own efforts? I do not say it is
impossible. But I believe it is not an easy task, and for that very reason
the present-day (*ima no*) Musashi Plain has an appeal for me. There are
probably quite a few who feel the same.[31]

Even if this area is significant in part for its historical associations
(and in that sense resembles the battlegrounds visited by earlier
writers like Bashō), the problem—indeed the narrator's interest in
the place—revolves around the question whether a modern (*ima no*)
man can truly appreciate it.

In other words, Doppo offers a new landscape refracted through
multiple perspectives; the question is how to piece them together.
A kind of resolution may be detected in what appears at first to be
decisive choices of one viewpoint over another. For instance, when
the narrator makes a trip with a friend to Sakai, just to the west of
the Musashi Plain, they encounter an old lady in a teashop who
ridicules them for coming in summer since the area is renowned
for cherry blossoms in spring. The point, of course, is Doppo's
declaration of a conscious break with the *meisho* tradition of associating famous places with particular seasons. On the other hand, if
only as a form of denial, this older understanding of place remains
embedded in the text.

In the same way, Doppo's intention to privilege previously un-
acknowledged aspects of the natural world is clear when he de-
clares a newfound attraction toward the oak (*nara*) woods that are
a distinctive feature of the plain. His appreciation borrows from a
non-Japanese view of nature, specifically Futabatei's translation of
Turgenev's story "The Rendez-Vous," which depicts another deciduous tree, the birch:

It seems that until the present time the Japanese have never appreciated
the beauty of woods filled with deciduous oaks. When woods are spoken
of, it is principally pine woods that are mentioned in Japanese literature
and arts, so that one never comes across anything about hearing autumn
showers in the depths of oak woods even in poetry. I myself grew up in
western Japan, and it has been ten years since I first came to Tokyo as a

student. But it has only been recently that I have come to appreciate the beauty of these deciduous woods.[32]

To speak of a "Japanese" appreciation of woods reveals a certain stepping back from his own culture, and this distance provides Doppo room to reflect on a traditional Japanese view that has been found wanting; the novelty of this approach is understood by the narrator himself, who stresses his recent conversion to this view. And, undoubtedly, Doppo's own ambiguous sense of belonging leads him to question traditional understanding of place. In the final analysis, however, the oak trees gain significance only in the context of the earlier tradition. In short, their value lies precisely in their *not* being pine trees. In that sense, his "new" viewpoint remains essentially confined within that same tradition, albeit it radically transforms it and makes it more complex.

But a concern with nature is not restricted to natural phenomena like trees, and an understanding of the Musashi Plain does not arise simply from grafting together diverse, pre-existing appreciations of its features. To a degree, Doppo's work borrowed from opposing Sino-Japanese views of nature—human beings as minor players in a vastly greater universe versus a Confucian-inspired interest in people. It is, however, also important in the way it delineates a new form of landscape, the suburb (*kōgai*), where rural and urban sites are less easily distinguishable. The plain is described as a series of undulations like an ocean, with the troughs between waves forming shallow valleys:

There are mainly paddy fields at the bottom of these valleys. Most of the plowed fields are to be found on the elevated land, and this land is broken into various configurations of plowed field and forest. . . . As a result, rather than continuing in a single stretch, the forest extends perhaps less than three miles. The plowed fields, too, do not go on for ever but instead are broken up in such a way that a clump of trees is surrounded by plowed fields, and plowed fields are enclosed by forest on three sides. The presence of farmhouses interspersed between them breaks up everything even more.[33]

Although dotted with seemingly untouched remnants of forest, this land is clearly worked: presented to the reader as a single moment, but one that implies its gradual transformation by the slow

(human) hand of time. But if the landscape resembles the patch-
work form of the text itself with its separate images of human labor and "natural" woodland existing side by side, a more comfortable harmony of complementary support is evoked in the way its
features artfully surround and fit into one another. The narrator
explains why he is drawn to such places:

Why do such places make such an impression? I can answer in a few
words. The reason is that, somehow or other, such scenes on the city's
outskirts give people the impression of seeing society in miniature. In
other words, one is led to feel that those houses conceal several stories capable of exciting the interest of people from both countryside and city;
insubstantial stories, stories of great pathos, or hilariously funny stories.
Characteristic of such places is the way traces of city life and remnants of
country life seem to blend together in gentle swirls (*uzu o maite*).[34]

Takitō observes that Doppo is attracted to seeking out the stories of others in order to "escape the quagmire of his own ego,"
which does not know where to locate itself.[35] It is certainly true
that this landscape and its stories offer a prospect of relief to someone who could settle nowhere. What is more, this world in "miniature" promises a degree of containability and control; even the split
into the extreme poles of countryside and city engenders only restless movement between the two. In the end, these stories represent
a hybrid extracted by modern man from rural and urban experience to reveal the tentative weaving of a newly shared national
identity "capable of exciting the interest" of all.

Doppo may have been attracted to the suburb as a new feature
of the Japanese landscape, but his sense of nature was also affected
by William Wordsworth, whose poetry made a strong impression
in the emotional and intellectual realm. The English poet became
known to Doppo and his contemporaries in the early 1890s, and
Koshoshi produced the first Japanese critical biography in October
1893.[36] Wordsworth's works were Doppo's indispensable companion during his stay in Saeki, and he even claimed to see physical
links between the Lake District and the Kyushu countryside,
which he described as equally rich in mountains, valleys, and stories of everyday life.[37] Reflecting on his experiences at this time,
Doppo outlined the poet's importance in providing a means to

clarify his shift toward nature in opposition to the "unnaturalness" of urban life:

As long as I was still a believer of Wordsworth, I was unable to think only of people in society apart from nature. It was precisely because people existed in this mysterious and exquisite natural world, which acted in concert with people, that the lives of ordinary men in an ordinary environment appeared to me as an extraordinary reality.[38]

There is an unresolved tension here: Doppo may claim a preference for man's relationship with the "exquisite natural world," but he did not go so far as to sever his ties with "society" entirely, and the suburb attracts him precisely because it is a possible point of contact between the two. Nevertheless, this is further confirmation of Doppo's discovery of value in ordinary people and their surrounding landscapes, already discussed in connection with "Unforgettable People."

But Doppo's attention to "ordinary men" also underlines his adherence to the new current of literary realism, which profoundly affected his representations of nature. In the essay "Written Depictions of Nature" ("Shizen o utsusu bunshō," November 1906), he contrasted his writings with a then-prevalent literary style to emphasize his own texts as an exercise in highlighting specific natural features:

There is a bad habit among people who are excessively skilled in writing—people who have read many travel sketches and can use lots of Chinese characters—to be carried away by their writing so that, contrary to expectations, their depictions of nature are spoiled. In order to depict one's observation of nature, one must write about it exactly as it is seen, exactly as it feels. . . . But people who are excessively skilled in writing, that is, people who use a lot of words and adjectives when forming sentences, end up with works that have exceeded that degree. The result is that, if you take away the nouns and place-names, a description of a Shinano landscape becomes indistinguishable from a scene of Sichuan's mountain paths . . . "The Musashi Plain" may be a poor example of writing, but it most certainly describes directly and without embellishment what I felt.[39]

It is not surprising that tired allusions to Chinese poetry will no longer suffice for a writer keen to question the assumptions of an earlier tradition, although this also implies his willing acceptance of new systems of perception coming from the West. Doppo spelled out the kind of "excessively skilled" writers he was reacting against when, claiming Wordsworth as his literary mentor, he denied any influence from Ozaki Koyō (1867–1903), associated with the Ken'yūsha group of writers, and Kōda Rohan (1867–1947), both of whom drew their inspiration from Tokugawa literature.[40] Moreover, as Kitano Akihiko has pointed out, Doppo's rejection of decorative stereotypes of nature as serving only to embellish a novel's characters may be seen as part of a general movement shared by others such as Tōson and Tayama Katai to "individualize" nature through attention to minute detail and introduce into their literature the "local color" of the regions they had only recently left.[41]

Clearly, Doppo and these other writers shared a concern usually identified with the school of Naturalism. Doppo's emphasis on viewing nature "exactly as it is seen" (mita mama) carries strong echoes of the frequent Naturalist calls for depictions of reality "just as it is" (sono mama). For this reason, late Meiji Naturalist critics were happy to promote him as an exponent of their own theories. But Doppo did not feel comfortable with this label, and in a 1907 article he questioned any connection between himself and this school, which seemed so powerful at the time.[42] Under pressure to seek common ground, he published a more conciliatory article a year later, but still ascribed his distinctive approach to the pervasive influence of the English poet:

At the very least, Wordsworth was unable to view people and nature from a detached position. It was impossible for him to think of mysterious great nature (fukashigi naru daishizen) and human life as entirely separate. For the present Japanese Naturalists, however, the main concern is for people and human life; even though they look into what has been hidden until now in the world, that is, in society, they appear not to look into the bosom of nature, which is the greatest reality for mankind.[43]

In other words, whereas Doppo was always of two minds about how to reconcile the contradictory attractions of nature and human life, the Naturalists solved the problem—wrongly, in his view—by discarding half of the equation to concentrate only on the "hidden" details of social reality.

By their refusal to "look into the bosom of nature," the Naturalists were excluded from the emotional aspect of what Doppo saw as the proper observation of nature, that is, writing "exactly as it feels." For instance, in "The Musashi Plain" he quoted with approval Futabatei's translation of a Turgenev story in which the narrator's depression is described in terms of a cold windswept landscape at the approach of winter:

A timid crow flapped its wings heavily. Cutting through the wind with great force, it flew past high above me. It suddenly turned its head, glared at me briefly, then soared steeply upward crying as if it would tear its voice before disappearing into the woods beyond. A large flock of doves flew vigorously from a granary, but suddenly they danced upward as if to form a pillar, and immediately scattered over the whole surface of the field. Ah, autumn! Someone seems to be passing by the bare mountain, and the sound of an empty cart echoes throughout the sky.

Of course, this is a Russian landscape, but for Doppo the sight of Musashi Plain at the same season is "more or less the same thing."[44] In any case, the natural scene evokes an emotional outburst—Ah, autumn!—while the empty cart's echo engraves it with a human presence. It is precisely such appreciations of nature that led Katai, in a 1908 article on Doppo immediately following his death, to detect signs of sentimental Romanticism and lingering immaturity.[45] In fact, Doppo merely remained loyal to his understanding of the sincerity of expression articulated in his reading of Carlyle, while he continued to support Wordsworth's perhaps willfully naïve project to reinvest experience with emotion. At the same time, he acknowledged a spontaneous emotional response that echoes the "pure heart" of his native tradition.

If this were all there was to be said about Doppo's representations of nature, he might be characterized as a modern writer who, despite difficulties, rather skillfully constructed a landscape to compensate for the fractured experience of everyday life. However, set against this aspect was an entirely different view of nature obtained during his trip to Hokkaido in 1895. Although long home to the native Ainu, from the perspective of mainland Japan it was a frontier wilderness region in the process of being "developed" under the auspices of the Meiji government. The famous exhortation "Boys, be ambitious!" of William Smith Clark (1826–86), a charismatic American educator who served for nine months beginning in July 1876 as the first president of Sapporo Agricultural College (now part of Hokkaido University), neatly captures its significance as an exciting arena of new possibility. By the time Doppo arrived, the successful pursuit of this ideal had become questionable, but Hokkaido nevertheless retained its allure as a site where he could entertain dreams of a better life with his wife.[46] In the event, his experiences there added a distinctive edge to his portrayals of the furusato.

Doppo recorded his visit in "Banks of the Sorachi River" ("Sorachigawa no kishibe," November and December 1902), which describes a disorienting space with none of the familiarity associated with sites near Tokyo. For one thing, the narrator's movements are governed by a search for an elusive government official surveying the Sorachi River, who will provide guidance on land for purchase. He eventually finds the official but only after several false leads. After reaching the settlement of Sorachibuto, for example, he is advised to go back to Utashinai, where it will be easier to cross the mountains in order to reach the river. This crossing requires the assistance of a guide, which indicates a degree of helplessness absent from "The Musashi Plain," in which the reader is advised that, should he ever come to a spot where the road branches, just "stand your stick upright and follow the direction in which it falls."[47] This northern territory is even out of joint in terms of season—it is necessary to wear winter clothes in September, a time when the summer heat normally lingered in the capital.

The kind of relationship he develops with nature here is very different from his other experiences. The stark and dreary prospect seen from the train window limits the possibility of engaging with this land: "A frightening power of nature overflowed through fields and mountains. No love or emotion was to be found here."[48] It is not surprising, then, that he is forced back into himself, unable to find common links with his fellow passengers in a way at all reminiscent of "Unforgettable People." He describes his own mood in the third person:

He could not help but feel that an unbridgeable ravine stretched out between himself and the others; so that the train cutting across the plain of Ishika with its burden of himself and the others appeared exactly like the progress of his own life. What solitude! Although he had stepped beyond society on a personal search for it, at heart he could not really endure the feelings of solitude.

"Unforgettable People" depicted lonely characters too, but at least they were integral to the scenes in which they appeared. In Hokkaido, by contrast, the "grandiose scenery" is beyond the human scale, even antagonistic, "laughing coldly at mankind's frailness and transiency."[49] This is, moreover, a deliberate quest in uncharted territory—no comforting "society in miniature" here—a "personal search" into an impersonal and bleak universe. He experiences another form of nature altogether, the "mysterious great nature," already identified in relation to Wordsworth, which allows none of the subtle melancholy pervading "The Musashi Plain"; a place, in short, where, in Takitō's words, "people go beyond melancholy to quiver in fear."[50]

But if, to take up Soja's words once more, this encounter between landscape and man articulates the "existential dimensions" of spatiality and social being, respectively, the new technological environment created by the railway supplies the third aspect of temporality informing Doppo's perception of nature. His emotional isolation is as tight and as enclosed as the small man-made box trundling over the great plain in which he is traveling, and his separation from the external scene is confirmed by the transparent barrier of the window that frames the awesome landscape passing before his eyes. Indeed, the very mode of transportation shapes, quite literally, how his presence is felt. On the way to Sorachibuto, "the train ran along a single track, cutting through the great forest, which had remained untouched since primitive times, where no human had set foot for thousands of years."[51] In his keenness to highlight the "untouched" aspects of the place, Doppo completely fails to acknowledge the presence of the native Ainu, a common failure among people seeking to lay claim to "virgin" territory. But even in his own terms, the way in which he "touches" the land is a new phenomenon. In the Musashi Plain, the stroller gained his pleasure by following a maze of old tracks whose haphazardness mirrored its very contours. By contrast, the railway cuts across the plain "as if drawn with a ruler. . . . As the natural irregularities of the terrain that were perceptible on the old roads are replaced by the sharp linearity of the railroad, the traveler feels that he has lost contact with the landscape."[52] For Doppo, the "old roads" were located on Musashi Plain, but the point remains that Hokkaido represents a site where contact between people and place is much diminished.

Of course, the rural-urban dichotomy complicates matters here: a writer claiming to aspire to the "natural" world finds the suburbs more comforting, and his encounter with raw nature is made possible through a new technology emanating from Tokyo. There is, however, no doubt that Hokkaido embodies a particularly chilling manifestation of nature. At the end of the line, the train reaches a tiny station and delivers the narrator into

a solitary island surrounded by forest. Apart from the two or three buildings attached to the station, there was no other link with mankind. As the long wail of the train whistle reverberated unbroken through the forest and faded into the distance, the solitary island reverted to an unspeakably desolate silence.[53]

Hokkaido stands totally outside the traditional lexicon of place-centered signification; for him it has no history, no memories, and the whistle's wail can obliterate that awful truth only temporarily. There are no recognizable landmarks. Its status as a site of absence is confirmed when the narrator books a small room at an inn in Sorachibuto. In deepest gloom, he watches as the forest trees outside are battered by the strong autumnal wind and rain:

At such a time and in such a place, without a single friend or anyone to talk with, there was no pleasure at all in watching the ceaseless autumn rain from the window of my inn. I happened to recall my parents and brothers and close friends in Tokyo and felt all the more keenly the warmth of human feelings that had enveloped me until today.[54]

Rainfall in woods was a positive experience in "The Musashi Plain," but this episode offers none of the compensatory intimacy Doppo was able to glean there. The cost he has to pay for his deliberate quest for individual solitude is acknowledged in a comparison of the two places:

In the past, I have encountered autumn rains in the deep woods of Hokkaido, rendered all the more fascinating by the fact that they are great forests completely devoid of human trace. On the other hand, they lack the tug (*omomuki*), like whispers, of the autumn rains of the Musashi Plain, which evoke the presence of people long gone.[55]

Thanks to the railway, he has gained access to a form of nature previously unknown to him, but it leads to a horrifying emptiness, quite literally, at the end of the line. Hokkaido stands for nothing; its landscape is blank. As he contemplates the autumn rains from his lonely room, traditional associations tempered with the "warmth of human feelings" linger only as a memory that confirms his present exclusion from that earlier tradition.

But it is precisely here, where the hollowness of the ties between man and landscape comes to the fore, that a clue emerges to the principles guiding Doppo's construction of his furusato. For if Hokkaido suggests a virtual denial of communication, it does highlight the impulse to bridge that gap—much as the narrator of "Unforgettable People" had recourse to sympathy—and *make* something of it. The other travelers encountered during his trip may represent new and individualistic speculators, "a kind of person who could appear for the first time only in Hokkaido,"[56] but their kindness in advising him where to go and whom to ask for information is the sign of an embryonic society, a first step in rendering the unknown known. Likewise, when the innkeeper relates how he came to live in Utashinai, this constitutes a rudimentary mapping out of a newly expanded national history, the creation of a network of "human feelings" specific to place. In the same way, Doppo's furusato has no identifiable basis; rather, it emerges as an insistent presence from disparate forms of "nature," literary memories, and fragments of personal experience.

Ports for the Storm

In the Introduction, I noted Tansman's useful warning against equating literary texts too directly with sociopolitical developments. It would be wrong to suggest that Doppo's impulse to write was driven primarily by a conscious desire to articulate a new national identity. However, as a literary figure sensitive to the ideological currents of his age, he could not help but join this important debate, albeit, to quote Tansman, in a "more abstract and troped way." A close reading of two of his furusato texts sheds light on the emerging Japanese consciousness, particularly in terms of the relationship between people and place.

In both "River Mist" and "Let Me Return," the transitory nature of the furusato is brought out by depicting it as a temporary haven. In "River Mist," a forty-year-old man returns to his native place after spending half his life unsuccessfully in Tokyo: "From the sea of hopeless failure, he had drifted ashore onto an island of hopeless security."[57] "Let Me Return" provides a more positive metaphor, at least at the beginning of the story: the main character, still only twenty-seven, is returning home by train from the capital for the first time in four years, filled with a quiet excitement as he moves toward the "small peaceful happy port" of home.[58] In different ways, these stories reveal both the potential and the limitations of Doppo's furusato writings.

In "River Mist," spacing in the original text suggests a division into three sections. In the first section, Ueda Toyokichi is given an enthusiastic farewell by local townspeople as he sets off for Tokyo. Like many other aspiring youths of the early Meiji, he is aiming at social success. The only sour note is sounded by an unpleasant old man called "Whiskers of the Cedar Grove" (*Sugi no mori no hige*), who has an uncanny ability to see into the future; he confidently predicts that Toyokichi will come back a failure. Sure enough, after various business-related struggles in the city, Toyokichi cuts his losses and returns home. The second section describes his hesitant reappearance in the town and his warm and sympathetic acceptance by his family and friends. He is delighted by their suggestion that he set up a private school for the local children and throws himself into the task, believing that, at long last, he has discovered a worthwhile role in life. In the third section, on the very night before the school-opening ceremony, he comes across Whisker's grave and suddenly feels unable to complete the task. The story ends with him boarding an unmanned boat docked on the riverbank. He drifts off toward the sea, bathed in moonlight and enticed by a beckoning mist.

The significant features of the furusato become clearer in the second section, which first describes Toyokichi's first impressions upon returning and then depicts his attempts to reintegrate himself into local life. In the first part, the furusato is nostalgically evoked through the eyes of an observer who no longer quite belongs. It is the site of a slightly unreal experience: "He began to stroll around and pursued old fragmented memories as if walking through a dreamscape."[59] He experiences a certain enjoyment in revisiting the memories that sustained him during the long and difficult years in Tokyo. Noticing a well-kept garden in an old schoolmate's house, for instance, he feels satisfaction in his friend's success. And he knows instinctively that a boy carrying a fishing rod is going to the nearby river, where he, too, passed idyllic youthful days.

On the other hand, the pleasure he derives from the furusato gains substance through a tension between the prospect of what is desirable and an inability to engage with it fully. Upon his arrival, Toyokichi hides away from prying eyes in a grove as he tries to muster the courage to announce his arrival: he sees the boy with the fishing rod from behind a wall where he has nervously placed himself. In fact, even if the sensations engendered in Toyokichi are generally pleasant, the separation between observer and scene here is as complete as that found in "Banks of the Sorachi River" when the narrator views the natural landscape from the train window. Toyokichi plays out an impulse to try to enter this ultimately unattainable world when, seeing the boy pass by, he "could not help but follow him, concentrating all the time on the shadow cast by the youth. Although he was about twenty paces distant, in reality it was a distance of thirty years. Toyokichi was confronted by a clear vision of his former self."[60] This double view is available only to someone walking through a "dreamscape"; the boy is both a person in his own right and a visual projection of the older man when young. By retreading the path to the river, Toyokichi may revive a much-loved experience of thirty years earlier, but he also confronts his separation by that same distance of time.

Yet this separation does not entirely preclude the potential for the initially hesitant Toyokichi to insert himself further into the landscape. In narrative terms, the function of the boy with the rod is to lead him to a group of young friends fishing at the riverside, but the possibility of a more intimate connection with the scene emerges when the physical appearance of one of the other boys leads him to surmise—rightly as it turns out—that he has found his elder brother's son. Significantly, he does not reveal himself immediately but lingers at a distance in order to savor the furusato in the most graphic of terms. The nephew is fishing with the other boys:

A short distance from the boy, a traveler, sitting against a willow stump, his clothes and expression indicating his reduced circumstances and weariness, watches the youth as if in a dream. Further upstream above the willow, he sees how the stone wall of the distant hilltop castle has crumbled. Early autumn, and the air is pristine clear, the sunlight absolutely brilliant. This picture! How deeply meaningful it is.[61]

Although the "traveler" has a place of sorts within the scene, his isolated location makes him a witness, in contrast to the boy, who is completely integral to Toyokichi's long-remembered vision of the native place. Moreover, the boy's obliviousness to his own "meaning" for the older man associates him with the "people-as-landscapes" in "Unforgettable People." In any case, this lyrical high point in the text encapsulates the essential desirability of the furusato. On the other hand, if the "picture" gains vivid clarity through the lens of Toyokichi's bitter experience in Tokyo and his much-enhanced nostalgic evocation, it also keeps the newly returned man irretrievably on the outside, since his appreciation is dependent on a visual image as framed and as distanced as a Hokkaido landscape seen through a train window.

The only possible way into this landscape is through a reconfiguration in which dreamscape gives way to reality and history reasserts itself. A fundamental change takes place when Toyokichi engages the boy in conversation and reveals himself as his long-departed uncle: "The youth's face changed color, and he threw down his rod. Then, without saying anything, he dashed off to the old mansion where he lived."[62] At a stroke, Toyokichi's earlier fanciful projection of his own experiences onto the boys is no longer admissible, since each character, including himself, is now revealed as a separate being with its own history relative to the place. A positive aspect of this change is that he can reaffirm himself as a living presence in the genealogy of his family. But as he does so, the furusato as an idealized site becomes unsustainable. For once his covert presence is common knowledge, the privacy of his vision is undermined, and he becomes visible to the local inhabitants and equally susceptible to their scrutiny. While he laments that the pretty girls he used to court are now married with children, they see him as pathetically aged. If the furusato embodies all that Toyokichi lacked during his dark years in Tokyo, participation in its real life involves a loss; indeed, his final failure suggests he returned to a barren land.

Doppo's depiction of the furusato as incapable of compensating fully for the disappointment of city life arises not only through this conflation of landscape and history but also through the personality of the character himself. Toyokichi is described as a good man, with talents,

but he lacked staying power (*kon ga nai*), or, rather, he had quite a bit of staying power but there seemed to be something shadowy (*kage no usui*) about him, and he never quite hit the mark whatever he did. . . . Toyokichi was a good man, passionate. But, being timorous—fainthearted might be a better word—he was essentially like a sea anemone.[63]

Toyokichi's lack of "staying power" (literally, "he did not have a root") hints at the rootlessness experienced by the author, but Yamada Hiromitsu notes that a positive attribute of the sea anemone is precisely its ability to stick fast to a rock while awaiting the arrival of food, just as the premodern rural peasantry were characterized by hardy perseverance in times of adversity.[64] It was this very stubbornness that empowered Toyokichi and allowed him to survive so long on memories of home. However, in the modern world, where only more aggressive personalities thrive, such passive virtues no longer suffice. This helps explain the image of the shadow in the passage quoted above and elsewhere in the text. When Toyokichi trails the boy with the fishing rod, his attention is fixed on the boy's shadow; and, on the fateful night he decides to abandon his native place, he is depicted as pensively walking along, "following his own shadow."[65] Despite his attempt to reconnect with the "real" native place, it remains essentially intangible, a site where only shadows are pursued.

In short, Doppo's "River Mist" portrays a furusato that is less than ideal, that promises more than it can deliver. Toyokichi, his "well of vitality" (*seikon no izumi*) dried up,[66] simply has no roots left to put down. Takitō remarks that, although the metaphor of a port indicates an opportunity to replenish one's energy before setting off again, it is debatable whether this hero has enough energy left to leave his "island of security."[67] In the event, he does act, but only passively, by allowing himself to be carried away by the river. Doppo may generally have been torn between the attractions of society and the "natural" world, but here at least the final choice is to abandon the complications of human life, even those associated with the furusato, and give himself up to "mysterious great nature."

At forty-five pages in the standard *Collected Works*, "Let Me Return" is almost four times the length of "River Mist," and not surprisingly, in it Doppo offers a more complex version of the furusato. It is a love story centered around a young man, Yoshioka Mineo. Although returning to the native place ostensibly to visit his father's grave, his main purpose is to sound out a young local woman, Ogawa Aya, about the possibility of marriage. Upon arriving home, he is surprised and a little suspicious to hear from his aunt, now living in the family home, that a Japanese of his own age and resident in Korea is staying at the lodge attached to the Ogawa house, where Mineo had intended to spend the summer. Only after the visitor leaves can he move in. Once settled, Mineo and the younger members of the Ogawa family visit an offshore coral island, Kanade no iso, where they used to play as children, and Mineo finally has an opportunity to speak to Aya alone for the first time. Although interested in his suggestion that she come back with him to Tokyo, she hints that there are problems. Just then, Gorō, an orphan brought up in the Ogawa house, rudely interrupts their intimate talk, which clearly angers Aya. Mineo is plagued with doubts about her feelings and lies alone at night in a boat by the seashore. His solitude is disturbed by a drunken Gorō, who reveals that Aya is promised to the man from Korea and makes rude insinuations about her. The two fight, and the next morning Mineo abruptly leaves, distraught that he has lost his chance. He travels round the region for two weeks and drinks himself into a stupor in an attempt to forget his misery. When he returns to bid his aunt farewell and go back to Tokyo, he is horrified to hear that Aya is dead.

The Ogawas made another trip to the coral island, this time with the man from Korea, who had returned to finalize the wedding plans. When the weather suddenly turned bad, the party decided to return to shore. As Gorō was helping Aya into the boat, it rocked violently, and the two slipped into the sea and drowned. Mineo is unsure about the truth of this account and visits Aya's grave with her sister. She reveals that Aya had always been the first to read his letters from Tokyo but began to doubt his intentions when he did not return the year before. She felt she had no choice but to accept her father's plans for her marriage, especially since Gorō had been making unwanted advances for the past year. It was only when she and Mineo had recently spoken on the island that she appreciated his true intent, but it was too late. Convinced that Gorō engineered both their deaths deliberately, the devastated Mineo returns to Tokyo.

This bare outline does not do justice to the wide variety of approaches employed by Doppo to articulate the promise, and ultimate failure, of the furusato. If nature in "The Musashi Plain" emerged from views drawn partly from outside the tradition, the same is true of the native place during Mineo's first week stay with his aunt. He eats lunch and, forgoing his siesta, climbs a nearby hill that gives the best prospect of the surrounding area. Intoxicated by the beauty and peacefulness he knew as a child, he settles down to read Samuel Johnson's *The History of Rasselas* (1759), an English text in use at the time in Tokyo schools:

I read on and on, and before I knew it I forgot I was in my own valley, and my mind was wending its way through that happy valley in Abyssinia. Was it such a good thing that even young ones living in the happy valley followed their blood's urge to flow out in search of an even happier plain? Caught up in these thoughts, I realized that Johnson's pen had seized me unawares, but not in an unpleasant way; it was more like an untrammeled view of the spring sea, or mist. Thus, I forgot the passage of time.[68]

Johnson's story describes how Rasselas, a prince of Abyssinia, is brought up in a spacious valley cut off from the outside world by steep mountains, with the only way out firmly barred. The valley is rich in vegetation and animal life, and all the prince's needs are catered for by musicians and dancers. When Rasselas reaches twenty-six, however, he feels discontented with his perfect home and, together with his sister and a guide, tunnels out through the mountain side in order to explore the "real" world with all its blemishes and hardships. After several years, having failed to find an answer to life's problems from the various sages he meets, he finally concludes that the "happy valley" is as good as any other place to fulfill his wishes. The implication is that Mineo, after several years in the debilitating environment of Tokyo, might equally well seek self-fulfillment in his native home.

The contents of this foreign text imply a shift in thinking about the native place. Although Mineo is thrilled to re-experience the surrounding prospect, which reminds him of his happy childhood, his view is profoundly shaped by his western learning; a view so naturalized, in fact, that he compares its effect to the "spring sea, or mist." There is some irony in his expression of anxiety about separation from the furusato and the desirability of its rediscovery through a western story, but this indicates the extent to which "foreign" and "native" views had become blurred. In an article published in 1897, Doppo elaborated on the significance of the hilltop experience:

Although the sun was sinking slightly in the west, this was precisely the time at summer's peak when the sun was at its hottest. The wind appeared to die down, while the cicadas slept. Overwhelmed by light, the grass and trees became dispirited and faded at their core. Ah, where is the happy valley? At that moment a single clear thought entered my heart like a breath of wind. The happy land I am thinking about, it's here! Here in this place where I am reading a book shaded by trees on a summer's day. This sun should never sink, this sun should keep going for ever.[69]

This article reinforces the desire that the moment should "keep going for ever," and in "Let Me Return," Mineo allows himself the pleasant illusion of stepping outside history to "forget the passage of time." But in reality the sun always does sink, and things change over time. The characteristics of the furusato strike Mineo so sharply upon his return precisely because he lives in Tokyo. But other factors beyond his personal experience challenge his preferred vision of a native place isolated from the shifting realities of the outside world. Aya's family has business dealings with Korea, and 70 percent of the men from a nearby island are working there.[70] Moreover, Mineo's lament that people are tempted to leave their home in search of "an even happier plain" is prompted by an earlier conversation with Unosuke, a villager his own age, who reveals he might follow friends and relatives to work in Hawaii.[71] In other words, Mineo may envisage a perfect furusato in the fullness of the moment, but, as Rasselas found, it gains meaning only against the background of its potential loss and eventual recovery over time.

Just as in "River Mist," the wistful vision in "Let Me Return" of a timeless native place is set against the inevitable intrusion of history. In fact, both texts should be read as part of contemporary literary currents in which "furusato literature" was an important element. To clarify this, it is worthwhile to compare Koshoshi's *Returning Home*, the first example of the genre, with Doppo's own approach to the subject. Koshoshi and Doppo shared similar personal histories. Both came from the provinces and took courses in politics at the Tokyo senmon gakkō, and each developed a strong interest in Christianity to compensate for their disappointment with the *risshin shusse* ideal. This religious element led them to participate in Tokutomi Sōhō's Min'yūsha, with its egalitarian approach to political, social, and economic matters. In April 1897, they also collaborated with Tayama Katai and Yanagita Kunio, among others, in a poetry collection entitled *Lyrical Poems (Jojōshi)*, which drew on Wordsworth in a deliberate challenge to the Ken'yūsha's representations of nature, although the collection's significance was eclipsed by Tōson's groundbreaking *Young Leaves* (*Wakanashū*), which came out in August of the same year. Given these common interests, it is probably inevitable that Doppo's literary portrayal of the furusato should echo Koshoshi's work.

On the other hand, Kitano Akihiko notes how different childhood experiences contributed to distinct Romantic evaluations of the furusato. If Doppo's early life was characterized by constant movement, Koshoshi's sense of home was firmly rooted in the wealthy Kyushu household in which he grew up. As a result, Doppo drew on his Yamaguchi years, but essentially he yearned to escape his present difficulties by articulating a freer but as yet unrealized world, whereas Koshoshi attempted to recapture the native place he actually knew.[72] Koshoshi's narrator returns to a safe and comfortable environment still inhabited by friends and family, whose actions confirm a warm, loving community in contrast to his experience of Tokyo. Things even go well in his encounter with his lover. Togawa makes a more subtle distinction when he suggests that the value of Koshoshi's *Returning Home* is not in its articulation of a simple "country = good, city = bad" formula, which was in any case becoming a commonplace among urban youths of the time. Indeed, the narrator knows that his role is now largely that of an outsider—the locals treat him as a source of fascinating information about the progress of civilization (*bunmei*) in the city—and the furusato can be enjoyed only through an urban perspective as a consciously aestheticized construction. Nevertheless, it still provides a continuing source of consolation when life in the city becomes unbearable. For Doppo, on the other hand, the betrayal of the initial promise of the furusato makes his characters outsiders and renders them uncomfortable; in the end, they have no option but to leave.[73]

Compared to Doppo's, Koshoshi's depiction shows a greater concern with details of a native place based on real experience, but this does not preclude him from drawing on a wider literary context. Apart from references to Johnson and Chinese poets, he quoted from Laozi and the *Book of Songs* (*Shijing*) and alludes to the Japanese tale of Urashima Tarō.[74] The Christian element is particularly strong. The narrator describes the experience of city life in terms of having tasted the forbidden fruit of knowledge, which now excludes him from re-entry into his "Eden."[75] Section Two even likens his first moment back home, when he jumps from his carriage to kiss the ground, to an arrival in the holy city of Bethlehem. Koshoshi's main interest is to revive youthful experiences that reconfirm a strong sense of self-identity related to place; these extra references add layers to his literary landscape. In that sense the effect is somewhat reminiscent of Doppo's collage-like construction of the Musashi Plain.

In "Let Me Return," Doppo likewise gives further depth to his *furusato* by drawing on other literary sources. His high evaluation of the rural life as the site of a "happy valley" specifically relates to Johnson, although it is more generally reminiscent of Wordsworth. He also shares Koshoshi's strong interest in the poetry of Tao Yuanming (365–427), best known for his prose story "Peach Blossom Spring" ("Tao hua yuan ji"). It tells the story of a fisherman who follows a stream through a blossoming peach grove until he arrives at a small cave-like opening. He passes through it to discover a completely isolated rural utopia created by a group of people who abandoned the conflicts of the outside world six hundred years earlier. Having revealed its marvels to him, the friendly inhabitants permit him to leave, on condition that he never disclose its location. When he attempts to return at a later point, he cannot find the entrance. The theme struck a chord with various Japanese writers over the ages. One Edo period example is Suzuki Bokushi's (1770–1842) *Trip to Akiyama* (*Akiyama kikō*), which describes the narrator's search for a similarly fabulous place.[76]

"Let Me Return" resembles this Chinese tale in some respects but not in all. Whereas in the Chinese work the fisherman's passage through the cave is relatively brief, Mineo experiences a long and complicated journey from a crowded Shinbashi railway station in Tokyo to his quiet family home. Two trains take him as far as Hiroshima; he then travels by boat through the Inland Sea to Yanaizu and walks over the Taburogi pass. In both cases, however, physical movement describes a clear shift from one world to another. In addition, the same Daoist element that informed Tao Yuanming's philosophy of life is evoked by Mineo. Delighted to have left the city and its pressures, he reflects: "I have emerged from bustling reality into a peaceful world of dream; or perhaps one might say that I have suddenly awoken from some unreliable, oppressive dream and returned to the calm, long days of the real world."[77] This must be a reference to Zhuangzi's famous anecdote of a man who dreams he is a butterfly only to awaken and wonder if he is a butterfly dreaming that he is a man.

Doppo also picks up the strong pastoral element in Tao's work, in which the cave opens onto a broad plain "where houses and huts stood neatly, with rich fields and lovely ponds, mulberries, bamboos, and the like. The field dykes crisscrossed; chickens and dogs could be heard from farm to farm."[78] The same natural abundance is apparent in Doppo's text. When Mineo has almost reached home, he sees a view of lush, green paddy fields and is informed by a farmer that there will be an "exceptional harvest."[79] Doppo demonstrates his attraction to the pictorial aspect of the pastoral as Mineo, after drinking from a well surrounded by a grape arbor, pauses to look around:

A family of chickens emerged from the grove, guided by the lordly cock. The cicadas emitted their shrill and resolute cries from grove and hills. Little by little, the sun began to blaze. I looked up to see the sky was high and clear today, and intensely blue, blue the color of deep azure. Ah, summer! It really is summer! I felt my body well up with overflowing good health.[80]

If Tao created a utopia in which "history's temporal course is replaced by Nature's timeless cycle now running undisturbed,"[81] Doppo also eulogizes a seasonal high point when all things come together, held in a perfect moment.

But the Chinese poet's personal experiences reveal a more specific connection with Doppo. Also living at a time of great social and political unrest, Tao assumed public office on several occasions in order to involve himself in the defense of his state against foreign invaders. Like Doppo, however, he was torn between the conflicting attractions of society and those of a quieter, "natural" life. His increasing sense that public engagement was futile led him to retire and return to his rural retreat. Doppo's indebtedness to the

Chinese poet is revealed in the title of his own work, which he borrowed from the opening line of one of Tao's poems on the theme of returning home:

> Let me return!
> My farmstead will soon be overgrown with weeds:
>   why not return?
> It was I who made my heart my body's slave;
> Why should I be dismayed and grieve in solitude?
> I realize the past cannot be helped,
> But I know the future may still be regained.

The subtext of this poem suggests why Doppo's title was particularly apt. The poem was written to commemorate what Charles Kwong describes as the "key decision of [Tao's] life": he finally realized that a commitment to public service was no longer viable and that his only option was to retreat so as "to preserve his integrity."[82] Although Doppo's story was written in 1901, it is loosely based on his return to Yamaguchi in 1891, after he had withdrawn from university and was considering the rural option as an answer to problems identified with city life. Mineo in effect articulates the author's struggle at the time. His appreciation of *Rasselas* leads him to a more general consideration of his "future" life:

Isn't true freedom itself the real promised land? Is not true freedom first obtained by people like me who, having made some preparation in their heart, take up the pastoral life (*den'en no seikatsu*)? I have property, which means I am free of cares about food and clothing. I am fond of reading, which means I have comfort for my spirit. I am surrounded by nature, which means there is a pasture for both mind and body. These are all gifts given to me from Heaven (*ten*), so why should I suffer by throwing them away and settle for flinging myself willingly into city life? "For the sake of work," "to carry out one's duty," "for national profit and private wealth," "for the sake of humanity": these may be true enough. . . . But don't let yourself be bound by a fine reputation! Do I enjoy city life without any sense of being bound? No, not at all! I am nothing but a slave to vanity, a servant of extravagant play.[83]

The call for personal "freedom" and the references to "spirit," "pasture," and "Heaven" point to a Christian influence, but his desire to reject his self-imposed "slave" mentality in favor of the "pastoral life" reflects that of Tao. Here Doppo is seriously weighing the furusato as a response to the slogans of an earlier Meiji generation and finding them hollow. And yet, it was this desire for individual liberty against the background of continuing traditional restrictions that contributed to the new Japanese identity during Meiji.

In the event, Tao took the step of returning home and, more important, staying there for the rest of his life. But if Doppo toyed with the same idea through Mineo, his text also spells out why such an impulse was not viable. When visiting relatives in a neighboring village, Mineo suggests he might come back to live in his native home, but they advise him to give up these foolish thoughts; the fact is, all the village youth are trying to get to Tokyo.[84] And, in a conversation with Aya's father, who similarly dismisses the idea out of hand, he is reminded that his learning (*gakumon*) separates him from the local men who cannot be successful in the wider world (*shusse*). The older man may be using the rhetoric of an earlier period that no longer resonates with Mineo, but the point remains that, like the youth in Koshoshi's text, he has eaten of the fruit of knowledge and can never be fully accepted back home. It might be more correct to say that, from the beginning, there never was a place for him to return to. Like Koshoshi, Tao was at least able to center his pastoral fantasies on a distilled version of farm life he grew up with, but for Doppo the native place essentially remained an imaginary site, even if he experienced some approximation of it for a few years.

There are serious questions, then, surrounding the extent to which Doppo was able to embrace the furusato in his literature, and these problems pervade his general sense of identity in the modern world. While Mineo still had hope, he told Aya's father that if things did not go well in the city, "I can always wipe the dust straight away from my feet and come back to my native place,"[85] but Aya's death destroys that illusion along with his future well-being. Mineo finds himself at dusk standing heartbroken outside an empty junior high school in Yamaguchi, where he had spent several happy years. His only option is to return to the city and start again. For Doppo, it seems, the furusato is at best a temporary retreat. In tracing a fundamentally unstable relationship with place, his texts highlight this restless impulse toward constant reinvention as a defining characteristic of his generation.

The Heart of Unfulfillment

In "Let Me Return," the ideal furusato is portrayed as brimming with sensuality and the fullness of life. However, its vitality depends entirely on Mineo's imaginative faculty, in stark contrast to his experience of daily life in Tokyo and its environment of uncompromising harshness that seems to preclude creativity. This chapter concludes with an examination of Doppo's furusato literature from a different angle, namely, the modern crisis in language itself. My aim is not only to highlight the fundamental problem of trying to reconstitute the native place through text, but also to relate the literary process to an evolving national identity.

I am certainly not the first to point out that one of the main areas of literary interest in Meiji was the contentious relationship between language and representations of reality. Karatani has written on the essentially modern consciousness in Meiji that perceived tensions between the spoken and the written language and sought to bridge the gap between the two.[86] Of greater interest in the present context, however, is his attention to Doppo's use of the term "membrane" (*maku*), since it helps to conceptualize the idea of one side separated from the other and permits more general observations about the relationship between people and environment. Karatani quotes from Doppo's short story "Death" ("Shi," 1898), in which a friend's suicide forces the protagonist to ponder the physiological process of dying:

While I was thinking about these things, I developed a feeling that I was enclosed in a kind of membrane. It struck me that my perceptions of all aspects of reality were somehow separated by a single layer of skin. Even now, my anguished self firmly believes that if I cannot confront facts and all aspects of creation face to face, directly, then "god" and "beauty" and "truth" amount to nothing more than a kind of game in which illusions are pursued. This is all I believe.[87]

The same metaphor appears at the end of "River Mist": Toyokichi, about to set off down the river to the sea, feels that nothing more than a "single half-transparent membrane" separates himself from his deceased friends.[88]

Karatani's main concern is to argue that "interiority" emerged in mid-Meiji. He begins by citing Jean Starobinski's suggestion that Jean-Jacques Rousseau privileged self-consciousness (in the form of the inner voice) as the only kind of knowledge that was immediate and therefore "transparent" to oneself. Everything else, including writing and even speaking (seen as secondary to the inner voice), is a derivative and opaque phenomenon best characterized by the word "obscurity."[89] In Karatani's view, Doppo's "membrane" is analogous to the separation between "obscurity" and the transparent self and was instrumental in the Meiji "discovery of interiority."

But it is also possible to understand this membrane as a metaphor for the problematic relationship between man and landscape. In the train journey across Hokkaido, for instance, the young man's despair arises from a deep sense of gloomy isolation predicated on the intervening window (membrane) that precludes full contact with the exterior world. The natural landscape of Hokkaido may be less than inviting, but this membrane denies the possibility of knowing "god," "truth," or "beauty." It is precisely this sense of frustrating isolation that informs a conventional understanding of the loneliness of the modern individual, and this is an important reason behind Karatani's and others' identification of Doppo as one of Japan's first modern writers.

On the other hand, although the membrane suggests an unbridgeable distance, it can also function in a more dynamic manner. Mineo's experience of city life leads him to feel no longer part of the native place, but the very language of his response belies the complete lack of fulfillment he overtly expresses. As Mineo and Aya's father enjoy a drink to celebrate his first night back at the Ogawa household, the young man laments that "in Tokyo, it is simply not possible to relax and feel the touch of the sea breeze, to take your time over a drink and speak from the heart, not even if, like now, it has become late."[90] Mineo speaks the truth in a practical sense, and it is precisely because he no longer has daily contact with the native place that he sings its praises at such enormous length during his temporary visit. Yet the impulse to lovingly describe its attractions would not have arisen without the previous separation. The young men who have never left are indifferent to the place where they live. By contrast, just as the intensity of Toyokichi's charged vision of the boy fishing in "River Mist" depends almost entirely on his position as a virtual outsider, Mineo's long separation drives him to reproduce the native place through language. At a more conceptual level, the separating membrane implies a creative tension by which lack itself engenders production. To put it in a different way, language comes forcefully into existence to make something out of nothing, to fill a void. Likewise, it is this play between plenitude and lack that leads Doppo to associate the membrane with the equally pivotal contrast between life and death.

It is also possible to trace the productive aspects of this metaphor along a more literal trajectory by considering the native place as synonymous with the *natal* place; that is, to envisage the membrane as a womb-like protective cover, intimately linked to the reproductive process of birth itself. A Chinese parallel can be found in Tao's "Peach Blossom Spring"; Hirakawa Sukehiro suggests that the physical shapes of the secret cave and enclosed plain of the fertile rural utopia recall an erotic or maternal image in their resemblance to the female uterus and womb.[91] In the Japanese context, Jennifer Robertson cites the term *ofukuro* (which she translates "bag lady")—an affectionate expression for mother used almost exclusively by males—as useful when outlining links between native place and the maternal image, since both concepts suggest themselves as "repositories" of traditional values. She goes on to emphasize the gender implications of the term, which she sees as

a throwback to the historical reference to women as *ohara*, or "womb ladies," indicative of a belief in procreation as a monogenetic phenomenon—that is, the belief that the male role is the generative and creative one, and that the male alone is responsible for the identity and subjectivity of a child. Female bodies, literally and figuratively, are the containers for male-identified "babies," from human infants to things such as values and ideologies. In this context, native place-making is a "recuperative project": a paternalistic attempt to reconstruct an authentic, ontologically secure past in which is prefigured the shape of the future.[92]

Robertson's specific concern is the nostalgic, postwar creation of furusato-like sites, but her comments can be related to the ongoing reconfiguration of patriarchal authority since Meiji.

There is evidence of this maternal aspect in the stories of both Doppo and Koshoshi. In "Let Me Return," for example, Mineo explicitly sees the native place as a site that has nurtured him from birth. At the end of his long journey home, he walks down a narrow path through rice fields to a small valley surrounded on three sides by hills—perhaps another symbolic uterus and womb—and describes it as "the cradle (*yōran*) in which I was brought up. At the foot of the hill at the back of the valley, the white surface of a residence with walls built from stone received the direct sunlight. It was the house in which I was born."[93] Doppo's very positive identification of the land itself as a "cradle" may in part be compensation for his anxiety over his own origins. However, both he and Koshoshi undoubtedly seem far more interested in portraying mothers than fathers, who in both stories are already dead before the narrative begins. In a study of Koshoshi's *Returning Home*, Maeda Ai describes how the youth's initial stay with his mother is followed by a further trip back to the village where his grandmother still lives. This progression is likened to tracing the family tree, but only on the maternal side, an almost exclusive interest in the feminine underlined by numerous allusions to water and moonlight throughout the story.[94] Yamada Hiromitsu has sought to place the attractions of such an environment in the context of modern life by describing the site of the childhood home as "a twilight world related to memories of the period when one was young, a world that has broken loose in order to confront the reality of modernity pressing in like waves."[95] The fact that Koshoshi depicted his real native place strongly supports the argument that we should read his furusato literature as a longing for the remembered "womb," as well as a fundamental search for the source of life. Even Doppo successfully creates a "twilight world" that functions as a shelter, providing a familiar and protective landscape, at least until the fantasy is shattered by Aya's death.

Both writers, then, may be described as drawn to the ideal of a womb-like furusato surrounded by a protective membrane. Yet they differ in the way they work out this attraction. The image adheres most closely to Koshoshi's text in the sense that the native place he recovered has been a known quantity from the very beginning; relatively speaking, it engenders less conflict and has no need of further development. Doppo's work, in contrast, is driven by a dynamic restlessness; consequently the membrane as a barrier against the intrusive world becomes problematized. In concrete terms, both writers describe young men returning home for the sake of love, but the tragic outcome in Doppo's story requires that another resolution beyond the furusato be considered. Moreover, whereas Koshoshi's youth is welcomed home by a mother's embrace, Mineo must make do with his aunt, since his mother now resides in Tokyo, thus compounding an unresolved gulf between city and native place.

For Doppo, the membrane is less an impermeable barrier between fixed environments than a site of potential movement, figuratively speaking, from one side to the other. The journey down the river in "River Mist" may be seen to evoke the passage down the uterus, the very moment of birth, which promises that the "half-transparent membrane" will finally rupture and allow Toyokichi to be fully reunited with his friends, albeit in another realm. "Let Me Return" offers a solution still connected to this life although equally transformative. Mineo's sense of utter desolation forces him to reassess the most fundamental impulses that validate his continuing engagement with the world: "Struggle! That's right, human fate boils down to struggle. Struggle itself is human fate. Let us go on. Let tomorrow come, tomorrow!"[96] With the promise of the furusato now destroyed, Mineo's only option is to contemplate himself in an as-yet-unrealized form, seeking his own reproduction through language by a powerful act of will.

Edward Said's comments on Joseph Conrad's articulation of a western crisis of confidence in the powers of language are relevant to the representation of the unrepresentable in Doppo's literary furusato.[97] For Said, Conrad shared a common concern with Nietzsche, Marx, and Freud in attempting to reveal the duplicity of language. It was precisely because of his outstanding command of language that Conrad was forced to confront its limitations and discover that "the chasm between words saying and words meaning was widened, not lessened, by a talent for words written." A similar anxiety about the deficiencies of language is outlined in Doppo's posthumously published *The Wretchedness of Isolation* (*Koritsu no hisan*, 1912), in which he lamented our mistaken belief that we are more capable of communication than the rest of the animal world:

The birds and beasts have no words; so that they lack the minimum means of relating their thoughts to one another. This is even more true of plant life. And yet the truth is that people, too, for the most part lack this means. One of the imperfections in people is the actual deficiency of such a means.

What isolation! And yet people have created society. The isolated element and the social element of people have not yet come together. People remain isolated while they live in communities. They deal with each other, while things that cannot possibly be understood by others remain tucked away in their hearts. In their exchanges of words, people deal with others, while cherishing things that it is impossible to express. What misery! Most misery in the world arises from this deficiency, made even worse by the fact that people are not aware of it.[98]

According to Said, Conrad's perception of words as a powerful medium that ultimately fails to deliver amounts to "the alternation in language of presence and absence." This expression resonates closely with the Japanese writer's attention to the equally contradictory poles of life and death. Doppo's anxiety about the efficacy of language is reflected in "Let Me Return," where Mineo's only option is to engage in similar "exchanges of words" as he attempts to substantiate the lost furusato, an endeavor that, perversely, confirms the impossibility of its full expression.

Moments of linguistic impasse that reveal an inability to get exactly to the point are to be found in the works of both Conrad and Doppo. In Conrad's *Heart of Darkness*, Marlow travels into the

African interior in search of the mysterious figure Kurtz. Said notes how the narrative takes the shape of a series of approaches to and radiations from the "center," that is, the narrator constantly draws the reader toward a central point—the center of Africa, the central truth—with the intimation that all will be eventually revealed. However, the closer the center, the fewer the words available to describe it: "Hence the eerie power in Conrad of minimal but hauntingly reverberating phrases like 'the horror' or 'material interests': these work as a sort of still point, a verbal center glossed by the narrative and on which our attention turns and returns." The reader is borne along on a narrative flow like the winds of a hurricane, only to find that at the very core—the hurricane's eye, as it were—language loses its capacity to carry us forward. A somewhat similar operation takes place in Doppo's "Unforgettable People," in which the narrator encounters the man on the island, the singing youth with his horse-drawn carriage, and the monk playing his lute. In each case, although the reader is invited to pause and observe them, and despite the fact that Otsu gains some kind of communion with these three through a sympathetic understanding, in the final analysis none of the characters can be fully known; we can only, quite literally, read *about* them before moving on to the next encounter. Such moments fascinate and hold us temporarily, but do not entirely satisfy.

The "heart" of Conrad's *Heart of Darkness* ultimately remains unspoken. And in a similar fashion, the process by which Doppo delineates the furusato in his texts highlights perpetual contradictions; of presence and absence, satisfaction and denial, life and death. But if sympathy is one way by which Doppo tries to bridge the gap, Takitō also suggest that the writer's earlier belief system centered around an ideal of sincerity gradually shifted toward an interest in wonder (*kyōi*) as a means of experiencing reality more directly.[99] To this end, he deliberately sought out moments that recaptured the freshness of a child's first encounter with the world. In "Unforgettable People," the fish market where the monk plays his lute is drenched in sunshine so that "extra light was thrown on everything with color in it, which made the congested scene even gayer." Otsu suggests why his senses should be so heightened:

"Since I was simply a traveler and had no ties or affinity with this place, I did not know anyone or recognize anyone's bald head. As a result, the sights before me somehow created a strange feeling, and I sensed that I was watching a world made more vivid than normal."[100] The "strange feeling" arises because, if only for a moment, the dulling of sensation concomitant with adulthood fades away to re-create the childhood condition associated by Doppo with a "face to face" experience of truth and beauty, an experience he had despaired of ever regaining.

Strictly speaking, "Unforgettable People" does not address the furusato, but the same principle applies in "Let Me Return," in which place is frequently described in terms of visceral sensations tied to childhood memories—the blue summer skies, the cicadas' cry, the "exquisite fragrance of mushrooms"[101]—in confirmation of what Takitō calls a "return to the furusato of existence." However, most important for an understanding of the furusato in the modern context is the fact that, whether the locale in question is Hokkaido or the native place proper, Doppo's characters are obliged to travel in order to overcome the ennui of the familiar and seek out these new experiences. This fluidity recalls details of the writer's life, in which inner restlessness contributed so much to the shape of his furusato. It also suggests links with representations of nature in "The Musashi Plain," which emerge from a conscious process of selection driven by need. There is, in short, nothing natural about the native place.

How, then, may the struggle for linguistic expression be placed in the context of an emerging national identity? Doppo may have, as Karatani asserts, been the first to articulate his "discovery" of an individual modern interiority through the transparency of an inner voice, but this soon became a *common* practice. Likewise, Doppo and his fellow writers were equally engaged in trying to make sense of the "obscurity" of the external world in which they found themselves by constructing what Clifford Geertz describes as "maps" of social reality, and the literary reproduction of the furusato served as a useful map to address this need. The concept of the native place as natal place also overlapped with an interpretation of the Japanese sense of self in a broader context. In "Let Me Return,"

Mineo's praise of the "cradle" that nurtured him goes beyond individual memory. Rather, it confirms Anthony Smith's suggestion that any national landscape must be seen to constitute the historic cradle of the people as a whole.

Some comments by Liah Greenfeld on the western genealogy of the term "nation" shed further light on the process by which a shared self-consciousness initially restricted to a literary elite evolved into a more general bond of national consciousness. Her concern is with the embryonic history of the term before it developed its more familiar connotations, but the word carries traces of previous incarnations even when translated into the Japanese context. It originated from the Latin *natio*, meaning "something born," and for a long time its primary implication remained derogatory: "In Rome the name *natio* was reserved for groups of foreigners coming from the same geographical region, whose status—because they were foreigners—was below that of Roman citizens." In the Middle Ages, this sense of a group of foreigners coming together was extended to denote temporary student communities from loosely affiliated regions of western Christendom. For example, students at the University of Paris from England and Germany were considered members of the "nation de Germaine"; the term ceased to be relevant to them once they had completed their studies and returned home. During the period of their study, however, the derogatory connotation took on a more positive tone: "Owing to the specific structure of university life at the time, the communities of students functioned as support groups or unions and, as they regularly took sides in scholastic disputations, also developed common opinions. As a result, the word 'nation' came to mean more than a community of origin: it referred now to the community of opinion and purpose." Since universities would send representatives to Church councils to offer opinions on ecclesiastical problems, the nation as a "community of opinion" was commonly used to describe the "ecclesiastical republic" from the late thirteenth century on. Because the participating individuals represented both religious and secular interests, the word's significance broadened further to denote "representatives of cultural and political authority, or a political, cultural, and then social elite."[102]

In Meiji Japan, the writers of furusato literature originated from a variety of places, but all of them felt equally foreign in the landscape of modern Japan and sought to overcome this sense of displacement through writing. Moreover, their privileged social position afforded them cultural authority, and they came to constitute a "community of opinion"—a kind of proto-nation—that prefigured the more general emergence of a national identity. The writers' common discovery of individuality and the impulse to break through the isolating "membrane" pushed them toward an imaginative re-engagement that would ground them as modern Japanese. But texts are not so much artifacts as signs of involvement in the needs and expectations of a wider environment; in this particular Japanese context, they spoke to the concerns of an equally displaced readership. Doppo was undoubtedly expressing his own anxieties in highly individualistic terms, but more broadly he was articulating the national search for a subjective identity.

TWO

Shimazaki Tōson:
A Distant Perspective

The Transforming City

Born only one year after Doppo, Shimazaki Tōson (1872–1943) grew up in a similar world of rapid social change that would color his literary articulation of the native place. Like Doppo, Tōson's sense of belonging to a specific locality was complicated by disruption; he spent only eight years in Magome, his birthplace in Shinshū (or Shinano, roughly equivalent to modern Nagano prefecture) before being sent to Tokyo to study, and he did not return to the region until 1899, when he took up a teaching post there for six years. He also shared with Doppo an early interest in politics, which began with a reading of Napoleon's biography around the age of fourteen. During the years 1887–91, when he was a student at the Presbyterian-run Meiji gakuin, however, his interest shifted to works of Japanese and western literature. He read widely—from Shakespeare and Dickens to the latest Japanese stories such as Mori Ōgai's (1862–1922) "The Dancing Girl" ("Maihime," 1890)—and it was during this time that he first came across a collection of poetry by Wordsworth in a Ginza bookshop. Together with Koshoshi's *Returning Home*, the Englishman's verse helped stimulate his attraction to nature as an inspiration for writing. He later recalled that by the time he left school, "the ambition to become a politician had completely disappeared . . . and it was inevitable that the path I trod would be that of literature."[1] Such words echo Doppo's equally important decision to abandon his desire to become another Napoleon and instead seek to express himself through literature.

However, although both writers wrote about the furusato, this subject accounts for only a small part of Doppo's output, whereas Tōson returned to the topos again and again. This may in part be explained by the fact that whereas Doppo was drawing on a set of real experiences from one relatively stable period of his generally rootless childhood, Tōson was revisiting a site to which he felt a far more fundamental attachment since it was the actual area of his birth. This is not to say, however, that personal ties to an "authentic" native home make the link between writer and place less complex; indeed, it is the tension surrounding Tōson's desire to "go home" and his inability to fully realize that aim which underlines the complexity of his literary endeavor. The implications of this caveat are explored in this chapter.

Compared to Doppo, Tōson could piece together a picture of home by drawing from a richer bank of memories, which, far from being limited to a few years of his own childhood, reached back through generations. His father, Masaki, was headman (*shōya*) of Magome. Although still a peasant, his position in the village was a prestigious one with a long pedigree; he was the seventeenth successive head of the family to hold this post.[2] What is more, the Kiso Road, on which Magome stands, was a section of the Nakasendō, one of the five great premodern highways (*go-kaidō*), and until 1868 the Shimazaki house served as the local *honjin*, an officially designated stopping place for feudal lords traveling to and from Edo during their alternating years of residence (*sankin kōtai*). The Shimazaki family benefited both financially and socially from this arrangement.

But if at one level this family background ties Tōson to the history of the locality, his novel *Before the Dawn* suggests that a sense of historical continuity had already become problematic for the previous generations. Specifically, his father's tragic fate was a firsthand warning of what might happen to those who could not find a place in the age of Meiji. Based loosely on the Shimazaki family's fortunes, the work reflects how his father's positive expectations of political and social change during the Tokugawa-Meiji transition were gradually destroyed. As a young man, Aoyama Hanzō (the father's fictional persona) had taken the side of those who sought to restore the Kyoto-based emperor to a position of authority over the Edo shogunate in order to remedy the enormous social and economic problems of the latter years of the Tokugawa period. The philosophical ideas of what came to be known from mid-Meiji as the National Learning (kokugaku) movement, based on the writings of Tokugawa scholars such as Motoori Norinaga, were an important intellectual support to this movement. These scholars had concerned themselves principally with articulating a Japanese national character clearly distinguished from the elements of Chinese culture then pervading many aspects of Japanese life. Although part of a long-term search for a national identity, the arrival of aggressive westerners in 1857 stimulated this endeavor. It is no coincidence that Hanzō is particularly attracted to the ideas of Hirata Atsutane (1776–1843), whose followers ranged from samurai to Shinano peasants and for whom "the place where the ancient gods most actively manifested virtue was not Kyoto but the rural villages."[3] Hanzō's predilection for this strand of National Learning set him against the centralizing tendency of much of Meiji politics.

Hanzō's expectations of better things to come after the Meiji Restoration are continually disappointed. He is shocked, for instance, to hear that his old National Learning teacher Kansai, who had sponsored his membership in the Hirata school, has been making money by trading silk to foreigners in Yokohama. Only a short while before, the restoration movement had been spurred by the anti-western call to "revere the emperor and expel the barbarians" (sonnō jōi). Hanzō's disillusionment intensifies when Kansai, perhaps from shame, does not call on his eager pupil when passing through Magome. Hanzō understands that a new era requires dramatic social change, and he realizes that "the age centered on the samurai was at last passing away" and the changes now required "the renewal of life from the very roots."[4] His bitterness arises from his growing awareness of his own naïveté in having believed that the political struggle was "an opportunity to restore all things to [the forms of] antiquity."⁵ Life was renewed in Meiji but not in the way he had anticipated, and his feeling of exclusion from the times finally reduces him to a state of mental instability.' Like Tō-son's father, Hanzō passes his last days confined like a wild animal in a guarded hut.

If the Shimazaki family history reveals a less than settled relationship with the furusato, Tōson's personal relationship with the furusato was equally ambiguous. His memories, which tied him both to the native place and to Tokyo, were at least as instrumental in determining the particular nature of his later attempt to "return" home through literature. In the next chapter, I examine the way in which he incorporated aspects of idyllic early childhood memories into his work; the present chapter considers how his perception of the native place was shaped in a rather more "negative" sense, namely, through his removal from it as a boy and his experience of growing up in Tokyo. An examination of Tōson's personal circumstances reveals not only the experience of a displaced individual but also the prototype for an emerging national subject consciousness.

Okuno Takeo argues that for some city-based writers, the native place they had left was an original or "primal landscape" (*genfūkei*), a set of memories "intimately linked to the flesh and blood production of the self, which might be described as the deep layer of consciousness."⁶ The extent to which this fundamental landscape endured was suggested by Tōson himself in the introduction to *Furusato* (1920), a collection of short pieces describing various aspects of the childhood home: "Just as people never forget the taste of what they ate as children no matter how old they become, they never forget the place where they were born."⁷ Okuno, however, tends to see memory as based on facts and overlooks the evolution of the metaphorical landscape through a process of continual reinterpretation. Tōson's recollections are, after all, predicated on the fact that they are no longer immediately available; temporal and spatial distance serves to sharpen their intensity. Indeed, temporary juncture and movement were characteristics integral to the post station that served as Tōson's native place. In any case, Tōson's initial separation created not so much a fixed landscape as a fluid dynamic, in which his earliest memories, which provided a core sense of self but were also inextricably bound up with his later experiences of displacement, were then repeatedly revisited with the aim of over-coming that fracture. Hence, it is insufficient to explain Tōson's re-lationship with the native place as the result of a simple dichotomy between a lost rural idyll and the alienating city to which he was exiled. Rather, those initial memories took shape only through the perspective of his experiences in Tokyo, themselves more fluid than fixed; in other words, both the furusato and the urban phases of his life worked on each other in the constantly changing "pro-duction of the self."

In fact, moving from the provinces to the capital was far from a rare event in Meiji, but the difference in age between Tōson (eight) and Doppo (sixteen) when they experienced this move ensured that the nature of their attachment to Tokyo was somewhat differ-ent. A strong parallel to Doppo's first engagement with the place is found in Tokutomi Kenjirō's (1868–1927) novel *Footprints in the Snow* (*Omoide no ki*, 1901), a vivid portrayal of a young man driven by a rather naïve belief in the virtues of self-help and hard work and fired with ambition to move to the capital, get a first-class edu-cation, and gain successful employment. Finally reaching Tokyo in 1887 (the same year as Doppo), the youth soon discovers that the city cannot live up to his expectations. Gazing over the city from the viewpoint of Atago Hill one evening in autumn, the disap-pointed youth contemplates the fateful attractions of this "terrify-ing vortex" and half plays with the idea of returning to the place he left behind:

However, men must live, and fight in order to live. They must gain fame and earn money; they must engage in a life or death struggle. The gulf be-tween town and country is so great that once someone has tasted the city's rice, he can never again settle in the countryside. And so, emaciated, consumptive, almost with pickpocket's eyes, like a living corpse, he toils unceasingly in the city. Yet countless young men in their prime are drawn here year after year so as to fatten the capital's cavernous belly. I had done the same myself.[8]

This passage evokes Mineo's lament in "Let Me Return" not only in its suggestion that Tokyo has the power to enslave—Mineo feared urban life might make him "a slave to vanity, a servant of extravagant play"—but also in its reluctant acknowledgment that any ambitious person who has tasted urban life can never again seriously contemplate returning to the native place. It is this contradictory set of attractions that Doppo articulated in his work.

Although Tōson was certainly not adverse to strong criticism of life in Tokyo as well as high praise of the furusato in his writings, the fact that he was still a child when he first arrived meant that his relationship with both city and furusato was inevitably more complicated. Like the figure in Tokutomi's novel, the sixteen-year-old Doppo's move to Tokyo was the culmination of a long-held ambition; the eight-year-old Tōson, by comparison, had far less say in the matter; it was his father who decided to send him there. As a result, the city made a far stronger imprint on Tōson's intellectual and emotional development as he grew into a young man. In his first ten years there, he moved between Kyōbashi, Ginza, Nihonbashi, and Hamachō, and his experience of living in the very heart of the city must have been almost as instrumental as his Magome years to the "flesh and blood production of the self." Watching the city change over time, he also changed with it. For this reason, it is worthwhile considering the general significance of Tokyo during Meiji since it not only contributed to the growth of Tōson's personality but also engendered a correspondingly profound reevaluation of the native home.

The possibility of economic advancement in Tokyo exerted an enormous pull on people from rural areas. For instance, the head of the Yoshimura family, who was entrusted with raising the young Tōson, originally left Kiso-Fukushima in Shinshū "to seek his fortune" in the city.[9] Tokyo also set the latest intellectual trends and drew many who wished to be part of these new developments. Tōson's father identified his son as a "spiritual heir"[10] to his own innate love of learning and, as did other country families, sent the younger generation to Tokyo to obtain the best education.[11] Tōson first went to Tokyo with his elder brother Tomoya in 1881 and, except for a few years, he remained there until his move to Komoro back in his native Shinshū region in 1899. By the time his first major novel, *The Broken Commandment* (*Hakai*),

came out in 1906, the population was undergoing a radical transformation. Between 1898 and 1907, for instance, 40,000–60,000
people moved to Tokyo each year, and "1908 is considered to have
marked only the beginning of a decade of intensified urban migration that continued through the end of the First World War."[12]

But this surge in population was also indicative of Tokyo as
symbol of wider cultural shifts during Meiji that would influence
Tōson. "From the beginning of Meiji," wrote Tayama Katai in 1917
as he reflected on many changes he had witnessed during his life,
"Tokyo was gradually built up as the capital of the new Japanese
empire."[13] Edo was transformed into Tokyo not only by a physical
reconstruction of the city but also, and just as important, by a new
set of aspirations. Beginning with the construction of the Ginza
shopping district with its brick buildings in the 1870s, Tokyo
served, among other things, as a showcase for western fashions and
innovations.[14] The term *miyako*—with its associations of traditional culture in the style of the older capital of Kyoto—did not
suit a new city that was "a challenge to be met with modern technology and practical learning." Instead, it was given the title *teito*
(imperial capital), a term that suggested an emerging nation taking
its place among other "advanced" nations of the West, an effort in
which aggressive imperial designs seemed a necessary element. And,
as part of this drive toward self-determination rather than subser-
vience to the West, western learning and concepts of self-help became intimately woven into the domestic culture of the city.[15]

The correlation between physical change and transformations in
the cultural makeup of the city was strong. For example, a clear
sign of the different economic needs of Tokugawa Edo and Meiji
Tokyo was a shift from dependency on the waterways, especially
around the important Shitamachi area, to the development of the
city into what has been called a "land metropolis" (*riku no tō*).[16]
The introduction of more efficient western technology such as the
railway meant that the canals of Edo gradually fell into neglect as
land-based forms of transportation took over. A change in the emphasis of river policy from access for boats to flood control fur-
thered this tendency. But such developments had an effect on more
than the economic sphere, for the network of canals in Edo "did

not occupy simply an important position in navigation: great bustling open spaces and celebrated sights that drew people existed
alongside the water, and many theaters of the Edo period and the
early modern period were set up on the waterside. All the vigor of
the city was concentrated by the water."[17] With the shift toward
the land, the social and cultural activities that had, together with
trade, evolved in close relationship with the waterways of the Edo
period were adversely effected.

Not surprisingly, these cultural changes drew the attention of
creative artists. Some writers felt uneasy and lamented that the fla-
vor of the old city was being lost. An outstanding example is Nagai
Kafū (1879–1959), whose *The River Sumida* (*Sumidagawa*, 1909) lovingly creates a highly selective and nostalgic image of earlier times
as Meiji is drawing to a close. Another of his works, *Cloudy
Weather* (*Donten*, 1908), portrays a narrator walking through Ueno
Park, where his view is marred by an exhibition hall. In his eyes,
the building represents the way modern planners are almost willfully destroying the former landscape: "After a great deal of hard
thought about how the inexpressibly melancholy view of the park
in autumn might be destroyed, the massive Meiji building must
have been built as a symbol to express 'disharmony' and 'disorder,'
the great ideals of the new age."[18] Despite such protests, however,
the city underwent an irreversible physical and cultural reconfiguration. Although the Shitamachi district remained a commercial center, the geographically higher area of Yamanote increasingly became
not only an important site for government and banking but also an
alternative base for writers and artists. Some may have found the
breakup of the old city dismaying, but it led to the birth of a new
Tokyo, a place that others saw as filled with innovative and exciting
possibilities. And one of the major groups of writers who emerged
to meet that challenge as new national subjects were people like Tōson who had moved to Tokyo from the countryside.

A sense of the confusion and excitement a country boy experienced on his arrival in the big city with its masses of people is provided by Yamamura Bochō (1884–1924) in a short piece entitled
"After Reaching the Capital" ("Jōkyō-go," 1911). It is the story of a

child coming to study in Tokyo. After his first railway ride, he and his elder brother disembark in Ueno Station:

"Ueno! Ueno!"
The platform attendant's voice was lost in a confusion of noises. I drew up to my elder brother, and as we walked, we were swept along by human waves. The clatter of clogs, cries of every kind, the train whistles and beams of light that stuck our eyes—bewildered by all these things, I was terrified I might have set foot in Hell.[19]

The boy would have known the sound of clogs and the cries of merchants in the countryside. In the city, however, the sheer quantity of those sounds magnifies beyond recognition—especially within the confined space of a railway station—to create a "confusion of noises" that neatly parallels the boy's psychological mixture of excitement and apprehension. Human beings have lost their individuality and form an impersonal force of "waves." Add in unfamiliar elements of the new technology, such as the "train whistles" and "beams of light," and the boy feels that all his senses are under violent attack. This is not the world he left behind; it embodies all that is fearful and unknown, a "monster's cavernous belly" in the words of Tokutomi. With no control over this environment, his only option is to act passively, to seek protection from his brother and be borne along on these "human waves."

This inability to comprehend what Raymond Williams has called the "crowded strangeness"[20] of urban life is emphasized further when the two take a rickshaw in the darkness to the house of an uncle with whom they will be staying:

We passed through a roadside district with its numerous, low-set houses where people were doing side-jobs in the gloomy lamplight, and with its shops selling sundries; then on past another street built up on only one side with a ditch smelling of mud set up in front, until we suddenly came to a place where dawn seemed to have broken. The clamorous streets and the sounds of the samisen blended together and produced within me an odd feeling.[21]

Crossing a landscape too large and diverse to know in total, and populated by people whose lives can be perceived only piecemeal in visual snatches, the boy's mind shifts hungrily from one sensation to another. The pungency of the mud gives way suddenly to the shock of a street so brightly lit that dawn seems to have arrived. The boy of this story is clearly an outsider overwhelmed by the novelty of the environment and yet to put down roots in the city.

Tōson also drew on memories of his arrival in Tokyo, but the way in which he dealt with such experiences indicates a complication of his sense of home. His semi-autobiographical *When the Cherries Blossom* (*Sakura no mi no juku suru made*, 1919) tells the story of a young man, Kishimoto Sutekichi, who attends a Christian college in Tokyo (closely based on Tōson's time at Meiji gakuin). After saying goodbye to his mother, who has paid a brief visit and then returns to the countryside, Sutekichi falls into a depression, which he seeks to overcome by taking a stroll around the city's bridges:

An unusual feeling welled up in Sutekichi's heart. He recalled vividly the childlike expectation he had felt the day he came from his distant hometown to pursue his studies in Tokyo, the first time in his life when he saw a great city. It was the day when the horse coach they had taken along the Nakasendō stopped at the side of the Mansei bridge; when, under the guidance of his elder brother, he and another youth, who had come to Tokyo for medical treatment on his eyes, had stepped down together from the horse coach. And he saw clearly the scene of the music halls and inns close to the avenue of trees where the carriage had stopped at the plaza.[22]

Since in 1881 Tōson traveled to Tokyo by road, he does not evoke the overwhelming chaos highlighted in Yamamura's description of the railway station (not built until 1883). Nevertheless, he presents a similar picture of a young boy from a small town awed by the great city, and his attention is likewise drawn to the sheer quantity of things in the city with its numerous "music halls and inns." A major difference, however, is that Tōson explicitly frames the description of his arrival as something that took place years ago. Both passages offer a child's first encounter with an urban landscape, but what was once unknown to Sutekichi has become the stuff of a familiar and recoverable memory. For this reason, a simple contrast between an unthreatening countryside and the fearful city does not do justice to his feelings. Indeed, it is the uncomfortable awareness of the dual aspect of his past, stirred by his mother's visit, that disturbs him. This becomes clear when, following the recollection of his first arrival, Sutekichi seeks to overcome his depression by "taking a walk through the streets in which he was brought up long ago."[23] Here he is referring not to the streets of his native place but those of the urban district of Tsukiji, where his second family, the Tanabes (corresponding to the Yoshimuras in real life), had raised him. In other words, his experience of Tokyo speaks of a conflict of identity: it is at once a site undeniably integral to his sense of self and a painful reminder of his separation from the original furusato. This very conflict was a major characteristic of the emerging Japanese identity.

The Views from Tokyo

The daily routine of urban life strongly colored Tōson's personal development, but the intellectual currents that pervaded the capital were equally vital in giving shape to his understanding of literature. These currents became even more important when, against the wishes of Yoshimura, who had reared him in the expectation that he would enter the family business, Tōson developed the desire to become a writer. With regard to these broader currents, although I suggest above that his first encounter with Tokyo was of a different kind from Doppo's, the emergence of furusato literature as a means to articulate the perceived shortcomings of city life turned out to be at least as important in effecting the direction of his work. This is perhaps not surprising, since his own literary debut took place in 1892, just two years after Koshoshi published *Returning Home*. The first of a series of translations and introductory pieces by Tōson began to appear in the magazine *Jogaku zasshi* from January 1882. But the native place was obviously not something Tōson lived on an everyday basis, and any attempt to write about it required that he learn how to see it; this was something that needed time and study. Indeed, in the preface to *The Greenleaf Collection* (*Ryokuyōshū*, 1907)—his first collection of short stories, most of them written between 1902 and 1904 during his tenure as a teacher in Komoro—he recounted how it was only in spring 1899, when he returned to this region, that he first came to understand the meaning of the term "countryside": "It was from that time that the 'countryside' (*inaka*) first really began to appear before my eyes. And so, starting from my immediate surroundings, I determined to try and represent things exactly as they appeared to me, exactly as they felt."[24] In other words, Tōson himself acknowledged the conscious effort required to reappropriate the countryside—in this case, including his own furusato—as a literary construct.

Above, I touched on the specific lessons Tōson learned during his stay in Komoro about conceptualizing this rural landscape. But such "ways of seeing," to borrow John Berger's phrase, began much earlier, in the 1880s, when he started to draw on various intellectual trends that stimulated his literary ambition. These wider discourses, discussed below, were equally influential in providing new perceptions and an empowering perspective that would help him refocus on the lost home and interpret his own origins.

LANGUAGE REFORM

Tōson's determination to represent the things of the countryside "exactly as they felt" (*kanjita mama*) brings to mind Doppo's emphasis on describing nature "exactly as it is seen" (*mita mama*). This common concern in turn reflects the contemporary debate over language itself—particularly its supposed potential to represent external phenomena unproblematically. According to Yoshida Seiichi, the 1894–95 Sino-Japanese war gave a strong impetus to socioeconomic changes in Japan, as capitalism became more deeply rooted into society. One effect of these changes was to prompt writers to seek literary forms that allowed them to articulate their growing consciousness of discrepancies between a sense of self and society at large. Many were attracted to Realism (*shajitsushugi*) as a way to depict the external world more "honestly" in comparison to earlier literary forms; it was precisely this question of realistic representation that Doppo used to differentiate his output from what he saw as the excessively ornate writing of Ozaki Kōyō and Kōda Rohan. The idea of Realism as the highest literary value would prove to resonate deeply in the modern Japanese literary tradition, and a line of development can be traced to the emergence in late Meiji and Taishō periods of what Edward Fowler has called the illusory "transparent text" of the I-novel (*shishōsetsu*), in which Realism is assumed to equate with the writer's sincerity.[25] In mid-Meiji, it helped produce various novelistic categories that often overlapped in content and still escape exact definition. All of them, however, can be characterized as aiming to represent everyday lived experience more "truthfully."[26] The pressing question of the time, however, was ultimately less a particular novelistic form and more the nature of language itself, that is, the medium in which the external world was to be depicted. This debate over language falls under the general rubric of the *genbun itchi* (correspondence between the spoken and the written languages) movement.

Much has been written on this movement, to which Tōson made an important contribution. Nanette Twine, in her useful article,[27] summarizes the four main literary styles available to the Japanese as the Meiji period began: *kanbun, sōrōbun, wabun,* and *wakankonkōbun.*[28] These styles were based on Chinese or on Heian-period court Japanese, or a mixture of both, and effectively limited the readership to the literary elite. With the change in social and cultural expectations in Meiji, however, the need to master western technology and educate the general population required a far less cumbersome and time-consuming means of written communication. Religious sermons were being published in colloquial Japanese as early as 1810, but it was not until Meiji that the utilitarian case for a writing system based on the colloquial language was made. In general, exponents of *genbun itchi* appeared to gain the upper hand, and, for example, children's school texts changed from *kanbun* to a more colloquial style in the mid-1880s. But the argument was not always one-way; minor newspapers devoted mostly to entertainment (*shōshinbun*) used colloquial until around 1879, but then shifted to *kanbun*, since an increasingly educated readership was now considered able to handle more difficult and "cultured" written forms.

In any case, language reform was a major concern among writers and intellectuals. In 1886, Mozume Takami, a professor at Tokyo University, published the influential essay "*Genbun itchi*," which was actually written in colloquial. In the literary arena, Tsubouchi

Shōyō's (1859–1935) groundbreaking *Essence of the Novel* (*Shōsetsu shinzui*, 1885) suggested that dialogue should be written in colloquial even if descriptive passages retained older literary trappings. One of the writers most closely identified with the movement was Yamada Bimyō (1869–1910), who emerged from the Ken'yūsha literary group; he began his career by writing in the *kanbun* style of Kyokutei Bakin (1767–1848) but came to eschew its sinicized language and adopted a style closer to contemporary speech. He wrote widely in support of colloquial—in fact he helped coin the term *genbun itchi*—and was inspired by Mozume's article and the appearance of the first installment of *Floating Clouds* in 1886. This work by his childhood friend Futabatei Shimei inspired him to start publishing his own *genbun itchi* novel in 1887.[29] So many other writers were drawn to experiment with a style closer to spoken Japanese that 78 percent of the novels published in 1905 were written in colloquial. By 1908 that figure was virtually 100 percent.

For some, a rejection of earlier Japanese literary forms in favor of what Tayama Katai famously championed as "bare-boned description" (*rokotsu naru byōsha*)[30] signified a wholly welcome and revolutionary transformation of the literary arena, but distinctions between progressive and conservative forces were not always so clear. For instance, the language of Kōyō's *Confessions of Love* (*Ninin bikuni iro zange*, 1889)—premodern Japanese for the narrative parts and a more colloquial style for the dialogues—hardly differed from what Shōyō had proposed in 1885, yet it was still "considered retrograde by the most progressive" critics.[31] In fact, it is hard to imagine that any writer aware of the contemporary debates would not at some point consider the question of what language style—or styles—might most effectively mediate his experiences. What is more, at a time when the very definitions of "modern" and "traditional" language styles were being hammered out, few writers could be identified exclusively with one camp. Rather, individual writers were distinguished by the degree to which they drew on varying combinations of classical and colloquial forms, and this sense of appropriateness might change over time.

In this connection, two essays by Tōson's friend Yanagita Kunio are particularly instructive since they reveal a single writer considering the *genbun itchi* question from both ends of the argument. In "Sketching and the Essay" ("Shasei to ronbun," 1907), Yanagita examined the "sketching" (*shasei*) techniques expounded by the haiku poet Masaoka Shiki (1867–1902) and concluded that there are great advantages in borrowing heavily from colloquial Japanese. His description of sketching as writing echoes both Tōson and Doppo: writing "just as you see (*mita mama*), just as you hear (*kiita mama*), without embellishment or artifice. Writing like this is not so difficult. The result is that anyone—anyone who has an idea—can write."[32] Only two years later, however, he had reached the opposite conclusion. In "The Distance Between Speech and Writing" ("Genbun no kyori," 1909), he called into doubt the possibility of conflating the two into a single form of communication; indeed, the existence of each seems predicated on the distance that separates them. In his account, Japan, in contrast to the West, seldom incorporated colloquial speech into written work, and this led him to believe that the Meiji call to write only in the colloquial will certainly fail. In fact, Yanagita went further with a novel twist to the usual meaning of the term "correspondence of the spoken and the written languages" by suggesting that the education system should be used to train a new generation of Japanese to speak in a style closer to the written language![33] To a certain extent, these essays indicate that Yanagita was still working out his own position on the subject; they also demonstrate his sensitivity to the complexities of language and his ambivalence about the idea that any writing style is capable of expressing all aspects of reality. In any case, his questioning of a simplistic correspondence between spoken and written Japanese required some boldness at the time, when the kind of Naturalism expounded by the likes of Katai was at its most influential.[34]

Yanagita was certainly not alone in doubting the representational potential of language. In western literary debates, the interrelationship of language, meaning, and representation has become a particularly major concern in the past few decades. As my discussion on Doppo in Chapter 1 notes, Karatani draws on these discourses to argue that in Japan the concept of an external world vis-à-vis a describing subject's interiority emerged in Meiji. But

Karatani also challenges the argument that the *genbun itchi* movement represents a fundamental shift in the relationship between spoken and written Japanese. He identifies an 1866 petition to the Tokugawa shogunate from Maejima Hisoka, an interpreter based at a shogunate school in Nagasaki, entitled "The Reason for Abolishing Chinese Characters," as the first sign of the *genbun itchi* movement. Maejima was interested more in abolishing kanji than in the unification of the spoken and the written languages, but Karatani suggests that the two aims are intimately linked. Denying any inherent correspondence between the spoken and written languages, since "the spoken word and the written word are fundamentally different," he locates in Maejima's attraction to the "economy, immediacy, and democratic nature of phonetic writing" a clue to how *genbun itchi* helped engender a completely new ideology. He argues that if, in the western context, Saussurean linguistics tends to view phonetic writing as secondary to the speech that it transcribes, then something similar occurred in Japan when Maejima assumed that "writing should be in the service of speech." As a result,

once this became the established understanding, the question of whether to abolish kanji actually became irrelevant. The reason was that kanji were now viewed as being in the service of speech, and the choice was simply one of using either kanji or native kana. When writing came to be viewed in this way, Maejima naturally turned his attention to the spoken language, with the result that the gap between the spoken and the written languages emerged as a problem. Until this time, there has been no "problem."[35]

Karatani's approach has its own problems. His attempt to trace a native Japanese genealogy for "modern Japanese literature" is to be commended, but he apparently feels obliged to find Japanese versions of earlier, "original" western developments, be it the creation of visual perspective or a new relationship between the spoken and the written languages. This does, of course, beg further questions relating to critical revisionist approaches by Japanese scholars and who has the authority to make use of "western" discourse. As a corrective, one might bear in mind Edward Fowler's alternative understanding of the intellectual "modernity" that emerged in Meiji, that is "no more—and no less—than the institutionalized process by which Japanese continue to apply traditional (and specifically non-western) modes of thinking to contemporary social, economic, and political issues."[36] The insistence by another critic, Miyoshi Masao, that the term *shōsetsu* be retained as a translation of the term "Japanese novel" (with its implication of imitating a western model) highlights further the difficulty of negotiating a modernity that acknowledges both native and universal (i.e., western) influences.[37] The danger here is that retention of the Japanese term might lead to an essentialist, *Nihonjin-ron* reading in which the Japanese tradition is considered unique. As the efforts of these three important critics show, however, the issues of modernity, representation, and language that arose in mid- and late Meiji are complex; the fact that they remain the subject of critical debate even today indicates the importance of this period as the starting point of a modern literary and, by extension, national subjectivity. This was precisely the time when Tōson came of age as a writer.

THE POETIC IMPULSE

Like many of his literary peers, Tōson developed a strong interest in language reform, although both he and other critics thought his first major prose work in the colloquial language, *The Nap* (*Utatane*, November 1897), an artistic failure. But his particular sensitivity to the evocative powers of language is demonstrated in a short piece from his *Furusato* collection, "Words of the Native Place" ("Furusato no kotoba"), in which he considered certain phrases found only in the Magome region—*wayaku na*, for example, meaning "naughty" or "mischievous"—which for him immediately recalled his childhood and presented the illusion that his grandparents "are still alive in those words."[38] Given this affinity for linguistic resonances, it is perhaps not surprising that he first emerged as an important literary figure in the area of poetry with the publication of his first collection, *Fresh Greens* (*Wakanashū*, August 1897). This volume began to take shape immediately after he escaped various problems in his relationships with his extended family and moved to Sendai to teach at the Tōhoku gakuin in September 1896,[39] where he stayed for almost a year. The poems were written between September 1896 and March 1897, but the intense creativity of his first two months there, when eighteen poems, or one third of the total, were completed, merely underlines why this volume was seen to represent the vigor and youthful innovation of a new generation, and was widely greeted as "truly like the break of dawn."[40] Three other major volumes of poetry were to follow—*A Leaf Boat (Hitohabune*, June 1898), *Summer Grasses (Natsugusa*, October 1898), and *Fallen Plum Blossoms (Rakubaishū*, August 1901)— but it was *Fresh Greens* that identified Tōson as the leading Romantic poet (especially following Kitamura Tōkoku's death in 1894) with a fresh and lyrical style that initiated "a new epoch in the history of Japanese letters."[41]

It is difficult to overestimate the importance of Tōson's poetry, and it deserves more attention than I can give it here, but I will keep my comments brief since I am principally concerned with his later role as a novelist dealing with the native place.[42] As Yoshida Seiichi notes, even though *Fresh Greens* is Tōson's most lyrical poetry collection, it is still possible to find in it traces of traditional narrative *(monogatari)* as well as elements of tragedy and linguistic flourishes that suggest a Shakespearean influence. In other words, even the volume most closely identified with Romantic lyricism hints at a potential novelist seeking narrative forms beyond simple lyricism.[43] But two other important elements in the poetry, which also have a direct bearing on the furusato landscapes in his later prose, are that his material is drawn from daily life experiences and that his verse features something closer to ordinary language than did most contemporary poetry.[44] This not only indicates Tōson's attraction to realistic representation but also confirms Kitano Akihiko's observation, mentioned above with regard to Doppo but just as relevant to Tōson, that writers originally from the provinces often represented the "local color" of the regions they had left behind. In addition, this experimentation with everyday language suggests the influence of Wordsworth, the icon of Romanticism of literary Meiji.

Shinbo Kunihiro's outline of differences in Doppo's and Tōson's appreciation of Wordsworth deserves attention, since it helps clarify Tōson's distinctive understanding of the relationship between himself and other writers, which in turn effected his perception of the external world.[45] He places both writers in the context of the groups to which they were primarily associated. In Doppo's case, the link was with the liberal Min'yūsha. Once the Freedom and Popular Rights movement began to falter, Tokutomi Sohō and the others used their magazine, *Kokumin no tomo*, among other things, to articulate an ideal of the country gentleman (*inaka shinshi*). This new political and ethical subject was contrasted with the undesirable subject they saw being shaped by urban pressures and industrialization in the Meiji state. Wordsworth, as a rural poet (*den'en shijin*), was assigned the role of antidote to the modern world. This becomes clear in the 1893 biography written by Koshoshi, another member of the group. After a general outline of the poet's life, Koshoshi compared Wordsworth and Tao Yuanming to emphasize that both struggled in adverse conditions to gain spiritual freedom through integration into rural life. Doppo's adulation was even more fulsome, and he viewed this English poet almost as a personal mentor who had lived a full and spiritual life in an increasingly complex and "unnatural" modern world.

Tōson, on the other hand, is associated with the Bungakukai, a literary society founded in 1893 that published a journal with the same name. For the young contributors to this journal, Wordsworth personified a more recognizably Japanese-style tradition of seclusion (*inton*) rather in the mold of the group's leading light, Kitamura Tōkoku, who had become increasingly introverted and cut off from society. In fact, Tōkoku seems not to have warmed to the English poet, perhaps because the apparent calm of Wordsworth's verse did not fit with his own ever more desperate state of mind. Tōson was more amenable and was encouraged by descriptions such as "the homely poet of Rydal" and "recluse" that he found in the works of English critics like Matthew Arnold to imagine Wordsworth in his older years as a poet who had attained a kind of spiritual enlightenment (*satori*).[46] Whereas most Bungakukai members tended to forget Wordsworth as they moved on to other things, Tōson's interest continued. He may have been stimulated by Natsume Sōseki's article "English Poets' Conception of the Universe and Nature" ("Eikoku shijin no tenchi sansen ni taisuru kannen," 1893) as well as Koshoshi's biography. But by spring 1895, the angle of his interest changed. At a time when Tōson was

seriously beginning to address his creative side, which would cul-
minate two years later in *Fresh Greens*, general admiration gave
way to a more practical interest in the *Lyrical Ballads*, in which
Wordsworth expounded his theories on poetry. In any case, Tōson
was never as much in thrall to him as was Doppo. Doppo took
Wordsworth as the greatest teacher of his life; Tōson accepted him
as a literary sage from whom he could draw important lessons, but
ultimately he was only one sage among others.

The various reasons have been given for Tōson's turn from poetry
to prose, the most obvious being that, although he could not make
a living as a poet, "it was at least theoretically possible for novelists
to support themselves through their writing."[47] The fact that educated people like Shōyō and, later, Sōseki were willing to put their
names to their own writings must have helped remove some of the
stigma traditionally associated with writers of fiction. And Tōson
learned much from his own reading; especially during his stay in
Komoro, he covered the whole range of European novels in English translation.[48] Shimoyama Jōko also suggests that by 1897 he felt
unable to express all he wished through poetry. His frustrations
may have been compounded by Shiki's review of *Fresh Greens*, entitled "Poetry and Painting in *Fresh Greens*" ("*Wakanashū* no shi to
e," 1897). Shiki found much to praise, but he also complained that
the lyrical element was too conceptual and stereotyped. Feeling (*jō*,
nasake) may be the main concern of lyrical poetry, but it can properly come alive only by making almost physical contact with
things in accordance with specific concrete conditions. Tōson was
probably harboring a similar desire to find a more suitable means
of expression, since it was in November of the same year that his
first novel came out.[49]

The shift to prose was not instantaneous but part of a lengthy
process during which prose and poetic elements continued to inform each other. The narrative elements detectable in *Fresh Greens*
became increasingly noticeable in his other three volumes of poetry.
The third collection, *Summer Grasses*, is characterized by the length
of some of the verse; in fact, *The Plowman (Nōfu)*, a poem that tells
the story of a man returning home from war to find his wife dead,
takes up half the volume. And the fourth collection contains several

prose pieces as well as poetry.[50] Miyoshi Yukio agrees that Tōson's famous announcement in the preface to *Tōson Anthology* (*Tōson shishū*, September 1904), a poetry selection from earlier volumes, that "the new age of poetry has finally arrived" may be seen as the clearest clarion call for Romantic self-confirmation (its conventional reading), but it also hints that he has finally moved on to prose and that he writes now as a novelist looking back in a farewell to poetry.[51] Nevertheless, although it is true that *The Broken Commandment*, written mostly during his stay in Komoro but completed after his return to Tokyo, was widely acclaimed largely because of its successful use of a lean writing style that speaks of his engagement with *genbun itchi*, even here there remain sections reminiscent of lyrical poetry. And William Naff points to an even greater complication in this overlap between genres when he notes that *The Broken Commandment* emerged out of Tōson's poetic prose experiments in *Chikuma River Sketches* (*Chikumagawa no suketchi*), a work he began in Komoro, but also shows that by the time the collection was published in December 1912, some of these pieces had been rewritten to reflect what he had learned from the experience of writing novels.[52] As this brief outline suggests, Tōson's stay in Komoro was instrumental in his development as a writer and in the way he would come to "read" the native place in the context of a new national landscape. To this end, a very important technique he encountered during that time was "sketching."

"SKETCHING"

So far, I have spoken of "views from Tokyo" in the metaphorical sense of various intellectual frames that gave shape to Tōson's literary endeavors. With "sketching," the emphasis is more closely related to the specific faculty of sight, but even this involves more than meets the eye. Tōson moved to Komoro, located at the eastern edge of his native Shinshū but fifty miles from his birthplace, to teach at the Komoro gijuku, a school run by his former teacher Kimura Kumaji, between 1899 and 1905.[53] It was during this stay that he was inspired by "sketching" to "represent things exactly as they appeared," and *Chikuma River Sketches* was the work that emerged to give clearest concrete shape to such efforts.

What did Tōson understand by this term, which is sometimes translated as "sketching from life"? "Sketching" ("Shasei," 1907), an essay from the *From Shinkatamachi* (*Shinkatamachi yori*, 1909) collection, relates it to "seeing things" (*mono o miru*), but this is not merely the passive exercise it might at first seem: "For example, even when watching charcoal smoke rising deep in the mountains, it takes quite a bit of practice in seeing things before one realizes that the scene contains people who live and die. I adopted the 'sketching' method as a means of gaining 'practice in seeing things.'" That is, the process involves not simply the recording of involuntary visual stimuli but also a recognition that other levels of reality, including the human presence, are integral to any full appreciation of the scene. In the concern for a human element, it somewhat resembles Doppo's use of "sympathy" to overcome the impersonal distance (or membrane) that he felt separated himself from the characters in his literary landscapes. And certainly Tōson reveals Romantic, antiscientific credentials when he warns against the danger of excessively analytical (*kaibōteki*) perspectives, which lead to "treating living things as dead objects." The clue to a successful representation of life (*sei*) is a more conscious, mobile vitality (*seiki*), as he emphasizes through the organic analogy of a tree: "Millet says that 'things must always be observed from their roots, for this is the only basis of authenticity'; sketching at its finest would involve the ability to observe things from their roots, and then move freely to the branches and leaves."[54]

Although my main concern is with Tōson's use of "sketching" as a literary effect, this reference to Jean-François Millet (1814–75), the French artist famed for depictions of peasant life, hints at the extent to which Tōson was influenced by theories of painting. The term *shasei* itself is taken from the Edo vocabulary of visual representation, but his indebtedness to the French painter is underlined in *Chikuma River Sketches*. Having described a peasant woman with unkempt hair and a rustic, sunburned face, he mused that "she looked like a figure who came from a picture of farmers by Millet."[55] Tōson's familiarity with pictorial concepts developed through his association with the watercolorist Miyake Katsumi (1874–1954), a friend from his days at Meiji gakuin and a fellow teacher in Komoro. He encouraged Tōson to produce his own sketches, both visual and literary. But Tōson's interest had in any case been stirred by an earlier reading of John Ruskin's (1819–1900) *Modern Painters*, translations of which appeared in 1896–97 during his stay in Sendai.[56] And he was also familiar with the work of the modern western-style painter Kuroda Seiki (1866–1924). After returning from France in 1893, Kuroda caused a sensation by exhibiting his painting of a female nude in Kyoto in March 1895. Shinbo suggests that Tōson learned effective literary "sketching" from Kuroda's use of perspective and his application of light and shade to capture a partly drawn object.[57] In addition, Marvin Marcus has cited Tōson's association with Arishima Ikuma (1882–1974), writer and painter and younger brother of Arishima Takeo (1877–1923), to suggest that the coterie (*bundan*) "encompassed artistic and literary activity, and it was not at all uncommon for painters to write (about art and otherwise) and for writers to paint."[58] In other words, this was a time of flux between visual and literary arts.

The single most important Japanese figure to influence Tōson's understanding of "sketching" was Masaoka Shiki, whose principal interest was the transformation of haiku into a modern poetic form. Shiki and fellow poets began publishing a journal, *Hototogisu*, in 1897 to put into practice their literary experiments. In particular, Shiki spoke of the need to gather poetic material from a real landscape. This in itself was a new concept in a poetic tradition that drew heavily on celebrated localities (*meisho*) laden with seasonal and other associations, which rendered the need for an actual visit largely redundant. The object now was to write down what was visible to the eye in a sketchbook; this "real" observation, which shows Shiki's adherence to Realism as a literary value, formed the basis for the writing of "literary sketches" (*shaseibun*); it appears to approximate the exercise described by Tōson as "practice in seeing things." Karatani believes that the kind of description practiced by Shiki "was something qualitatively different from simply portraying the external world. The 'external world' first had to be discovered."[59] Since, according to Karatani, Shiki had come to accept as commonsensical the assumption seen in Maejima's petition that writing was phonetic in nature, an analogy can be made between

Shiki's literary practice and his understanding of the written and the spoken languages.[60] Both reveal a belief in the possibility of transcribing separate categories that emerge for the first time in Meiji; the author (subject) transcribing an external world, or the written script as transcription of spoken language. In any case, Shiki's literary experiments can be seen as part of a more general concern, shared by Tōson, to breathe new life into what had become a stale language. What is more, Tōson's aim of depicting ordinary events and people echoes Shiki's concern with real landscapes.

This is not to say their understanding of "sketching" was identical. Etō Jun's interesting distinction between the ideas of Shiki and those of his pupil Takahama Kyoshi (1874–1959) also helps clarify Tōson's interpretation of the term. Etō refers to Kyoshi's recollection of an incident in which he and Shiki disagreed about the proper way to appreciate the simple moonflower (*yūgao*). In Shiki's view, all literary associations with the flower extending back to *The Tale of Genji* were "fanciful" (*kūsōteki*) and should be expunged to allow for a completely new and fresh vision. From this, Etō surmises that Shiki's aim in "sketching" was the production of precise, concrete representations of external phenomena based on something close to "the objectivity of natural science." In other words, the moonflower "is not the word 'moonflower' but an accumulation of impressions 'that one sees before one's eyes in the form of the flower.'"[61] By this objective approach, Shiki aimed at a transformation of consciousness in order to break the conventional literary relationship between observer and object. Sōseki expounded a similar concept of distancing in his article "Literary Sketches" ("Shaseibun," 1907), in which he defined the main characteristic of the technique as the author's mental condition (*shinteki jōtai*). If the relationship between writers and the characters they describe is comparable to that between parent and child, the authors of "literary sketches" stand out for their comparative lack of emotional engagement; they tend to "describe someone crying while not crying themselves" even while remaining sympathetic.[62] Granted that Sōseki's work abounds in experiments with a wide variety of narrative voices, it may be that in this article at least he is articulating a need to counter the intrusive narrators found in earlier examples of "frivolous writing" (*ge-*

saku), much as Shiki's search for a modern literary voice seems to necessitate a violent rejection of past practices.

But Kyoshi's view of "sketching" took the concept a stage further, with important implications for modern realistic fiction. He felt that Shiki's extreme belief in the virtues of objectivity left something to be desired: "To completely dispense with the fanciful interest is to destroy half the flower's beauty, and this is no different from obliterating the historical associations of celebrated localities and old ruins (*meisho kyūseki*)."[63] In other words, it is precisely because the moonflower has been integral to human consciousness for generations that it gains much of its aesthetic value. As Etō says, by insisting that words "cannot be pure signs," Kyoshi rejected Shiki's attempt to reduce "sketching" to the "simple accumulation of impressions of things." In Kyoshi's mind, words, which constitute the building blocks of "sketching," emerge from the numerous contributions of others over time; they are not merely the individual efforts of a single writer. By emphasizing this literary process as a selection based on a communal imaginative function—that is, by insisting that history and human affairs be fused with Shiki's ideal of objectivity—he instilled "sketching" with a new and highly significant "living" style (*ikita buntai*). It is this style that, in conjunction with reforms in colloquial prose, gave shape to the modern realistic novel.[64]

It is now possible to clarify Tōson's difference from Shiki. Tōson's aversion to an excessively "analytical" viewpoint that threatens to reduce living things to "dead objects," as well as his "fanciful" concern for historical links between landscape and people, places him on the side of Kyoshi in his understanding of what "sketching" signifies. If Etō's argument is correct, Tōson's position in the vanguard of modern Japanese fiction should come as no surprise.

BACK TO NATURE

The ways in which Tōson, like Doppo, insisted on emotional links with the landscape were impulses that Motoori Norinaga would surely have identified as distinctly Japanese. Yet Tōson's upbringing at the center of modern capitalist Japan as well as the strong

influence of western intellectual currents on his work also contributed to a new level of Japanese self-identity appropriate to the age
in which he lived. An examination of his literary engagement with
nature confirms the complexity of this identity.

One day in 1890, while still a student, Tōson attended a confer-
ence on Christianity at Meiji gakuin. Looking back at this event in
1909, he described how the profundity of what he heard that day
translated later that evening into a memorable encounter with nature when he took a stroll and, for the first time in his life, "really
began to visually take in the beauty of a sunset."[65] The experience
is treated in greater detail in *When the Cherries Blossom*:

Suddenly something unexpectedly beautiful spread out before Sutekichi's
eyes. The color of the sky was in the process of change. The beauty of the
evening sun was reflected in his eyes for the first time in his life. Wanting
to share the surprise with his friend, Sutekichi ran off to Suga's place. He
stood again on the edge of the mountain, this time with the friend he had
invited along. The sky had changed color once more. The heavens were
red like a sea of flame. An astonishingly expansive world, unknown until
that day, glittered before them.[66]

Stimulated by the general atmosphere of Meiji gakuin with its Pres-
byterian ties, Tōson, like many of his generation, was drawn to
Christianity as a way of expressing a young man's sense of religious mystery. He was baptized in Tokyo by Kimura Kumaji (who
got him the teaching post in Komoro) in June 1888 at a church in
Takanawadai, but his formal ties with the religion were brief. In
1892 he transferred to a church in Kōjimachi led by Uemura Masa-
hisa (1857–1925), a major figure in the history of Christianity in Japan who had a close relationship with Meiji gakuin, but he broke
relations with this church, too. Tōson's break was partly due to his
inability to resolve the conflict he experienced between spiritual
teachings and his own instinctual feelings; he was particularly con-
fused by strong sexual urges.[67] However, the immediate reason was
a problematic romance that developed with Satō Suteko, a student
at the Meiji Girls' School (Meiji jogakkō) where he began to teach
in 1892. As a result of this incident, he left the church, resigned
from the school, and undertook a ten-month journey of self-
reflection in the Kansai region beginning in January 1893.

But in the world that "glittered before them," Tōson perceived not only a religious theme but also the promise of Romantic self-fulfillment. This very Romanticism was behind his attraction to Suteko, in itself part of a more general search for the (frequently thwarted) spirit of personal liberation that could develop from either the Meiji Enlightenment project or Protestantism. The presence of the Romantic mood during this period in Tōson's life is understandable since the school in which he taught was headed by Iwamoto Zenji (1863-1942), a man noted not only for his connection with Christianity and the improvement of women's social position but also for his contribution as publisher of *Jogaku zasshi*, a magazine that did much to introduce Romantic literature to Japanese readers.[68] Indeed, Tōson published several articles in this journal in 1892 before he joined the group centered around *Bungakukai*. On the other hand, although the influence of these two western forces, religious and secular, are clear in the powerful natural image that engages the young Sutekichi, this should not obscure the fact that other, more native literary traditions are also at work. Wordsworth led Tōson to a special appreciation of nature as a means to give shape to his feelings, equal attention should be given to Bashō, another literary sage closer to home.

In the afterword to *Chikuma River Sketches*, Tōson mentioned some of the western authors he was reading—Tolstoy, Flaubert, Ibsen, and so on—as he struggled to formulate a Japanese literary style for the modern age. But he also remarked that this reading had led him to a deeper appreciation of his own literary tradition. He found himself "amazed that my growing familiarity with modern works of literature taught me to reread works that had existed in my own country from ages passed."[69] Sei Shōnagon's *Pillow Book* is given particular mention, but he might equally well have referred to Bashō since, as Naff notes, "Bashō was the writer most frequently quoted in his juvenilia, and echoes of Bashō's works are to be found on almost every page of the travel portions of the Sketchbooks."[70] Yoshida, too, detects traces of the earlier poet's style in "The Deceased" ("Kojin"), one of Tōson's first literary works, which appeared in the August 1892 edition of *Jogakusei*. His interest in Bashō was at its peak during the years 1892–93, when his

pieces in *Bungakukai* are concerned not only with western influences but also with more traditional Japanese aesthetic terms like
"elegance" (*fūryū*) as shown in his essay "A Consideration of Elegance in Human Life" ("Jinsei no fūryū o omou," 1893). The 1890s,
after all, were a decade when a general reawakening of interest in
pre-Meiji literary forms, particularly the work of Ihara Saikaku
(1642–93) and Chikamatsu Monzaemon (1653–1724), was evident.[71]
As Takitō Mitsuyoshi has pointed out, apart from works on drama,
most of Tōson's publications in *Bungakukai* during his 1893 travels
in Kansai are related to the *haibun* style associated with Bashō.[72]

An important lesson that Tōson gained from Bashō, which also
had implications for his interpretation of the relationship between
people and place, was the concept of the writer as traveler, in both
a real and a metaphorical sense. Miyoshi Yukio demonstrates a
very concrete need for Tōson as a young poet to take on the role
of traveler, since it was only when away from Tokyo—whether in
Sendai, Koromo, or Kiso-Fukushima, where his sister lived—that
he managed to produce lyrical verse. The reason, Miyoshi suggests,
was that this style of writing required a particular state of mind
unavailable to Tōson in the city: "The place that served as the
womb for Tōson's lyrical poetry was, at the same time, a 'place of
tranquility' in which he was able to become conscious of himself as
a traveler. It goes without saying that the rise of this awareness of
himself as a traveler was related to his distance from Tokyo."[73]
And in his later years Tōson would note that traveling endured as
a more general metaphor for personal development throughout life:

My life first began with aimless travels in my youthful days, after which I
went to Sendai, and then to Komoro in Shinshū. Each time, I broke
through a personal impasse, I studied things, I grasped my own heart in a
new way, and little by little I was able to make myself anew. Similarly, although my three-year journey to France was very lonely and painful,
when I got back to Japan I understood that it had certainly not been a
worthless endeavor. It seems that, during my encounters with various
people on a gradual journey through this world, my own small mind has
opened up almost imperceptibly.[74]

The idea of traveling as a means to a deeper understanding of oneself, notwithstanding the loneliness this involved, is not new in the

Japanese tradition and is particularly associated with Bashō. However, Tōson's article "Concerning Bashō" ("Bashō no koto," 1924) from the *Waiting for Spring* (*Haru o machitsutsu*, 1925) collection, reveals the extent to which travel is identified in Tōson's own mind as a metaphor for spiritual progress. He idealized Bashō as a sage whose rootless wanderings, "step by step created a spiritual life in which he sat quietly above the tumult of life (*dōyō no ue ni seiza suru*)."[75]

An equally important element Tōson borrowed from Bashō was a perception that life, a transitory affair laced with suffering, gained value precisely through endurance. In "The Words of Grasses" ("Kusa no kotoba," 1928) from his *In the Town* (*Shisei ni arite*, 1930) collection, Tōson imagined a dialogue between a fragrant lotus (*kaorigusa*) and a banana plant (*bashō*, which not incidentally is the plant adopted by the Edo poet as his sobriquet). The banana plant's—and by implication Bashō's—resilience is underlined by the fact that, despite its short life span compared to the lotus, it has "lived life as fully as possible." And both plants feel that harsh experience also has benefits: "If we did not endure this snow," reflects the banana plant, "we would not be able to welcome a new spring again." The analogy with Bashō is even clearer when the lotus's ability to withstand winter without special precautions is compared to the fragile banana plant's need for a straw wrapping and even a straw "hat" in order to survive.[76] Miyoshi links the plant's appearance with a traditional traveler dressed in straw raincoat (*mino*) and hat (*kasa*) to evoke the "vivid image of a traveler who endures winter while awaiting spring" and suggests that it was not until late Taishō or early Shōwa that Tōson came to fully identify himself as a "naked figure bearing the hardship and groans of human life" after the image of his literary mentor.[77] But the seeds of this shared understanding are to be found earlier in his struggles to find value in literary work against the background of a turbulent personal life. In addition to Kitamura's suicide, he suffered severe economic difficulties as a writer, which led indirectly to the death of three daughters in 1905–6.

The fact that Tōson turned to the world of nature for his analogy—in the same way that he picked out a tree to elucidate the "sketching" technique—suggests that nature was important in articulating his own place in the world. But more generally, this conscious appropriation of traditional Japanese flora echoes Shiga Shigetaka's concern with natural landscape as the basis for a national identity. In both cases, an interest in native phenomena should be read as part of a more complex modern reconfiguration. Tōson's literary representation of nature emerged in part from a reaction to Christian teachings, but like Tōkoku and Doppo he never felt at ease with the idea of a personal god. He became increasingly interested in expressing spiritual feelings in terms of a more general pantheism. As Sasabuchi Tomoichi notes, Tōson came to view god not as something other than oneself but as something residing within; less a person than an abstract, limitless phenomenon. In short, god meant Truth (*shinri*), and Christ as savior was reinterpreted as an embodiment of that truth. Certainly, Christ was a sage of great significance, with the power to inspire, but ultimately he remained (merely) one among many outstanding human beings, a category that included Bashō and Wordsworth. Moreover,

the qualities of the universal and the abstract in Tōson's Truth recognized no difference between nature and people. There was no essential difference between elegant nature (*tsukihana*) and flowing water as the epitome of limitlessness and the ideal, and Christ as the manifestation (*fuzei*) of god. Thus, if one assumed that god existed as an abstract truth within the manifold phenomena of nature, the conclusion is that there are no real distinctions between god, man, and nature, with the result that there is no god to which one ought to pray. This is a pantheistic position.[78]

It might be added that this view also emphasizes a humanistic element, since Sasabuchi notes that Tōson's reading of Goethe and Byron offered "a link with a lofty spiritual world"[79] even as he sought to affirm everyday reality through literature.

Tōson and Tōkoku shared an interest in the "spiritual" side of Romantic poetry, but their differences are equally instructive. Tōkoku's *Tale of Mount Hōrai* (*Hōrai kyoku*, 1891), a poem inspired by Byron's *Manfred*, exemplifies his use of the natural world as a manifestation of what he called the spiritual "inner life" (*naimen seimei*). The presence of Mount Fuji in his poem—in imitation of Byron's use of the Alps—serves not only as a dramatic backdrop but also as a sign in nature of an ideal metaphysical world, and his move toward suicide speaks of an increasing inability to deal with what he perceived as the imperfections of the mundane world.[80] Tōson, on the other hand, tended toward greater inclusion of human feelings; the passion for life that he witnessed in the western Romantics translated into the incorporation of natural human desires, warts and all, into his work.

This interest in all aspects of human experience, both good and bad, also relates Tōson to another contemporary current of literary thought, Naturalism, which helped flesh out his understanding of the relationship between people and natural landscape. Japanese readers were first introduced to Emile Zola's experimental and observation methods in an 1889 essay by Mori Ōgai, entitled "Concerning the Novel" ("Shōsetsu-ron"). Takayama Chogyū's (1871–1902) suggestion in his *Aesthetic Life* (*Biteki seikatsu*, 1901) that man's basic instincts differed little from those of other animals stimulated writers like Tōson and Katai to focus more clearly on how man and nature might be connected. Critics have categorized these writings, along with assorted texts by Kosugi Tengai (1865–1952), Oguri Fūyō (1875–1926), and Nagai Kafū, under the rather vague terms "Zolaism" or "pre-Naturalism" (*zenki shizenshugi*),[81] but it was not until the period stretching from the close of the 1904–5 Russo-Japanese war to the end of Meiji that Naturalism became really influential and was hotly debated in journals such as *Waseda bungaku*, *Bunshō sekai*, and *Taiyō*. Tōson's *Broken Commandment* and Katai's *The Quilt* (*Futon*, 1907), as well as the novels of Tokuda Shūsei (1871–1943), were among its most important fictional products. In sociological terms, the coterie (*bundan*) centered around this movement has been described as "Japan's first youth subculture" and characterized as displaying "scepticism toward the established order, pained introspection, a fellowship of anomie and *taedium vitae*";[82] in other words, characteristics presaging the more introspective mood of Taishō youths. It was an intellectual shift neatly encapsulated in Hasegawa Tenkei's (1876–1940) iconoclastic *Art for the Age of Disillusionment* (*Genmetsu jidai no geijutsu*, 1906), in which he coined the neologism *genmetsu* to argue that Japan's old discredited beliefs should be superseded by a more commonsensical scientific view of the world identified in Naturalism.[83]

It would be a mistake, however, to view Romanticism and Naturalism as completely discrete movements in the Japanese context, since they both appeared within the space of a single generation. The move toward an introspective "inner life" had already been prefigured in Tōkoku's Romantic musings, and Shiki's concern with "realist" representations based on scientific observation preceded the moment of Naturalist ascendancy. Moreover, whereas Naturalism in the West developed over an extended period in reaction to Romanticism, with the result that individual writers tended to be identified with one movement or the other, the literary work of their Japanese counterparts often incorporated elements of both. In Tōson's case, Romanticism provided important lessons on how to represent the natural world in literature, and Naturalism also had an influential role to play. The concern in Zola's novels with the effects of heredity and social environment on people may be seen as a reaction against the Romantic tendency to downplay the broader social dimension. In Japan, the relationship between the individual and society in its wider sense was pursued less rigorously, but the western Naturalists' objectivity and seriousness of purpose was highlighted, since it provided a means to address the pressing question of how to define boundaries between public and private space and the nature of subjective experience. It was in this context that the I-novel gradually emerged as a major literary genre and a means for mapping out an "honest" depiction of what was considered the only knowable world—the writer's immediate environment.

But the Japanese approach to Naturalism should be seen less as a simple misunderstanding than a creative misreading related to a distinctive cultural prerogative, which called for the reassertion of a native trajectory as a means of escaping an unproductive dependency on a foreign model. Indeed, it was precisely one such misreading that helped draw Tōson's attention to nature in his writings. Just as Tōson's shift from a personal god to a more general pantheism reflects the influence of the native tradition on imported concepts, Naturalism was likewise reconfigured into a form more amenable to Japanese needs at the time. Taking a cue from Tōson's preface to *The Nap*, in which lyrical poetry is compared to portrait painting and the novel to landscape painting, Miyoshi points out an important change of literary direction:

> Tōson's poetry consists of an extremely personal emotional fluctuation abstracted from the area of concrete, social life; it is a monologue of the isolated spirit. It is similar to the way many portrait paintings are images of solitary people in which a fixed background is considered unnecessary. What we see in a portrait is not the face of someone located in a certain place. We see the face of an individual separated from the strictures of place.[84]

The structure of a novel, however, usually requires people to be located in some concrete place. Without being situated in the mesh-like links that correspond to real life, no protagonist can carry out novelistic actions. One might say that, in Tōson's case, his turn from poetry to prose is a return to life.

Miyoshi is rehearsing here a familiar shift from poetry to prose as the preferred medium that parallels a similar move in the West from Romanticism to Naturalism, but he goes on to suggest a distinct divergence from the western pattern. Whereas Zola expressed his interest in the mesh-like links of the wider world in terms of the relationship between man and society, Tōson was more interested in figuring out complex links between man and nature; for this reason, he frequently depicted rural, rather than urban, landscapes. Miyoshi even hints that this renewed interest in nature developed just as Tōson was becoming dissatisfied by the youthful visions set out in *Fresh Greens*; this suggests that nature may have emerged as compensation for his disappearing youth.[85]

Tōson's "return to life" with its emphasis on ties to the natural world evolved from a variety of influences—a mixture of old and new, traditional and western. For instance, Sasabuchi's examination of changes in Tōson's religious perceptions hints that even Meiji writers influenced by Christianity were frequently more comfortable with a worldview closer to Buddhism, that no aspect of reality—human or otherwise—was greater than any other; in other words, that reality consists of a complex web of interrelated factors. Certainly, in "Concerning Bashō" Tōson considered that

cause and effect might play a role in weaving human nature into
the fabric of other natural phenomena when, reflecting on the particular severity of Japan's geographical environment—its floods,
storms and earthquakes—he wondered if "perhaps the land where
we live has produced our human nature (*tensei*)."[86] That is, the un-
predictable rhythms of nature, which cause sudden and unexpected
disasters, are physical signs of equally turbulent human affairs. A
suggestion of common ground between man and nature had much
earlier Japanese literary precedents, such as Kamo no Chōmei's
(1155–1216) *An Account of My Hut* (*Hōjōki*, 1212), whose opening passage dramatically depicts the breakdown of human order through
the metaphor of houses being swept away by floods. And it is precisely the effort to rise above such precarious conditions that led
Bashō to articulate a philosophy of life through poetry. Tōson
drew from the diverse ideas of Meiji to locate nature as a site where
the aesthetic, the spiritual, and the physical might come together.
As a result, his aim was to capture a natural landscape instilled
with "vitality," to speak not only of charcoal fires but also of the
histories of people past and present.

Tōson and Doppo grew up at the same time and shared a similar
concern with the furusato—together with the overlapping concepts
of countryside and nature—as a literary means to anchor themselves. In addition, their works may be read as indirectly addressing a broader ideological interest in an emerging national identity.
But whereas Doppo only occasionally drew on the furusato in his
writing, Tōson stands out for the sustained attention he gave it.
Moreover, compared to the relatively short-lived Doppo, Tōson's
long literary career allowed him to develop the theme through a
wider range of techniques and influences. In the next chapter, I examine these points in greater detail with particular reference to Tōson's problematic attempts to create a stable subject position centered on the native place.

THREE

Shimazaki Tōson: The Limits of Engagement

One of the illustrations by the artist Kaburagi Kiyokata (1878–1972) in the first edition of *The Broken Commandment* reveals much about the limitations of Tōson's attempt to reclaim through writing the native region he had left as a youth. Ushimatsu, a young schoolteacher anxious that his *burakumin* background may be disclosed, takes a walk in the countryside. The farmers in the background of the picture are fully engrossed in harvesting their fields, but the viewer's attention is drawn to Ushimatsu, who stands in the middle distance with his back to the viewer while he observes the farmers at work. In other words, Ushimatsu is situated in an ambiguous position; he is obviously part of the picture but not quite fully integrated into it.[1] The same might be said more generally of Tōson's involvement in the literary scenes he sets out. If the experience of growing up in Tokyo created a complex sense of belonging, the same dynamic made it impossible for him simply to retrieve the native place as if those intervening years had left no mark. He lacked the authority to speak fully on behalf of the place or to re-establish a complete intimacy with the lives of country people. Indeed, as in Doppo's case, writer and place should be seen less as fixed states and more as aspects of a dynamic interaction. In this chapter, I examine, through close readings, Tōson's attempt to engage with the lost home and the circumstances that thwart this endeavor.

The Railway as Rupture

Tōson had no option but to reconstruct a literary landscape of the native place through a vision strongly colored by his personal experience of city life and the contemporary intellectual environment. These intellectual trends are related to more general social transformations in which technological developments played a significant role. In this connection, it is useful to examine Tōson's depiction of the railway, which proved to be as effective in shaping the writer's understanding of his native place as the Nakasendō road. For the railway serves not only as a symbol of the new capitalist order emanating from Tokyo but also as a material link connecting the city and native place as well as an important agent of the changing relationship between the two.

During the Tokugawa period, Edo was already established as a major center of commercial and cultural activities and drew in many people from surrounding regions. As demonstrated by the decision of Tōson's father to send his sons to Tokyo to gain the best education, this trend continued, and even intensified, during Meiji.[2] By the end of the period, Tokyo stood at the political apex of the Meiji constitutional system: "From the center, comprehensive structures extended outward and downward to all parts of the nation. National geographical spaces had been redrawn with new systemic grids, administrative, political, industrial, and educational structures that overlapped each other."[3] An important technological sign of authority centered on Tokyo was the railway, which served as "the quintessential symbol of progress and civilization, the very epitome of modern industrial power."[4] The association between imperial authority and the formidable force of the steam engine was underlined by the presence of the Meiji emperor at the 1872 inauguration of Japan's first railway link between Shinbashi in Tokyo and Yokohama. Isoda Kōichi even argues that the fact that Tokyo's main railway station (completed in 1914) appears on contemporary maps as the Central Station (*chūō teishajō*) implies that it was the center not only of Tokyo but of Japan.[5] Moreover, the terminology applied to trains headed toward Tokyo ("up trains," *nobori ressha*) and away from Tokyo ("down trains," *kudari ressha*)

confirms the capital's place at the top of the railway (and by implication, the political) structure. The system grew rapidly in Meiji
thanks largely to the efforts of private railway companies licensed
by government. Between 1883 and 1903, total operating track rose
from 245 miles to 4,500 miles.[6] An attempt to integrate the whole
system began with nationalization of the railways in 1906, and operating track exceeded 5,000 miles by 1910.[7] The transformation of
Tokyo into a "land metropolis" was repeated on a national scale as
the railways weakened the internal water and coastal transportation systems that had played a major part in economic activity of
the Tokugawa period. As Meiji came to an end, the railway had
"emerged as a powerful agent of social integration, helping to create both a national market and a national identity."[8]

Railways were not universally embraced; some complained of
pollution, and farmers resisted the expropriation of their ancestral
lands. On the other hand, for many the railway symbolized a future of great potential, and inevitably it began to excite the cultural
imagination. From 1898 the publishing company Hakubunkan produced a series of popular stories entitled "Railway Stories, Train
Companions" ("Tetsudō shōsetsu, kisha no tomo"), most of which
were written by Ken'yūsha member Emi Suiin (1869–1934).[9] Railways also created new possibilities of economic prosperity for
inhabitants outside urban regions. For instance, Tayama Katai described members of one village eagerly awaiting the arrival of the
first train, keen to supply a demand next to the station for teashops
and tobacco vendors.[10] Existing trade centers competed to ensure
that tracks were located nearby in order to gain an economic advantage. In short, far from being an object of resistance, railways
were generally welcomed.

One such struggle, between Tōson's native Kiso Valley and
neighboring Ina Valley, appears in his writing. The first track to be
laid in the Kiso Valley illustrates the shift from water to land: it
was a hand-driven light railway, built in 1901 and used for moving
timber downhill in this densely forested area as a replacement for
the river transportation system of the Edo period.[11] However, the
dispute in question began in the early 1890s and centered on plans
for a far more major undertaking, the National Railways Central

Trunk line (*kokutetsu chūō honsen*). With the aim of serving the central silk-producing regions of Nagano, Yamanashi, and Gunma, it was to run from Tokyo through Nagano prefecture, where the two valleys are located, to Nagoya in Aichi prefecture. There was fierce competition and political lobbying in the Diet between the business interests of the two valleys. Kiso was finally chosen in 1894, and work on the line began in 1896.[12] This was a decisive victory for the Kiso Valley, which had suffered severely from a loss of trade caused by the collapse of the old Nakasendō route. The Ina silk industry, by contrast, fell into a long-term decline.

For a considerable number of rural inhabitants, even those who never left home, the railway opened up the possibility of direct and lucrative involvement in the new capitalist economy. It also promised improvements in the material conditions of life and stimulated expectations as profoundly new as the atmosphere of Tokyo. In the event, the promises sometimes went unfulfilled. Tōson's novel *The Family* (*Ie*, 1910–1911), which investigates tensions surrounding the extended family in late Meiji, portrays the impact of the railway on his native environment far less positively; indeed, it points to a tragic and intensely personal destruction of the place he remembered so fondly. The novel begins with the main protagonist, Koizumi Sankichi, visiting the country home of his sister, Hashimoto Otane. They walk to the back of the grounds surrounding her house to view the terraced vegetable gardens and tilled land belonging to the family:

Halfway up the hill were planted a variety of well-tended plants such as lilies and beans. Passing under a dark green pumpkin trellis, they came to a place where an old peasant was working. Close to the stone wall a delightful path ran through the flower garden. From there, they could see part of the town in the valley below.[13]

In this scene of rustic beauty and simplicity, people and land are blended together in a harmonious and productive whole. The peasant, placed unobtrusively among the pumpkins and flowers, appears to be part of an unquestionable natural order. The same order is described a few pages earlier: the relationship between the Hashimoto family and the clerks it employs is "like that of feudal master and servants" who "had been in service for two or three generations."[14] Through the slow passage of time, an intricate network of vegetable life has developed and created a settled landscape in which everyone fits comfortably. Otane may tell her brother that she does not go out much, but by pointing out the house of some friends in the town below, she confirms her sense of a fixed identity as an integral member of the local human network.

Twelve years later, toward the end of the book, Sankichi pays a second visit. A railway track is now under construction through the very landscape he had earlier enjoyed:

The decimated slope, the vivid red clay, the tracks under construction, the railroad works that cut through the garden's center: all these appeared before Sankichi. The *miso* storehouse that his sister had once taken him to see and the white walls of the warehouse with its upstairs windows where he had read Tatsuo's diary had all gone. The pear field, the grape trellis, the large stone well where Oharu had frequently come to draw water had all been reduced to nothing. Otane used the broom she held to indicate what was left of the obliterated garden to her brother. On the slope opposite only a single wooden hut remained. It was morning, and gangs of workmen shouldering pickaxes passed by under the cliff.[15]

The old order in which a close identification was felt between people and place, where Oharu and the well seemed so closely identified with each other that they constitute a single memory, has gone. The "vivid red clay," suggestive of a gash, not only disfigures the land but also speaks of a family wound; Otane's husband, Tatsuo, has run off with his mistress, leaving his wife destitute. Time-honored ties with the family, too, have been restructured; the family and clerks "were no longer in a relationship of master and servants. Everyone now worked for a salary."[16] In Tōson's eyes at least, the railway's advantages are tempered by the substitution of the impersonal and fungible monetary exchanges for long-standing and mutually beneficial relations between people. Money was by no means a Meiji novelty, but Tōson's point is that this new and harsher economic order has no space for a useless path that runs through a flower garden.

Tōson's portrayal of the mercenary nature of those who have benefited from these changes at his own family's expense is not subtle. During this second visit, Sankichi encourages his sister to abandon hope of a reconciliation with Tatsuo, who has now moved to Manchuria:

> "It's fine for you to say that, Sankichi, but it's impossible for me." She smiled forlornly.
> A deep rumbling arose under the garden below the cliff. It was the sound of the railway trucks piled high with rock. Otane listened until the noise faded in the distance, as if it had penetrated deep into her brain.

Buffeted by cruel fate, Otane cuts a pathetic figure shaken to her very roots along with her beloved garden. In contrast, the fortunes of her adopted son, Kosaku, and his wife, Oshima, have improved immensely following their takeover of the family apothecary business, which had been bankrupted by Tatsuo's misadventures. When Kosaku receives cakes from a man as an apology for attempting to copy the Hashimoto family's patent medicines, he offers some to Otane and Sankichi:

> "How about having some of the forger's cakes?" laughed Kosaku as he offered them to others and took some for himself. Otane looked pointedly at her young daughter-in-law. "Oshima, you have a sweet tooth. Why don't you eat several?"
> "Oh thank you." Oshima sat down by her husband's side.
> "Look how happy she seems eating them!" Otane forced herself to smile.[17]

Kosaku's casual manner displays a marked lack of respect to "his mother," who set him up in business, and Oshima's amiability suggests a shallow indifference to Otane's pathetically reduced circumstances. Otane demonstrates the depth of her emotional barrenness when she opens the front of her kimono after the young couple leaves the room: "She was nothing more than skin and bones, and her withered breasts hung uselessly. Sankichi saw there the sum total of Otane's life." The symbolism is clear: Oshima fattens herself on cakes at the expense of Otane, whose life is draining away. What is more, there is no means of reconciling the gap between old and the new, for Kosaku is a progressive businessman who has turned his back on the old ways:

> Kosaku was a practical man, and Oshima had come to him in marriage lacking any feeling for an old family. As far as Tatsuo and Otane were

concerned, they came from another world. The young married couple had no idea how to console Otane.[18]

Practicality, profit—virtues that allow the couple to make their mark in the new world—are interpreted by Tōson as signs of cold disregard for Otane's personal needs. These impertinent and harsh new ways jar against the writer's more intimate memories of the native home. For this reason, he was unable to depict this new generation as taking advantage of circumstances, just as his own family had benefited from the post-town trade in earlier times. In this way, the home, which has been literally torn apart by the railway, embodies a failure tied to the past rather than a promise for the future.

Despite this negative portrait, Tōson's symbolic relationship with the railway is less clear-cut. The destructive side he was at pains to depict was an undeniable feature of the brash modern world, yet the railway was also a material sign of an economic order emanating from Tokyo that granted him one form of power even as it was denying him another. For the same centralizing force that, by bringing him as a boy to the capital, deprived him of full knowledge of the native place was the very means by which he returned home on a path of productive rediscovery. Literally, the railway easily transported him back to his native region, where he could mourn its loss to the full, much as Mineo undertakes a train journey in "Let Me Return" to eulogize wholeheartedly the childhood site where he no longer resides. Figuratively, the railway evokes a Tokyo-centered social and economic hierarchy in which, as a member of a group of writers from the countryside now located in the center, he has authority—however limited—to give voice to the native site.

In discussing the problems a writer can face when trying to reconcile personal history with the more general trends of society, Raymond Williams locates a site of "negative identification," where

the exposure and suffering of the writer, in his own social situation, are identified with the facts of a social history that is beyond him. It is not that he cannot then see the real social history; he is often especially sensitive to it, as a present fact. But the identification between his own suffering and that of a social group beyond him is inevitably negative, in the end. The present is accurately and powerfully seen, but its real relations, to past and future, are inaccessible, because the governing development is that of the writer himself: a feeling about the past, an idea about the future, into which, by what is truly an intersection, an observed present is arranged.[19]

Tōson's distinctly unflattering representation of the railway's impact derives from his family's success in providing services to official travelers during the heyday of the old post-station towns. Indeed, some residents of these towns "were among the most vocal opponents of railroads."[20] It is not surprising that he should lament the passing of an age at precisely the moment when, by irrevocably tying his home district into the new economy, the railway destroyed a social hierarchy that had served his family well.

In any case, the old native place has gone forever and can never be fully retrieved. Tōson was certainly not the only urban dweller with a sense of dislocation, who felt a need to reach back fondly—if only in literary form—to a home town. The railway does speak of his tragedy, his break from settled patterns, his disrupted memories. But it is his very position as a partial outsider that offers a chance to break free as a writer and put those fractured pieces together in a manner more to his liking, even if such an undertaking must inevitably confirm his loss. In short, the railway is a sign of a historical rupture between past and present that has irrevocably transformed not only urban and rural sites but also Tōson's deepest sense of identity.

Multiple Perceptions

Given this fundamental break, the primary impulse of Tōson's furusato literature is less the reappropriation of an actual locality than the articulation of a deeply felt need to seek a site of plenitude and fulfillment to compensate for the loss he experienced in the city. Such an impulse was frequently a selfish one; it prevented him from re-engaging with all aspects of the native place, as, for example, when his personal history inhibited him from seeing the positive aspects of the railways. Nevertheless, there are times in his writings when other voices break through, working against the instinctive authorial voice, to offer different points of view. Indeed, it is this ability to approach the native place from a number of positions that prevents his literature from being a single-dimensional and sentimental reproduction of "home" along the lines of Koshoshi's *Returning Home*, and instead pushes him toward a complexity of perspectives.

Some hint of these alternative views is shown in *The Broken Commandment*, when Ushimatsu returns to Nezu village in the Chiisagata region of Nagano, where he spent most of his youth, to attend the funeral of his father, a cowherd who was gored to death. When the services are over, Ushimatsu and an uncle walk to the neighboring town of Ueda to witness the slaughter of the bull that killed his father. They are met on the way by Inoko Rentarō, a *burakumin* teacher of philosophy whom Ushimatsu greatly admires, and his companion, a lawyer sympathetic to the *burakumin* cause who is standing in the upcoming elections for the national Diet:

Each of the four men saw the countryside around him from a different perspective. Three of them spoke of things close to everyday life: the lawyer described disputes between tenants and landlords; Rentarō discussed the peasants' suffering and their consolations; Ushimatsu's uncle spoke from experience of farming plagued by all sorts of weeds, comparisons of soil and their effect on harvests, and how mountain people tended to be negligent compared to farmers living in the Kozuke plain. But when Ushimatsu outlined the same landscape in his heart, it was the product of a young man's ideas and seemed unrelated to the everyday countryside.[21]

Kimata Satoshi sees here a "plurality (*tagensei*) of landscapes in which landscape reveals a different guise depending on the viewer."[22] For the lawyer, with his eyes on a seat in the Diet, this is a site of political activity and perhaps of future influence. Rentarō, whose disadvantaged background has led him to champion the spiritual and material liberation of his own community and of downtrodden workers generally, sees the land in terms of the common people who inhabit it. The uncle's interest is directed more toward practical problems of working the land; for him the landscape amounts to a collection of elements—weeds, soils—whose value is determined largely in terms of agricultural production. These three do indeed express a range of views on how the surrounding environment should be "read," but Kimata perhaps exaggerates the differences, since they might equally be seen as representing a common interest, albeit slightly nuanced, in labor and livelihood. On the other hand, they certainly contrast with Ushimatsu, whose view is linked to Romantic childhood associations.

Of the four characters, Ushimatsu comes closest to Tōson in terms of relationship to the landscape, but it is precisely because no single figure can speak completely for the writer's understanding of the place that these alternative views emerge. Indeed, a closer examination of Ushimatsu's and Rentarō's reaction to the environment underlines the complexity of Tōson's struggle to fully embrace it. During the interval between the funeral and the trip to Ueda, Ushimatsu has a long-awaited opportunity to share a moment with his esteemed mentor by acting as guide to the beloved home of his youth. Nezu is set in a landscape of magnificent mountains, and Ushimatsu knows every detail:

Ushimatsu was long familiar with this place, whose nature had inspired him from youthful days, and he pointed out and explained each of its features. Rentarō listened and gazed on with enthusiastic eyes. He seemed particularly drawn to the sight of smoke rising from a group of houses on the Yaebara plain visible on the opposite side. Ushimatsu pointed out the level sunny spot at the bottom of the valley and named the hamlets of Yodakubo, Nagase, and Mariko dotted along the river; in a shaded part of the valley enveloped in thick blue mist, there rose the hot springs of Reisenji, Tazawa, and Bessho; and up there was the pleasure ground on the mountain top where peasants would gather from all around when the buckwheat flowers bloomed in order to forget their hardships.[23]

Out of consideration for Rentarō and his interest in "the peasants' suffering and their consolations," Ushimatsu traces a landscape that highlights human activities—homes, signs of food preparation, hot-spring resorts—rather than the physical terrain in which they are set. And he draws attention to the way the locals have adapted aspects of the terrain to the rhythm of their daily lives, such as their use of the hilltop as an occasional "pleasure ground." For himself, on the other hand, Ushimatsu generally seeks out the features of a less humanized landscape. When he first arrives, he has an overwhelming feeling of relief: "Deeply breathing the air exhaled by the mountains themselves, Ushimatsu temporarily regained the pleasurable sense of self-forgetfulness."[24] This isolated landscape of his youth offers a temporary respite from his fear that he will be exposed as a *burakumin*, an anxiety that he associates with human society in the town he has left behind.

Rentarō, in turn, reveals how his appreciation of the area has been affected by Ushimatsu's detailed guidance:

According to Rentarō, there was a time when he had felt unmoved by this mountain landscape. The Shinshū scenery certainly constituted a "panorama," but it was nothing out of the ordinary among the many pictures painted by nature. Undoubtedly they were grand, but they lacked any real appeal. The mountain ranges rose and fell like waves, but they offered nothing more than a sense of unease and confusion. The sight of them simply threw his mind into disarray. These were Rentarō's earlier feelings. But strangely on this trip his ideas had been completely overturned, and he really saw the mountains with fresh eyes. A new sense of nature spread out before him. He witnessed slopes exhaling their damp mist, deep and distant voices hidden in the valleys, the breathing of half-living, half-withered forests, and banks of cloud laden with shadow or light or tinged with passion as they passed by. He came to understand in a new way the words "Nature rests on the plains and moves in the mountains."[25]

Rentarō's engagement with the landscape is a dynamic one: the land has worked its way into his consciousness and transformed his understanding of it. He has come to see an intermingling of human life and life in "half-withered forests," and his "unease and confusion" have given way to an awareness of slopes that "breathe" and valley streams that have a "voice." This is a landscape that, as it were, speaks to Rentarō in a way denied his companion.

In this passage, it is Rentarō who represents Tōson's desire to engage as fully as possible with the landscape. By contrast, Ushimatsu embodies a different urge, namely, the attraction to the forgetfulness sometimes attainable when confronting overwhelmingly beautiful scenes of nature. In Iiyama, where he teaches, for example, his general depression is relieved by the view of surrounding fields lit by the evening sun as it sinks splendidly behind the mountains: "If only he could enjoy this rural scene without any care or suffering, how delightful his time of youth would be! The greater Ushimatsu's anguished sense of struggle in his heart, the more lively external nature appeared to him as something that pierced his very sense of being."[26] Natural beauty can console when its magnificence temporarily overwhelms internal anxieties, an experience that echoes Tōson's encounter with a sunset during his Meiji gakuin days when he was caught in the growing pangs of a young man. But merely redirecting one's attention to external beauty does not address the internal problems; rather, the intensity of nature's presence is predicated on the very depth of one's anguish. This failure of resolution is explicitly acknowledged after Rentarō returns to Tokyo, still unaware of Ushimatsu's *burakumin* background. The anguished younger man senses a "tide of youth" as he walks the light-filled landscape:

> Without doubt he possessed power; he knew that very well. But that power was trapped within him, and he did not know which path to take in order to unblock it. Ushimatsu walked around the mountain top, caught up in these endless recurring thoughts. Nature brought comfort and encouragement, but which way should man turn? Nature would not say. Ushimatsu's question got no reply from the fields, the hills, and the valleys.[27]

Because of the unresolved gap between the worlds of man and nature, the "tide of youth" fails to translate into action in his present circumstances. In fact, his wistful recollections of his childhood as a time of bliss are a kind of trap; his mind, enmeshed in "endless recurring thoughts," does not allow the deeper relationship with landscape now available to Rentarō. Ushimatsu's familiarity with the Nezu region enables him to name the sites of human habitation for the older man, but what really attracts him is its potential as a place emptied of the social pressures he fears so much.

And this is the source of the unresolved contradiction within Ushimatsu that results in a sense of power being blocked. Rentarō's newfound understanding of the landscape deepens his understanding of the social organization of the local people. He now sees a stronger relationship between the inhabitants and the land, which serves as a place for both work and play. Ushimatsu, on the other hand, must suppress the human aspect in order to locate a site free of social complexity. And yet it is only by engaging with society at large that he can confront the question of his *burakumin* background. As things stand, his insistence on an "empty" landscape is a denial even of his own *burakumin* family's place in it. His inability to speak of his background even to Rentarō, a *burakumin* himself, reflects his failure to locate his own history within the context of the place. In this sense, Rentarō sees a landscape beyond Ushimatsu's understanding. His outcast status has become a positive tool for developing broad sympathy with the needs of all disadvantaged people and the land they inhabit. Consequently he has found a place to operate from within society, even if in the role of a rebel. Ushimatsu's relationship with the landscape simply confirms his continuing exclusion from society.

Etō Jun may have depicted Tōson's shift to writing novels as a "return to life," but this did not preclude the author from a painful awareness that life sometimes remains at a tantalizing distance. On the other hand, "sketching" techniques drawn from painting provided the opportunity to develop an alternative "living style" linked to the haiku poet Takahama Kyoshi. To return to the harvest scene in *The Broken Commandment*, the distinction between Ushimatsu and farmers seems obvious:

From the outskirts of Shinmachi, he passed through several fields of mulberry trees, which were beginning to change color, and before he knew it found himself in a corner of open countryside. Sitting in the shade of piled-up straw bundles and stretching his feet over frost-withered grass, he drew the air of the fields into the very depths of his lungs and felt life stir within him.[28]

The harmony Ushimatsu feels with his environment is expressed in terms of the very essence of the countryside, its air, as it penetrates to the core of his body. In a similar passage in the "Kotatsu Tales" section of *Chikuma River Sketches*, the narrator directly links the mountain atmosphere and a sense of belonging. After his city lungs become accustomed to the cold mountain air, he describes feeling "an almost piercing kind of pleasure known only to people who live in this kind of place."[29] On the other hand, the scene that Ushimatsu witnesses next is possible only because of his distance from it, pictorially represented by the fact that he sits in shade while the "autumn sun shone fiercely" on the farmers. Ushimatsu watched the peasants, both men and women; some were parents and children, others were husbands and wives. All worked strenuously, completely enveloped in clouds of dust rising around them. The sound of mallets striking rice husks reverberated through the ground and blended with the threshing of rice, producing a stirring rhythm. Here and there white smoke rose up. Flocks of sparrows would sometimes soar into the sky, twittering loudly, to scatter almost immediately once more over the field's surface.[30]

His resting position emphasizes his isolation from the others, whose "strenuous" activity is dictated by a real and pressing need to gather the crops before they are damaged: a failure to do so would mean great hardship in the coming months. For Ushimatsu, however, even if the scene stimulates a sense of sympathy in him—among the peasants he is shocked to see the family of an ex-colleague named Kazama who has fallen on hard times—it provides an impetus for life to "stir within him."

Kimata has suggested that in this passage "the landscape appears in two guises: as a spiritual repose for the anguish of Ushimatsu, and as an object of agricultural labor for the people of the Kazama family."[31] This family is forced to work in the fields because the father, Keinoshin, recently lost his teaching job because of illness just six months before he was due to collect his pension. For the laborers, work in the fields relates directly to their livelihood, and for them the sparrows are probably a nuisance, as they struggle to bring in the harvest. Ushimatsu, on the other hand, stretches his legs and enjoys the scene as a diversion from the "real" world centered around his teaching and his fear of exposure; to his eyes, the birds provide a pleasantly lyrical touch evoking the rich pickings of harvest time. In its recreational aspect, there is common ground here with the scene in *The Family* in which Sankichi engages in rural labor: "It was the first time he had taken up a hoe to cultivate even a small area of land."[32] Both characters are concerned primarily with education, and for them working the land or simply watching others do so signifies pleasure in temporarily stepping outside everyday experience.

This harvest scene strongly evokes the Millet paintings familiar to Tōson, and Kimata is right to emphasize this pictorial quality by distinguishing the viewer or "painter" from the object of his gaze. Ushimatsu, he says,

gazes objectively at a landscape from the position of a painter, and he encounters a paradoxical situation whereby he is totally alienated from physical sensations other than the landscape. Ushimatsu's pity for the members of the Kazama family never intersects with his own anguish. The pity that he feels is made possible only through the act of gazing.[33]

Here, however, the critic fails to give due consideration to the dynamics by which Tōson draws Ushimatsu further into the picture. True, the scene depends on the central gaze of Ushimatsu. His view of the laborers as he rests comfortably in the shade highlights the absolute difference between himself and the world beyond him, and Tōson's use of light and shade suggests the influence of Kuroda's painterly techniques. Moreover, the Kazama family is described entirely in terms of Ushimatsu's feelings of pity toward them. When he learns, for instance, that the present Mrs. Kazama is a second wife who, despite her short-temper, feels duty-bound to do the work of a peasant to support her husband and stepchildren, the "knowledge aroused even deeper feelings of pity for Keinoshin in him."[34]

On the other hand, Ushimatsu's alienation offers the possibility of another, closer form of engagement with at least one detail of the landscape and suggests that Kimata is perhaps too quick to equate the gulf between "painter" and landscape with that between Ushimatsu's anguish over his situation and his pity for the family. Ushimatsu catches sight of Shogo, Kazama's son, working in the fields.

"Kazama, where are you going?" he asked.
"I'm going . . ." Shogo faltered. "Mother's over there in the fields."
"Your mother?"
"There she is, sir, that's my mother over there."[35]

From the generality of nameless "men and women . . . husbands and wives," Ushimatsu's gaze is drawn specifically to the Kazama family centered round Mrs. Kazama. In the sense that she has the "robust" qualities characteristic of women from northern Shinano, she fits easily into a rural activity alien to Ushimatsu, "moving her body back and forth as she worked away threshing the ears of rice." Nevertheless, only a short while before her family had been part of his own world, and she is still described as a "teacher's wife."[36] His pity is not for the regular peasants, who will always remain outside the orbit of his experience, but for the Kazamas, who stand in an ambiguous position—not quite peasants but no longer fully part of Ushimatsu's world. It is a pity that he could equally well apply to himself as a *burakumin* passing as a "normal" member of society. And it is precisely this shared experience of alienation from the environment that allows Ushimatsu to experience a level of compassion with this family that he cannot extend to the other characters in the scene. It also suggests a more subtle relationship between "painter" and landscape.

Ushimatsu's gaze, which is neither single nor static, exemplifies the mobile vitality Tōson identified with "sketching" as it moves from an overall view to a particular focus. Ushimatsu witnesses a little drama centered around the wife's irritability with Shogo, whom she considers lazy: "It's because your father's too gentle with you that you won't listen to anything I tell you."[37] This indirect attack on the absent Kazama, who is the cause of her presence in the fields, draws attention to the fact that she is not comfortably part of the landscape in which she finds herself, much as Ushimatsu's *burakumin* status excludes him from a full sense of belonging. In other words, although the wider landscape in which the peasants thresh can never be more than a charming background, Ushimatsu's closer scrutiny of this particular family is made possible by his personal experience, which enables him to sympathize far more fully with their tragedy. To be sure, this concentrated focus diminishes his ability to relate to the total landscape; after all, the very construction of the scene from Ushimatsu's perspective denies his inclusion in it. But by acknowledging the human element, which he considered fundamental to any proper understanding of "sketching," Tōson integrated Ushimatsu into the landscape in a way that casts doubt on Kimata's overly clear-cut distinction.

Tōson's attempt to bridge the gap between himself and the native place must be judged in terms of his success as a novelist. To this end, a consideration of his understanding of the concept of work is particularly useful since it challenges the seemingly obvious distinction between repose and labor in the scene above and throws new light on the relationship between people and place. Sasabuchi Tomoichi has noted Tōson's humanist side, which emphasized art not as a realm apart from everyday experience but as a secondary level of human life (*dai ni no jinsei*). Tōson's high evaluation of work was most likely influenced by a reading around 1892 of *Labor: The Divine Command*. Edited by Tolstoy, this book was a polished version of ideas by Timofei Mikhailovich Bondarev, a Russian peasant who argued that work was a sacred task; the more educated a person, the greater his or her responsibility to promote the value of work.[38] For Tōson, however, work was not simply physical labor but an activity related to the particular circumstances of life in which a person finds himself. This is made clear in the Preface to *The Greenleaf Collection*, in which he recalled seeing young men from Komoro as well as some of his Tokyo acquaintances joining up for the Russo-Japanese war. Although he did not enlist himself, he was stimulated to consider similarities between reporting a war and his ongoing work on *The Broken Commandment*: "Human life is a great battlefield. And the author is like a war correspondent for it. In this way, I comforted myself with the thought that my friends in the distant Manchurian plains and I who was applying myself to writing a novel were all engaged in the same task."[39] But most relevant to the harvesting scene are his reflections on work in a letter to a friend in which he recalled his ideas on Millet as an example of how to realize one's ideals in everyday life:

One example I gave of someone who completely blended this final aim and the carrying out of daily activities was the French pastoralist painter Millet. He retired to the countryside and engaged in farming, at the same time painting a series of works entitled "Cry of the Earth" based on farmers and shepherds. But Millet's aim was not to become a farmer, neither was it to paint pictures. His daily task was to work together with the other farmers and directly study the meaning of nature, to dig the earth through the sweat of his brow. It is such daily practice that gave birth to his pictures. Millet's artistic work is equivalent to the sweat of his spirit.[40]

Compared to Millet, however, Ushimatsu rests metaphorically on the labor of others, as he sits among the bundles of straw, although

Tōson did come closer to the ideal in *The Family* when he depicted Sankichi with a hoe. Nevertheless, just as Tōson saw his engagement in novel writing as a legitimate form of labor, Ushimatsu may be seen to stand for a particular form of intellectual work. Far from being merely a vehicle for his observations, Ushimatsu's perspective emerges from a selection of elements in the harvesting scene—the people, the autumn sunlight, the hard earth—with the deliberate aim of producing a pictorial sketch that constitutes a temporary antidote to personal troubles. That is, the scene is the result of a spiritual "sweat." This effort parallels Tōson's own, very conscious drive to reconstitute the most desirable features of his lost native place and suggests that, despite the gap that undeniably exists between author and landscape, there is, on another level, a real and productive relationship between the two.

A Writer's Market

If Tōson's texts reveal a struggle for his own subject position through a complex negotiation between people and place, they also responded to his readers' need to locate a more stable sense of identity. A closer examination of this relationship between readers and writer helps clarify the broader contours of an emerging national consciousness.

In a study of the influence of social and economic forces on the development of rustic landscape painting in England from the late eighteenth century on, Ann Bermingham notes that a distinguishing feature of John Constable's (1776–1837) painting is the explicit inclusion of the spectator in the scene. His *Hampstead Heath* (1821), for instance, shows laborers working in a gravel pit while strollers from the city walk the heath and take in its views:

Equally absorbed in their activities, the laborers and the strollers are both accommodated in a landscape whose mixed character makes it appropriately a place where some work and others merely watch. The spectator . . . is now portrayed so that his presence is casually taken for granted. In suburban Hampstead, the role of the spectator has become thoroughly unexceptional, disembarrassed of the burden of singularity and withdrawal. This landscape authorizes seeing as much as working. Consequently, rather than signaling our alienation from the landscape, our own role as spectators is what allows us to enter into it, much like the Hampstead strollers.[41]

Of course, Bermingham's concern is with a very different period and setting, and Ushimatsu's problematic relationship with the harvesting scene is characterized far more by "singularity and withdrawal" than the London spectators' unselfconscious gaze. Nevertheless, her observation of a landscape that "authorizes seeing as much as working" prompts the question of the extent to which Tōson's furusato literature invites the reader to adopt the role of "spectator" of the native place. This notion leads us beyond the writer's narrow personal need for a literary "home" to consider the more general demands of late Meiji readers.

To better understand how Tōson's individual impulses coincided with demands in the literary marketplace, we need to place him in the context of the wider range of voices emerging in the contemporary literary scene in Tokyo. Isoda Kōichi's distinction between the Tokyo dialect (*Tōkyō hōgen*) and standard Japanese (*hyōjungo*) serves as a useful analogy. According to Isoda, although the Tokyo dialect was used as the basis for standard Japanese, it held on to certain "slang" variants. For example, up until World War II, the standard Japanese *hikōki* (airplane) was still sometimes pronounced *shikōki* in Tokyo. A more profound difference was that "although 'Tokyo dialect' actually pertained to a living place, 'standard Japanese' was determined as the official and universal Japanese language," and this difference between local distinctiveness and central universality "produced psychological friction in modernization."[42] Among writers in Tokyo, a similar tension appeared between those who were concerned almost entirely with the local urban experience, and those like Tōson whose works showed interest in provincial as well as city life. This difference in geographical interests reflects alternative literary styles that were developing in response to the needs of urban readers.

Representative of the group devoted to urban life was Nagai Kafū, who came to write almost exclusively about the ambience of old Edo in a language rooted in the traditions and experience of the place. He resembled both Sōseki and Ōgai in being almost entirely concerned with the cosmopolitan experience; provincial life was treated with condescension. But as the Edo landscape began to give way before the encroachment of modern Tokyo, Kafū relied on a sensuous and lyrical writing style in order to compensate for the disappearance of an increasingly rare and exoticized culture. Like Tanizaki Jun'ichirō (1886–1965), Kafū was unwilling to discard the melodious quality of earlier literary forms, and both became identified with the Aesthetic school (*tanbiha*), following in the footsteps of authors like Ozaki Kōyō and Higuchi Ichiyō (1872–96). Both Tanizaki and Kafū considered themselves sophisticated urbanites compared to relatively recent arrivals like Tōson with strong ties to the countryside, and they were scornful of their aspirations for success and their angst-ridden search for an ethical life. As Isoda might put it, they shared a concern to remain sensitive to literary "dialects" rooted in place.

In contrast, writers from the provinces (who constituted the majority of the Naturalists) were forced, because of their varied backgrounds, to discard local differences in a search for "standard" elements that would bind them together in the city. Although they might be well versed in earlier literary writing styles, they tended toward a leaner, more straightforward prose in order to articulate their common experience of a new city, a sense of exclusion from the more traditional urbane sensibility expounded by Kafū and others, and their nostalgia for the rural sites they had left behind. Tōson's experiments in *Chikuma River Sketches* were important steps in this direction. At the same time, such innovations were unwelcome to writers like Kafū, whose claim to speak on behalf of the urban-based literary tradition as a whole became increasingly problematic. As Isoda notes, they grew increasingly defensive: "The reason why Tokyo people had to be essentially conservative is deeply rooted in the fact that the people who lent a hand to the destruction of 'Tokyo dialect' were provincials and the group of fanatical modernists who felt a yearning for Tokyo, the capital." [43] The uprooted provincial writers had everything to gain from discarding older literary forms and joining together in the city in the search for something new. Inevitably, their tendency to view Tokyo as a center of exciting potential involved a rejection of Edo, from which the Tokyo dialect had evolved. A common "standard" language, relatively uncluttered by the weight of literary tradition, was an invaluable medium for expressing their shared experience.

These very different writers disagreed over who could best respond to the varied needs of their city-based readership. A writer like Kafū derided what he viewed as the presumption of these newcomers that they felt they could speak for a city he considered his own. And he had good cause; provincial writers may have experienced alienation from both the urban landscape and their home communities, but as old Edo faded into an increasingly distant memory, Kafū, too, became a kind of exile in the new Tokyo. Isoda suggests that since adherents of more traditional literary forms found themselves bound together by their defensive stance, "in order to protect elements of 'dialect' from a modernization based on standard Japanese, it was necessary to create villages called *bundan* in Tokyo."[44] Naturalist writers similarly coalesced into groups. Kafū, with his interest in the Shitamachi area, was definitely marginalized, and the ability to speak for an urban tradition centered around the waterways was decisively challenged and reduced. But it would be wrong to see such a writer as merely trying to hold out against modernization. Rather, the arrival of new writers represents not a displacement of one group by another but a redistribution of authority to speak on behalf of the city. There grew up in Tokyo several distinct literary "villages," each addressing the needs of a particular and, sometimes, overlapping readership but, in an increasingly complex social environment, lacking the authority to speak on behalf of all aspects of the city. Whether "fanatical" modernists or conservatives, all were implicated in the configuration of modern literary Tokyo.

It is against this background that the character of Tōson's readership and its needs come into focus. Whereas Kafū addressed his readers' nostalgic tendencies by piecing together an imaginary and fanciful Edo landscape, an important function of Tōson's work was to provide his readers—many of whom had no memories of a rural native place—with access to his own native place. As Bermingham might put it, he gave them authority to enter as spectators into his personal *furusato*. In the following passage from *Chikuma River Sketches*, for example, Tōson described his experience of the Komoro region, where he had recently moved. It is addressed to Yoshimura Shigeru, a childhood friend from his early years in Tokyo:

Both men and women work very hard here. People like you who study in the city cannot be expected to know about holidays taken for the silkworm season. I think I once read in some book that in other countries, too, in wheat-producing areas, country schools have something called a "harvest holiday." Our silkworm season holiday is something like that. When the busy season comes, even schoolchildren must lend a hand at home.[45]

The Preface to this book mentions that Yoshimura once accompanied Tōson on a visit to his sister's Kiso home and stayed with the writer twice during his time as a teacher in Komoro,[46] and the region would not have been entirely alien to him. Nevertheless, Yoshimura represents a city person largely ignorant of rural life and, in that sense, stands for the wider audience targeted by Tōson: "Until now I have never written anything aimed especially at young readers. This is part of the reason why I wrote the present book."[47] In an attempt to familiarize such readers with the customs of Japanese rural life, Tōson resorted to comparisons with farm children "in other countries." The implication is that for many urban youths Tōson's native place is another "country," to be discovered through his texts just as other foreign places are accessible through "some book."

Given that this territory is unfamiliar to many of his urban spectators, the writer must carefully guide them through each detail of the novel experience. He describes a visit to the farm of a student called S, whose family is involved in dairy farming:

Have you ever visited a farmhouse? The yard at the front is so wide that you can pass directly to the backdoor from the side of the kitchen. Another feature of the farmhouse is that there is a large earth-floored room (*doma*) in front of the house itself. The earth-floored room of this house is directly connected to some grape arbors next to which a cattle shed has been built. They keep three milk cows.[48]

Such space, not to mention the grape arbors and farm animals, were largely unknown in the city; the novelty was compounded by the fact that dairy farming was a Meiji innovation. But Tōson opens up new vistas defined not only by physical dimensions but also by a type of person not found in the city. Visiting a home in Nezu village, he describes the mother of a student called O as "a large-framed, plump woman whose ruddy, glowing cheeks convey a sense of her simple cheerfulness. Women along the Chikuma River really work hard, with the result that they have strong temperaments. Since you are used to seeing only city women, you may find this impossible to imagine."[49] This is a picture of the native place in which uncomplicated needs are easily satisfied, where hard work gives women a strong inner resilience and an ability to accept life with "simple cheerfulness." The mother's contentment is manifest through physical well-being, which, the writer implies, is lacking in the urban environment.

Such a simplistic portrayal of rural life points to how Tōson's furusato literature functioned in part as an unproblematic antidote to the harsh realities of urban life, a temporary escape that certainly appealed to some readers. But his observations should be placed in the context of a more general interest in comparisons between urban and rural life. In 1907, for example, a book entitled *Garden Cities (Den'en toshi)* was published under the auspices of the Regional Bureau of the Ministry of Home Affairs (Naimushō Chihōkyoku). It addressed what were seen as the evils of modern city life and examined European ideas about garden cities as a means of combining the best, and avoiding the worst, elements of urban and rural life. Idealization of rural life is much in evidence, as in the following passage describing the experience of country people foolish enough to move to the city: "What they hear is not the music of water trickling through the paddy fields, but the roar of the factory whistle that simply deafens the ears; what they see is not the beauty of fruit trees and vegetable gardens, but only brick walls covered in soot and smoke."[50] There are echoes here of Tōson's idyllic vegetable garden in *The Family*, although in that story its attractiveness is enhanced by its imminent destruction. This government-sponsored text, however, praises the countryside's advantages without reservation. Anyone who journeys into the countryside discovers that everywhere you go is invested with a fresh scenic beauty. Fragrantly scented young green colors as far as the eye can see, unlimited amounts of beautiful sparkling sunshine, the light of the heavens extending to the ends of the fields and the margins of the woods, the shadow of clouds, even the forms of fluttering birds; all these are scenes unavailable in the city.

In comparison to this environment of boundless space and unlimited fresh air, "the majority of city people are forced to breath unclean and polluted air mixed with a mass of dirt."[51] It is hard to imagine why anyone would ever exchange the vigor of the countryside for the wretched life of the city. Such writing is at least as revealing of its author's unease with the relentless influx of people into the city as of actual living conditions.

Some of Tōson's work undeniably plays up to this idealized theme. Kären Wigen has noted a stereotype of residents of the Nagano region (*Shinshūjin*) as "famous throughout Japan for their penchant for argument [and] their passion for education,"[52] and Tōson confirmed this in his portrayal of Komoro residents, albeit in a somewhat humorous manner:

When they encounter a person accomplished in something, they try to absorb new knowledge from that person. In the region round Komoro, there really are many instances when famed people are welcomed. It is almost like one of those old internal customs barriers where they are loath to let such people pass through.[53]

Rural life as the superior choice is articulated more explicitly in the Preface to the *Chikuma River Sketches* in a way that echoes Bashō as he set off on his journey to the Deep North: " 'Isn't there a way to make myself more pure, more simple?' This was my mood when I fled the city air and went off to that mountainous area."[54] The countryside as a place of unadulterated delight is confirmed in *The Family*, when Sankichi's new wife, a new arrival in the countryside, notices a stream running past her home:

There was a narrow stream at the rear of the house. Oyuki bent down under a silverberry tree and scooped some cold water into her hand. Water poured down through grass from the nearby bamboo thicket, and rushed through the rocks before her very eyes. It was the first time Oyuki had ever washed her face in such a place.[55]

Tōson is giving voice to his readers' (and his own) nostalgic desire for a countryside that offers an easy abundance, a pure and constantly available source of the good things in life denied to the city dweller, a site where all the hardships of city life are expunged.

Tōson's negative evaluation of city life can be equally single-dimensional. His essay "The City" ("Tokai," 1925) presents an unsanitary environment that contrasts strongly with rural health and people with "ruddy glowing cheeks." After discussing Auguste Rodin's (1840–1917) comments about the debilitating effect of the city on its inhabitants, Tōson noted that the gray, lifeless color of Tokyo's vegetation is reflected in the complexion of its inhabitants. For seven years the writer had lived in the Asakusa region of Tokyo, an area that still retained the atmosphere of old Edo:

Nevertheless, if you ask people familiar with local matters, it seems that times are changing even if the buildings remain; the same names may hang above the shop fronts but the inhabitants are different, and households of three continuous generations have become most rare. Children are weaker than their parents, and grandchildren become weaker still. This is visible proof that the city debilitates people and causes their life force (*seikatsu ryoku*) to waste away.

It is this very "life force" that Tōson identified with the strong determination of country women. He next described how the urban environment causes this force to dissipate:

Although the great city is a site of human activity, to what extent does being in the city on the contrary deprive one of the life force? Urban life, in which countless people come together, robs the inhabitants of their individuality, equalizes and evens out their distinctive qualities, and uniformly pounds out their life force with a pestle invisible to the eye. By way of experiment, a simple look around will confirm that there are any number of families just getting by, living like parasites on the city. How pitiful it is to think of city inhabitants living in their narrow and cramped streets, and fighting over limited space and sunlight as they rest their eyes morning and evening on the most insignificant pieces of vegetation that they have claimed for themselves.[56]

There are no houses here with large yards or pleasant grape arbors. Not only does the concentration of people lead to a dehumanizing struggle for what small physical space there is, but it also deprives people of an ability to develop individual personalities. Separate "life forces" become fragmented and exhausted as they struggle to maintain themselves among the relentless stimuli of excessive "human activity."

But although such oversimplifications are undeniable, Tōson's roots in rural life ultimately differentiate his writing from the naïve rural discourse apparent in other texts of the time. William Naff suggests that an important section of his faithful audience consisted of readers who "found a reflection . . . of their actual experience in this country boy who had gone to Tokyo and made good through hard work and strength of character after years of bitter struggle."[57] Tōson's detailed knowledge of people and place gives his work an element of authenticity attractive to such readers. They may have moved to the city for a better life, but they were still keen to cast an occasional fond glance back at the home regions they had left behind, although their own insights meant they were unlikely to take excessively lyrical evocations at face value. For them, Tōson's writings might best be viewed as a collection of parallel memories that helped them retain and refine the increasingly distant image of the native place.

An example of Tōson's attention to more realistic elements can be found in the "Farmer's Life" section of *Chikuma River Sketches*. The narrator begins with a somewhat condescending desire to know as much as possible about the farmers, whose life "seems so open, plain, simple, half-exposed to the fields," but he raises the possibility that there is something more to discover:

> But the closer I get to the farmers, the more I come to feel that they have hidden and complicated lives, even though they all wear the same clothes, carry the same farming tools, and are engaged in the same farmwork. For instance, they have lives of extremely gray sobriety, yet there are any number of shades within that one gray color.[58]

Although the writer still approaches the farmers from the viewpoint of a relative outsider—to himself, as to many other city-based people, they all look the same—he is sympathetic enough to realize that there are other factors to their lives. In describing these lives as "hidden," Tōson was not implying a deliberate act by the farmers themselves; rather, he was acknowledging the urban dweller's lack of a deep enough understanding to make more than broad and often misleading generalizations.

In "The Home of a Tenant Farmer," he described activities that flesh out what these other "shades" of the farmers' lives might be and, in the process, raised doubts about any simple notion that the countryside is a carefree, harmonious environment. The narrator speaks to an old tenant farmer:

> From what he says, I find that what might be called small strikes sometimes occur among the tenant farmers in the Shinmachi area. He informs me that the reason tenant farmers get annoyed with landlords is that generally in this region a hundred *tsubo* is supposed to require one *shō* of rice, one *tsuka* is calculated as three hundred *tsubo*, and one *shō* of unhulled rice is supposed to be two hundred and eighty *momme*, but what is called one *tsuka* is not actually equivalent to three hundred *tsubo* of land. The extraordinary situation is that landlords and farmers share the difference fifty-fifty, and it is from this that the tenant farmers' grievance arises. The uneducated tenant farmers then decide to take their revenge on the landlords in various ways. They cause problems for them, for instance by putting stones in the straw bags when they weigh the rice, by dampening the sacks with water, or by taking greater care with the straw than with the ears of rice, and so on.[59]

Although the farmers are described as "uneducated," their livelihoods are shown to depend upon considerable numerate skills as they work against the equally calculating landlords. And no matter how crude the farmers' methods of revenge, the very mention of oppositional forces operating within the countryside indicates a complexity of relationships far beyond the "beautiful sparkling sunshine" and fluttering birds eulogized by the government ministry.

A similarly authentic depiction of rural life was presented by Tayama Katai, like Tōson a Naturalist and also from the provinces, in his 1909 novel *Country Teacher*. The teacher is Hayashi Seizō, a young man who yearns to go to Tokyo in order to study, but is forced to remain in Saitama prefecture to take care of his impoverished parents. As youthful expectations give way to melancholy reflections on his isolated predicament, his attitude toward his environment hardens:

He gradually came to see that, given the relationship between landowner and tenant and the extreme gap between rich and poor, even the country-side, where he had thought to live a life of pure ideals and be embraced in the calm bosom of nature, was after all an area of conflict and a world of greed.

He also came to understand that the countryside was unexpectedly obscene, wanton, and dirty. This sort of thing often came up in people's gossip. He was constantly hearing about what some girl had been up to, or how some young lady had been having an illegitimate relationship with a particular person, or about someone keeping a mistress somewhere on the quiet, or about endless arguments between husband and wife over another woman.[60]

Katai concentrated on the illicit, seamy side of life in conformity with his understanding of what Naturalist writing should entail. The important point to note is that, like Tōson, real experience led him to reject the idealistic fantasy of a countryside free of greed or conflict. Although particularly unflattering, this portrayal would be more recognizable to displaced urban readers than the idyllic picture produced by the Ministry of Home Affairs. Moreover, even as these more realistic texts may satisfy a desire to "go home" in one's reading, they also serve as a reminder that it may not necessarily be a desirable place to live in reality.

Tōson's furusato literature did more, however, than satisfy a readership curious to discover a world beyond its experience or hungry for authentic details of the world it has left behind; it also contributed to the construction of the native place as a modern myth. This function may well be the source of its profound appeal. In particular, his writing occasionally transformed his own fragmented personal history into an idealized version of family life; it was the response of an alienated individual yearning to belong, at a time when traditional family structures (including his own) were the subject of much dispute. Although he considered himself a member of sorts of the Yoshimura household, he nevertheless felt the separation from his true parents keenly. This is suggested in *When the Cherries Blossom*; letters from the country home to the young boy, Kishimoto, say that things are bad at home and encourage him to study hard in Tokyo:

Privation and hardship had seemed natural to him. He was never for a day able to forget the profound desire to keep other people in good humor and find happiness for himself. The willfulness of other youths who sat at their parents' knees and were able to do just as they liked was unknown to him.[61]

A barrier of politeness always remains between the boy and his adopted family. Deprived of what he sees as an unselfconscious intimacy between parents and their offspring, the boy is forced to seek fulfillment on a more personal level, to "find happiness for himself." In the same way, Tōson sought in his writings to overcome the initial dislocation of his life by recapturing that first intimacy of the native place, but his only option is to make such an effort through a consciousness that has been profoundly transformed by urban experience. He must somehow reconfigure his real family within himself.

An indication of how Tōson's contact with his real family became problematic once he moved to the city can be found in *Before the Dawn* when Hanzō comes to visit his son, Wasuke, in Tokyo. Contrary to Hanzō's hopes, Wasuke feels uncomfortable with his father and his country ways. He is acutely embarrassed, for instance, when his father, with his rural background and interest in Shinto, presents his school friend's mother with a simple mandarin orange instead of a gift more in keeping with sophisticated urban tastes: "To this youth, even to contemplate the idea of someone like his father being in the city seemed like an unbearable disharmony (*fuchōwa*)." This disharmony does not arise simply because of his father's physical presence and his ignorance of urban etiquette. Rather, the boy is uncomfortable with a discrepancy between his real family, embodied in the father, and the internalized image of that family that he has begun to construct for himself in its absence. The experience of "privation and hardship" has forced him to develop a vision of family that represents a willful restructuring of the original reality. Tōson spells out the kind of beautiful memory of the original family Wasuke now prefers to imagine: "His wish seemed to be that his father should remain deep in the mountains of Kiso; by the hearthside of the native home (*furusato*), he should pass the days quietly in the company of his grandmother, his mother, and the servant Sakichi."⁶² A barrier has grown up between Wasuke and the real country family, and resenting the father's attempt to cross that divide, Wasuke "wishes" him away. Meanwhile, the boy's longings for security have crystallized around an idealized mythical family of his own making.

The kind of idealized family Tōson has in mind is suggested in *The Family* when Sankichi receives a photograph from his sister of the Hashimoto family posing against the backdrop of the Kiso valley. The garden and the sunny slope that he witnessed earlier are in the background, suggesting "the tranquility of country life, even though it existed only as a scene within a photograph." It is a view that prompts him to recall his earliest days with his own family:

There were pine trees and peonies in front of his father's study. When the mornings grew cold, the whole family would take pleasure in gathering round the open hearth for a local delicacy, freshly baked potato cakes dipped in grated radish, still steaming as they tried to gobble them down. At night, the fire was enough to make their cheeks glow, while the old farmer making straw sandals told stories of the will-o'-the-wisp in the mountain depths.⁶³

Unlike the passage from *Before the Dawn* in which the physical presence of the father is an undesirable intrusion into Wasuke's inner life, Sankichi is in total control here as he contemplates a scene drawn from his own recollections. This process is somewhat similar to that found in the passage in *When the Cherries Blossom* in which Kishimoto's first arrival in Tokyo is remembered with the aid of the distancing effect of time, the result being that the initially fearful experience is to some extent brought under control. In both cases, recollection serves to cover up real blemishes and transforms actual experiences into more idealized versions.

A similar image in the "Lamplight Deep in the Mountains" section of the *Chikuma River Sketches* suggests Tōson is concerned more to seek out a native place that fits his inner needs than to recreate a rural site based on actual memories. In search of a "genuine" rustic experience, the narrator and a fellow teacher, W, hike up the slopes of nearby Mount Asama, where they intend to stay the night in a simple mountain hut. They are given a meal by the caretaker and his wife, Otake:

The caretaker came to the entrance to ask: "Are onions all right with the beef?"

W laughed and replied that onions would be fine.

"Oh yes, we have some potatoes. We'll put some potatoes in, too?" So saying, the caretaker went out to fetch some of the onions and potatoes they had stored. Presently we dropped down by the open hearth and used large chopsticks to encourage the sputtering wood fire by feeding oak branches to areas where flames were emerging. As the flames blazed, our faces turned red in the heat.

Once again, the hearth figures as a central sign of shared intimacy. As with Sankichi's recollection, this is a scene of great pleasure and plenitude as they eat to their heart's content. In both cases, the writer described an unabashed sensual satisfaction that he found lacking in relations with the city family. However, what is remarkable in this passage is not only its strong similarity to his recollections of the real family—the blazing fire, the red cheeks, the handling of hot food—but the fact that he is not describing his own family.

Tōson may have felt a kind of rupture from the reality of rural family life, but that does not stop the ideal family from emerging as a powerful image in his search for an unmediated experience of native place. The passage continues with a description of the relationship between the caretaker and his wife:

By habit he opened his mouth wide when he spoke, shaking his head, and laughed so much that he showed his tongue. The way he laughed was somewhat lacking in manners, but his straightforward attitude suggested a delightful young man with no hint of malice. One felt an immediate closeness with him. His wife was a plump young woman, known for her hard work, ruddy faced and with thick black hair, and with something of the girl still in her. They really were a well-matched couple.

The rustic simplicity of the father with his mandarin orange that jarred against the tastes of the urbanized Wasuke becomes, in the ideal family, a positive attribute, as the hint of crudeness is more than compensated by the caretaker's magnanimity. The "well-matched couple" stand in stark contrast to the bad marriages of his own family. Moreover, no threat of contamination by the urban experience is likely, since the hut is set apart even from the influence of the local rural town. As the wife says, "From my youth I was brought up in a lonely place, but it took me a long time to overcome the loneliness I felt when I first came here."[64] The writer who was excluded from the real site of familial intimacy at an early age has invented his own family. He has overturned the authority of the real family to become author of his memories.

Tōson could never reproduce more than fragments, fetishized remnants of earlier experiences through his writing. Nevertheless, the presentation of such moments to his readers hints at a shared identity through a common purpose. Shiga Shigetaka's reinterpretation of the native landscape as embodying "unique" Japanese characteristics set the Japanese apart through geography as an identifiable group among other nations. In a parallel fashion, access to the furusato provided Tōson's readers with the potential to develop a communal sense of belonging at the domestic level. His work may have overlapped with excessively simplistic portrayals of country life, but readers accepted it in the knowledge that fundamentally it was based on real experiences related to a specific locality. In that sense, he went beyond what Doppo was able to offer. Of course, Tōson's recollections of his own native place were personal and therefore outside the experience of most of his readers, but their most valuable function was to outline a distinctly Japanese homeland available to a broader society in flux. Indeed, it is this very tone of authenticity that Shiga Naoya would exploit with even greater success. The peculiar form of Japanese identity implied in Shiga's literary landscapes was strongly indebted to new ways of engagement between people and place that emerged during Taishō. One key to these changes can be found in the subject of the next chapter, Satō Haruo's use of imaginative fantasy to extend the boundaries of furusato literature.

FOUR

Satō Haruo:
The Fantasy of Home

A Place in the Sun

In the preceding chapters, I argue that the literary furusato is a highly amorphous concept, less the reflection of an actual locality than the product of writers' personal needs in conjunction with specific sociohistorical conditions. Moreover, their struggle to give shape to the native place and their response to the needs of their readers can be viewed as part of a larger debate concerning national identity.

For Satō Haruo (1892–1964), changing times provided the opportunity to seek a compensatory sense of belonging. The stories examined in this chapter were written just as the 1920s were beginning, a time when, according to Harry Harootunian, culture became synonymous with spirit (*seishin*), or "the world of nonmaterial values." As growing numbers of people came to live in industrialized cities and pursue an increasingly homogenized and standardized life-style dominated by the commodity, philosophy attracted a surprising amount of popular interest because it was seen as a means "to grasp a true or truer experience, an authentic movement unaffected by history and change." But philosophy served less as a critique of capitalist society than as a kind of

cultural consolation against the onslaught of the commodity. In this new vocation, it sought to realize this task by inverting the life of the masses for the poetic, mythic, even the natural. . . . The inversion thus worked to bypass the historical determination of memory completely by repressing the history that would in fact account for this move to make the appeal to a collective, accumulated, and unconscious experience appear natural.[1]

Without doubt, Satō would have recoiled from being described as a member of the "masses," but he was attracted to poetic and mythic themes as a way to break through what Doppo had experienced as a separating membrane, a way, moreover, that overlapped with Shiga's efforts to make the "unconscious experience appear as natural." Satō's distinctive contribution was to extend an understanding of the imaginary home into the realm of the fantastic. In the process, he also explored new possibilities of being Japanese in the modern world.

Satō grew up in Shingū in Wakayama prefecture. He moved to Tokyo in 1910 to pursue his literary ambitions and to enroll in the Department of French Literature, then headed by Nagai Kafū, at Keiō gijuku (later Keiō University). Compared to those of Doppo and Tōson, Satō's literary interests point to a new generation's greater familiarity with western writing. His close association with Ikuta Chōkō (1882–1936), a major figure of literary Tokyo of the time, ensured his personal interest in the translations of western works for which that writer was famous, including his seminal 1911 publication of *Also sprach Zarathustra*, and D'Annunzio's *Il Triumfo della morte* two years later. Satō shared Sōseki's disdain for the austere preferences of Naturalist writers, but his own interests were different. His attraction to Oscar Wilde—he even translated him—suggests that he found a light wit more congenial. Wilde's appeal revealed itself even in Satō's dress; he stood out from the other students at Keiō by wearing a red Turkish fez and a velvet suit and making acerbic comments in the vein of the Irish author.[2]

His first piece of fiction to gain attention in the literary world, "The House of the Spanish Dog" ("Supeinu inu no ie," 1917), shows both the extent to which western elements are integral to his literary creativity and his particular concern with the fantastic in depictions of home. The narrator and his dog come upon an isolated and vaguely western-looking house deep in the woods. Curious, the narrator "tries knocking in the western manner on the western-style door." No one answers. He peers through a window and sees a stone basin in the middle of the room from which water gushes onto the stone floor, reminiscent more of an enclosed Spanish courtyard than the inside of a Japanese house. Unable to restrain himself, he enters and notices a clock decorated with the moving figures of a western man and woman, as well as some books written in German on the table. Seeing a black Spanish dog lying in the room, he is afraid that it might bite him and leaves. When he looks back through the window, he watches in amazement as the dog transforms itself into a middle-aged man dressed in a black suit.[3]

Satō himself considered this work to be an example of traditional "hermit" literature along the lines of Kamo no Chōmei's *An Account of My Hut*,[4] but the Spanish touches—although it is unclear to me what a "Spanish dog" is—and the gloomy atmosphere, which is reminiscent of a German fairy tale, all in a Japanese location suggest that Satō's literary home amounts to an eclectic mixture of influences drawn freely as much from his readings of western literature as from "traditional" Japan. When it was published, the author noted that it was "a short story for people who like to feel as if they are dreaming,"[5] an indication that this patching together of diverse elements had engendered a deep sense of unreality. On the other hand, although the story's mysterious quality hints at a house that is not entirely comfortable to inhabit—the narrator is forced out by his fear of being bitten—"western" elements readily emerge as the means to give literary shape to that unease.

But why should Satō be drawn to write in such a fashion? Rosemary Jackson's comments on the wide variety of definitions of the fantastic as a literary genre might be of help here. Some western critics, for example, have a "transcendentalist" understanding and see such literature as attempting to "recapture and revivify" a "moral and social hierarchy" that has now been lost. To this, she opposes her own interpretation, that the literary fantastic cannot be read in isolation from its "historical, social, economic, political, and sexual determinants." This view parallels my own approach more closely. Her comments on the function of desire are particularly useful in relation to Satō's literary impulses. She suggests that fantasy, which is rooted in the conditions of its production, "attempts to compensate for a lack resulting from cultural constraints: it is a literature of desire, which seeks that which is experienced as absence and loss." Moreover, depending on the different meanings of the term "express," fantasy can operate in two ways: "it can *tell of*, manifest or show desire (expression in the sense of portrayal, representation, manifestation, linguistic utterance, mention, description), or it can *expel* desire, when this desire is a disturbing element which threatens cultural order and continuity (expression in the sense of pressing out, squeezing, expulsion, getting rid of something by force)."[6] The question is how this desire is expressed—in both senses—in Satō texts and, more specifically, how it relates to his representation of a literary native place.

Nakagami Kenji (1946–91), who was also born and brought up in Shingū, suggests a way of interpreting Satō's writings as a response to this "lack resulting from cultural restraints." He calls the Kii peninsula, where Wakayama is located, a "land of darkness" (*yami no kokka*), cut off from the rest of mainland Japan by its mountainous terrain and remote location and existing "on the underside (*ura*) of Japan. Japan may be united by a single sun in the sky, but there is nothing to unite it with this land of darkness."[7] In a powerful analogy, Nakagami describes the area as Japan's "private parts" (*kyokubu*), that is, a place with a "nature that cannot be subjugated, and a metaphor for sex."[8] Wakayama overlaps with the area traditionally known as Kumano, a region long associated with a sense of sacred wonder and otherness, as noted by Miyake Hitoshi:

From the ancient mythical ages to present times, the Kumano area has certainly been a land with the powerful characteristic of another world. On the one hand, it was thought of as another world belonging to the dead. On the other hand, it was considered to be a place visited by gods who had come from another world, or even the entrance into other worlds.[9]

Kumano as an extraordinary place set apart from everyday life is confirmed by its central significance for religious practitioners of mountain asceticism (*shugendō*) on the Kumano-Yoshino route, and it was also an important site for imperial pilgrimage. Its association with potentially disruptive forces can be traced at least to the *Record of Ancient Matters* (*Kojiki*), an eighth-century semifictional account of the founding of Japan. A major purpose of these chronicles was to legitimize the rule of the Yamato people over rival groups, and one of the stories describes Kumano's subjugation by the mythical Yamato emperor Jinmu during his expedition to the east. In other words, this area was stigmatized very early as a conquered site of defeat, and the possibility always lingered that it might at some time again challenge the "legitimate" rulers of Japan.

Nakagami situates Satō's literature in this broader cultural context by citing his 1911 poem "A Madman's Death" ("Gusha no shi"), which laments the execution of the radical Ōishi Seinosuke that same year for his part in an alleged plot to assassinate the Meiji emperor. Nakagami's acknowledgment of this region as a site populated by "the defeated, the despised, the crippled, the deformed, and the dead" is further underlined by his own status as a *burakumin*, but he finds common ground with Satō, who was not a *burakumin*. The poem's expression of sympathy for the radical— also from the same area—is read as a continuation of Kumano rebelliousness. However, the poem proves to be an exception. Nakagami suggests that Satō, like the late Taishō, early Shōwa Marxist writers, who were forced to renounce their political allegiances, ultimately felt obliged to commit a kind of *tenkō*. Satō, who reached Tokyo around the time of the trial, may have thought it wise not to eulogize his native place in literature. Like Ushimatsu in *The Broken Commandment*, the Shingū writer carried a secret that could not be readily broadcast. His apparent acceptance of this situation and his desire to overcome the specific roots that marked him as an outsider to mainstream Japanese writing constitutes his *tenkō*.[10] This is where Jackson's comment on the double-edged expression of desire comes into play. Having felt the need to express (*expel*) the fundamental reality of his own origins, he was obliged to find a compensatory expression (*tell of*) through the kind of fantastic "home" depicted in "House of the Spanish Dog."

Mention of Kumano as a metaphor of difference opens the way to a more general understanding of Satō's experience of lack in terms of national identification. I examine Shiga Naoya more fully in the following chapters, but a brief comparison between the two is useful here. If Satō may be seen to represent an axis of peripherality and otherness, Shiga, who grew up in Tokyo, stands on the side of orthodoxy and centralization: put another way, whereas Nakagami links Satō firmly with Kumano and its rebellious gods, Shiga is more closely identifiable with the sun goddess Amaterasu from whom the victorious Yamato line traced its line of descent. The circumstances surrounding the acquisition of property by Shiga's friend and fellow-writer Mushanokōji Saneatsu (1885–1976) as part of his New Village (*Atarashiki mura*) project helps clarify this point. Influenced by Tolstoy's philosophy, Mushanokōji was looking for a rural site where he could realize his dream of creating a community of artists and fellow-thinkers protected from what he saw as the corrupting influence of urban experience. His essay "The Earth" ("Tochi," 1920) describes the moment he first caught sight of the place where the village would finally take shape in 1918. After visiting various possible sites around Hyūga on the island of Kyūshū, he came upon a breathtakingly beautiful place where "the scenery seemed not to be of this world. A haze lay about, from which numerous hills appeared to float like islands." This description evokes an extraordinary and unearthly site detached from everyday life, an impression emphasized by Mushanokōji's comment that the place certainly resembled the site in Hyūga where the mythical Emperor Jinmu is said to have first descended from the High Plain of Heaven to Mount Takachiho.[11]

Mushanokōji enthusiastically linked the imperial Yamato myth to Hyūga—which is written with Chinese characters meaning "face the sun"—in order to provide greater legitimacy for the place where he would establish his own village. At the same time he may be seen as standing in symbolic opposition to the gods from whom Satō drew his support. He aligned himself with Amaterasu, primogenitor of the Yamato clan and the "single sun in the sky," which claims to stand for the whole of Japan, but whose rays (according to Nakagami) never fully reached the shaded land of Kumano. Furthermore, Jinmu was depicted not only as Amaterasu's grandson and the first god to descend to earth but also as the very emperor mentioned in the *Kojiki* as battling the forces of Kumano. Translating this into twentieth-century terms, Mushanokōji (and Shiga by association) side with the "single sun," the modernizing centralized state established under the authority of the emperor Meiji—which literally means "bright government"—and against which Satō and his radical countryman Ōishi, both inhabitants of the "land of darkness," rebelled. For this reason, the magnificent sunrise that concludes Shiga's novel *A Dark Night's Passing* (*An'ya kōro*, 1921–37) is particularly significant since it legitimates the main character's full re-integration into his world. In contrast, Satō's sense of lack was driven by the equal need to carve out a place for himself in the modern Japanese landscape and discover his own place in the sun.

Fantastic writings played an important role in this effort. Apart from Wilde, Satō was familiar with the writings of Edgar Allen Poe: the epigraph to his best-known work, "Rural Melancholy" ("Den'en no yūutsu," 1919) is a quotation from one of Poe's stories. Imported tales that subverted conventional western representations of reality were valuable tools in Satō's effort to rupture an apparently seamless authority and assert his own presence in the Japanese cultural landscape. He could also, however, draw on more native traditions of the fantastic. The influence of Edo fantastic literature is apparent in "Rural Melancholy": the narrator names his country cottage Grass Hut of Rain and Moon (*Ugetsu sōsha*) in honor of Ueda Akinari's (1734–1809) famous collection of mysterious stories, *Tales of Rain and Moon* (*Ugetsu monogatari*, 1768–76). In Chapter 1, I note Togawa Shinsuke's comment that furusato literature emerged among urban-based writers in the 1890s as an idealized fantasy to counter the disappointing experience of daily life. On the other hand, some writers moved toward the creation of what Togawa calls entirely "other worlds" (*takai*), best represented by Kitamura Tōkoku's more contemplative landscapes.[12] Wider cultural circumstances meant that it was simply not feasible for Satō to write his way back to the real native place. The only furusato available to him was precisely that found through the exploration of "other worlds."

Although Satō struggled to find a place for himself as a national subject within the Japanese tradition, this does not mean that he was untouched by the general developments of his age. In particular, the

shift toward introversion characteristic of many Taishō authors
provided the means to blend those "other worlds" and reality-based
"furusato" fantasies, which had remained more clearly differentiated
during Meiji. On this point, Ōkubo Takaki identifies a change in
representations of nature that took place between Meiji and Taishō
and shows that Satō came to envisage a landscape in which the
boundaries between internal and external worlds merged. He quotes
the passage from "Rural Melancholy" in which the narrator first
sees the neglected garden of his cottage in midsummer. A long hedge
is described, part of which has stopped growing completely:

This is because it was overshadowed by a large pine tree planted alongside
the hedge. What is more, wild wisteria tendrils growing unexpectedly
from the center of the bush had turned into vines thicker than a person's
thumb. Thrusting through the hedge, they climbed around and around
up the trunk of the large pine tree like a net with its captive prisoner, rising above to the very tip of the tree as far as the eye could see. But even
then they seemed not content. . . . Like crazed fingers in a state of physical anguish, the twisting vines rose frantically toward the sky, grasping at
nothing. One of these vines had crept over to a cherry tree even taller
than the neighboring pine and stretched far beyond any of its companions into the sky.[13]

In "Banks of the Sorachi River," Doppo also presented a picture of
nature that threatened to overpower, but a vital distinction between self and external remained intact. By contrast, Satō more
closely replicated Baudelaire's imaginary, distorted cityscapes in
which concrete reality and the poet's often grotesque fantasies appear as part of the same process. Likewise, the Japanese garden in
Satō's text points to what Ōkubo calls a "mental landscape" (shisō
fūkei); the chaotic vegetation expresses the writer's inner psychological turbulence as much as external nature.[14]

Ōkubo also shows how social changes created new possibilities
of integration between people and place in Satō's appropriation of
natural landscapes and the development of "garden cities" in Taishō. In 1918, around the time that "Rural Melancholy" was published, the entrepreneur Shibusawa Eiichi (1840–1931) helped form
the Garden City Planning (Den'en toshi keikaku) Company,
which would play an important role in the creation of Den'en

chōfu, Japan's first high-quality residential area, located in what is now one of Tokyo's outer suburbs. Shibusawa was inspired by the garden city concept, which first emerged at the turn of the twentieth century in Britain as a remedy for industrial pollution and overcrowding in city centers. The aim was to attain a better blend of urban and rural environments, but its social significance should not be underestimated: in contrast to authoritarian tendencies in Meiji, such developments were a physical manifestation of a middle-class claim to a more private space. At the same time, the word *den'en* underwent a subtle transformation in meaning. Its earlier use—a rural area in opposition to the man-made urban environment—gave way to closer associations with the *toshi* (city), as in *den'en toshi*; indeed, the Japanese term was frequently accompanied by *furigana* to suggest its pronunciation be anglicized. *Den'en* was now more closely linked to the concept of artificiality, an apparently natural landscape fabricated by human hands. Of course, the "naturalness" of nature represented throughout the Japanese tradition has been the source of considerable debate,[15] but the fact remains that the separation between the human and the natural world evident in Doppo's writing had much diminished by Satō's time. This blurring of boundaries and a greater concentration on private fantasies were major characteristics of his writing.

More personal factors also affected the way Satō gave literary form to his relationship with place. His texts stand out, for instance, for their attention to pictorial representations. The writer himself acknowledged a strong interest in the visual, and as a young man in Shingū, he had hesitated whether he should become a painter or a novelist. And his preface to the earliest version of "Rural Melancholy," which appeared in 1917 in the magazine *Black Current* (*Kuroshio*), urged his readers to think of the piece as an experiment in a new rococo style of literature that might be described, using the English term, as "decorative illustrations."[16] In any case, his decision to become a novelist did not preclude a continuing engagement in the visual arts. During Taishō, he hung several of his own oil paintings at major exhibitions.[17]

A personal predisposition to art constitutes one factor in Satō's writing, but even such individual preferences were partly shaped in connection with wider literary trends, as suggested in an interesting parallel from Charles Inouye's work on Izumi Kyōka (1873–1939). Inouye outlines the rise of sound-oriented forms of writing, beginning with seventeenth-century *kanazōshi*, which aimed to reproduce colloquial language in literature. Although illustrated books in the following century reveal some resistance to this trend, the development of a typographical culture and the final acceptance of movable-type printing in the nineteenth century led to the predominance of phonocentrism over an earlier pictocentric culture by the time of Meiji. Inouye argues that Kyōka was so attracted to pictorial images, especially in the illustrated fiction he read as a child, that in his own writing "he refused to rid himself of this influence despite the anti-figural nature of the discourse that came to dominate Japan's late-modern culture." In other words, Kyōka took a stand against the phonocentric conceit, most clearly articulated by the Naturalists, that it was possible to define what was "unambiguous and comprehensive."[18] Satō's similarly insistent privileging of visuality may also be understood as a preference for a determinedly ambiguous style of writing, as well as a more fanciful form of native place, in the face of phonocentric assumptions of certainty.

Satō wrote in a variety of styles and genres. During his early years in Tokyo, he was interested mainly in writing and translating poetry, and he associated with other poets like Yosano Tekkan (1873–1935) and Horiguchi Daigaku (1892–1981). In fiction, his interests ranged from futuristic novels to works heavily influenced by classical Chinese literature.[19] For the remainder of this chapter, however, I concentrate on three stories from 1919: "Rural Melancholy," "Beautiful Town" ("Utsukushii machi"), and "Okinu and Her Brothers" ("Okinu to sono kyōdai"). Satō's use of the fantastic to flesh out a version of the native place and his own identity as a modern Japanese set him apart from an earlier generation of writers like Tōson, who had never felt fully at ease with western influences. Indeed, Satō stands out for the way his writing clearly draws on earlier Japanese cultural practices yet seems unusually willing to engage with contemporary social, technological, and cultural developments in order to articulate an extraordinary sense of belonging. In particular, I explore three of his concerns: miniaturization, which corresponds to an impulse to escape; theatrical spectacle, which suggests the desire to reclaim the external world by reconfiguring it; and electrical lighting, which opens the possibility of communal reintegration through a utopian alternative.

Size Matters

In April 1916, Satō moved to Nakasato village in the Tochiku district of Kanagawa prefecture (present-day Kōhoku-ku, Yokohama City), then a rural area south of Tokyo. He was accompanied by the actress Kawaji Utako, with whom he had been living since December 1913 and would later marry. At first they rented a room in a temple, and later they moved to a country cottage, where they remained until they returned to Tokyo in December 1916. The stay provided material for several important works, including the final text (1919) of *Rural Melancholy*, the product of several earlier versions.[20] Its plot, such as it is, reflects real events and can be simply stated. The narrator and his wife flee the turmoil of Tokyo to a small, run-down cottage in the nearby countryside. He is unable to find peace of mind, and his mental state becomes increasingly unstable and susceptible to fantasies. In the end, he loses control over himself altogether. For the most part an exploration of the narrator's inner thoughts, the story is told almost entirely from his viewpoint.

The cottage stands in a quiet backwater surrounded by three urban complexes: "It was close—only sixteen or seventeen miles—to the great cities of T(okyo), Y(okohama) and H(achiōji) and might be compared to a void created by the borders of three fierce whirlwinds. Tossed away by the changes of the century, forgotten by the world, and swept aside by civilization, it lay there dejected." The village is represented as entirely cut off from modernizing influences, yet it is only through its opposition to threatening "whirlwinds" that its full significance is realized. That is, the "void" makes sense only in terms of a wider expression of unease in Taishō with urban life and the search for a site of potential respite. The narrator then suggests why the village best suits his present needs through a comparison with his actual native place (which, although never named, is apparently Wakayama):

On the tip of a peninsula far to the south, his hometown had been a dramatic landscape of wild excesses. Rough seas and jagged mountains clashed fiercely together, while squeezed between them people lived out the small details of their prudent lives in a small town. By its side ran a great and swift-flowing river, bearing rafts unceasingly as it pushed and jostled its way toward the churning sea. In comparison, this stretch of hills, and the village with its sky, its plains of miscellaneous trees, fields, paddies, and skylarks was a far more prosaic affair. If the former was nature as a harsh father, the latter was a mother, indulgent to her child.

There are echoes here of Doppo's "Let Me Return" and Mineo's relief when he returns to the "cradle" of his youth, but the passage also hints at a broader identification with what Smith calls the wider "historic land" of the nation. Satō rejected the dynamism of his real hometown in a way that appears to confirm Nakagami's remarks on his *tenkō*. Instead, he showed a preference for a relaxed and undemanding landscape—a mother figure, as he described it— where moods and whims could be indulged, and he could enjoy "a feeling of boundless joy and a rare ease of mind."[21] However, the ease with which he transferred his sense of belonging to another region suggests that, although he might have opposed aspects of the modern centralizing state, the very process of homogenization gave him license to select the region most suitable for putting down roots (however temporary) in a broader national landscape accessible to the Japanese imagination as a whole.

Satō established this form of self-identification unrelated to place of birth through extraordinary attention to minute details. With microscopic precision, the narrator's mind becomes focused on ever-decreasing areas of bounded space; from outlying cities to the rural area to the village to the cottage and, finally, to its enclosed garden. And this process continues even within the garden itself. Taking a stroll among the plants, he notices a newly hatched cicada clinging to a tree, its wings still shriveled and incomplete. Coming yet closer, he sees how "the very center of the insect's flat head was exquisitely inlaid with a minuscule patch of red even more brilliant than ruby." This observation, together with his earlier attention to a procession of ants on the ground, leads the narrator to observe how the garden's quiet isolation has given him the chance to revisit those distant "childlike pleasures" when he felt closer to nature.[22]

In this connection, Susan Stewart observes that the metaphor of the child may overlap with the miniature

not simply because the child is in some physical sense a miniature of the adult, but also because the world of childhood, limited in physical scope yet fantastic in its content, presents in some ways a miniature and fictive chapter in each life history; it is a world that is part of history, at least the history of the individual subject, but remote from the presentness of adult life. We imagine childhood as if it were at the other end of a tunnel—distanced, diminutive, and clearly framed.[23]

In Satō's case, the text reproduces a visual tunnel in order to relocate a childlike frame of mind and thereby overcome the pressures of adult life associated with city life. Moreover, just as Kyōka rejected a supposed phonocentric certitude in his stories, Satō recreated a childhood "home" through pictorial configurations that refute the logic of chronological distance.

Aspects of the traditional Japanese garden offer a clue why Satō articulated a sense of belonging in spatial rather than chronological terms. The garden in *Rural Melancholy* is not only unkempt but filled with exotic flora introduced by a previous owner, including plants such as "camellias, Chinese black pines, begonias, black bamboo, and weeping cherry trees."[24] This is very different from the traditional Japanese garden, which requires an extraordinary amount of time and energy for maintenance and "is not a botanical garden used to exhibit a large number of unusual plants."[25] On the other hand, there are closer links:

Within the garden confines, all elements that might serve as reference for normal-scale comparison are eliminated. Instead, the visitor enters a miniature world of intricate detail: A stone becomes a mountain; a clump of moss is a forest; a pond turns into an ocean. More than anything else, the Japanese garden is a model landscape in which the mind can wander through miles of countryside.[26]

Although the precise nature of the symbolic reductions found in the traditional garden differ from the narrator's close observation of tiny details in Satō's garden, this space also provides the mind with the opportunity to travel, albeit in a distinctly whimsical way. Listening to the rustling of trees in the wind, for instance, the narrator recalls a childhood nursery rhyme, which in turn takes his thoughts back to the dark woods behind the ruins of an old castle in his hometown where he once came upon an unnatural and mysterious black lily.[27] A feature of the garden—the wind—has set off a series of memories. To put it another way, the seeds of personal memory are located within particular phenomena in the garden, just as the writer's chosen home is constructed as a set of increasingly small spaces, each better suited for individual fantasy than the last. If Satō's garden does not highlight the illusion of great physical distance, it nevertheless allows for the expansion of an inner, imaginary landscape that cuts through the separation of time.

The potential for the garden as a magical locus of escape, fantasy, and spatial reconfiguration was examined by Rolf Stein, whose discussion of container gardens—known as *pencai* in China and *bonsai* in Japan—suggests how miniaturization is more than a simple aesthetic preference:

In fact, the more altered in size the representation is from the natural object, the more it takes on a magical or mythic quality. To set up a park holding specimens of all the typical things and beings of the universe is already a magical act, concentrating the universe into its center, the capital, the residence of the king. But reducing the whole thing in size, making it manageable, accessible to handling—this raises it from the level of imitative reality and puts it in the domain of the only true reality: mythical space.

Stein exemplified this point with the story of a Taoist magician of the Chinese court, Xuan Jie, who has been forbidden by the emperor to return to his home province. He makes his escape by shrinking to a tiny size and flying into a nearby small wooden sculpture located in a tray representing the Three Mountains of the Sea (Penglai, Fangzhang, and Yingzhou). A few days later, a report reaches the emperor that the magician has been sighted flying through the air on a yellow mare far from the capital.[28] The sculpture is both a tiny representation of something else—the "real thing"—and a "real" mythical world in its own right. It is this Chinese understanding that miniature objects are a source of magical power, transmitted to Japan in part through the practice of cultivating container gardens, that finds expression in Satō's story in which elements like the wind provide immediate and "magical" access to other worlds of past experience freed of normal chronological and physical distancing.

Satō's interest in the changing shape of things encompasses gigantic as well as tiny objects. Both interests come together in *Rural Melancholy* as the narrator begins to slip increasingly into an unreal world and encounters beautiful, tiny things. Lying in bed one night unable to sleep, he experiences an extremely detailed hallucination of a city street:

The miniature street was constructed in tiny, delicate dimensions and appeared clearly before his eyes right above his nose as he lay there on his back. It was a marvelous street that did not exist in reality. Although he had never seen it, he nevertheless felt sure that an identical place must exist somewhere in Tokyo. It was a lamp-lit night scene. The five-storied western buildings were only a little more than half an inch tall. And yet these and even tinier houses of less than a half or a third the size were all fitted with entranceways and windows from which brilliant lamp light escaped. Nearly all the houses were a pure white color. The green window hangings were so minute that they could hardly be imagined, let alone measured, by ordinary people. . . . But strangely, although it was a marvelous street scene at night, there was no sign of human activity, let alone vehicles, of any kind. . . . The moment he stared with all his concentration, the whole street slipped far away from his nose and became even tinier as if about to disappear.

The crushing crowds that made him flee to the countryside have been expunged from this idealized version of Tokyo. Fundamentally, this is a fantasy of power regained, in which the narrator reclaims the city by reducing it to manageable dimensions and containing it within his overpowering gaze. But his grasp of power becomes more tenuous when the hallucination undergoes a dramatic change:

Then, as he watched, the scene expanded with enormous speed to its previous dimensions. It then changed into something extraordinarily large, almost to life size, and grew seamlessly into a gigantic form, as if to cover the surface of the whole world. . . . He watched in a stupor as the street then quietly shrank and returned to the tiny miniature perching on top of his nose. For several minutes—or was it several seconds?—he felt as if he had been in the fairy tale in which one soars back and forth between the land of tiny people and the land of giants. When it was a city street in the land of giants, the space between his own eyes all at once widened. This made him feel as if he himself had become a giant, and there had been a corresponding expansion of his field of vision. At times he would be paralyzed by the thought that this illusory street had by chance grown enormously to natural size. Sometimes he would wonder if he might not really be in that street, and anxiously fumble around to strike a match in the darkness in order to look around at the sooty ceiling of his own house.[29]

Even though the city street becomes enormous, there is a corresponding growth of his own head and the scene finally remains "manageable, accessible to handling" in Stein's words. But Stewart suggests that the gigantic carries disturbing associations. Our most fundamental relationship with the gigantic

is articulated in our relation to landscape, our immediate and lived relation to nature as it "surrounds" us. Our position here is the antithesis of our position in relation to the miniature; we are enveloped by the gigantic, surrounded by it, enclosed within its shadow. Whereas we know the miniature as a spatial whole or as temporal parts, we know the gigantic only partially. We move through the landscape; it does not move through us. This relation to the landscape is expressed most often through an abstract projection of the body upon the natural world. Consequently, both the miniature and the gigantic may be described through metaphors of containment—the miniature as contained, the gigantic as container.[30]

In Satō's story, the narrator's head expands to remain in control of the "spatial whole," but the fact that he needs to strike matches to light his way back from a disturbing world suggests that his own power to contain threatens to disintegrate.

Satō noted that such sudden shifts in size are indicative of an uneasy relationship between the self and external phenomena. In *Rural Melancholy*, the hallucination is followed by the narrator's consideration of how his head sometimes feels as small as a bean and then expands as if to fill the whole universe. Satō examined the sensation more fully in an essay, "Concerning Refinement" ("Fū-ryū ron," 1924):

In an instant when you are mentally or physically exhausted, have you never experienced being seized by an odd feeling that a part of the body, such as a hand or the head, suddenly seems to expand to infinity, and all at once suddenly shrinks to the size of a poppy seed? I have frequently experienced such a phenomenon. And I have interpreted it to my own satisfaction: could it not be that, at a time when our ancestors and we ourselves were so young that we were hardly aware, the instant of surprise when we unconsciously realized the greatness of nature and the minuteness of humanity has now been engraved so deeply into the recesses of our hearts that this is the first thing to be instinctively recalled when the mind is left to its own thoughts? Surely that unpleasantly large palm of the hand, and the palm which, to one's consternation, seems to be about to disappear, are symbolic of the universe and humankind.[31]

The writer is anxiously addressing the fundamental question of how a seemingly insignificant self can be integrated into the awesome reality of elemental forces.

Clearly, it was not easy for Satō to attain a sense of full integration even in a fantasized form, and he acknowledged as much in his story "Beautiful Town." It concerns the artist E., who meets an old schoolmate after a separation of many years. The friend, Kawasaki, is of mixed parentage and has returned to Japan from America with wealth accumulated from his deceased father's mining interests in South America. His overwhelming ambition is "to invest all of his fortune in the building of a beautiful town somewhere."[32] He hopes to purchase the Tokyo riverside district of Nagazu, and he hires an old architect, T., to provide the designs. With Kawasaki's financial backing and E.'s artistic contribution, the three throw themselves wholeheartedly into the first stage of the task, working for three years from evening until late at night to construct an exquisitely fashioned town made of cardboard on a tabletop in a rented hotel room in Tsukiji.

Above I mentioned Shibusawa Eiichi's contribution to the creation of Japan's first garden city, but his concern with improving life was also shared by the government, which was turning its attention to inferior housing conditions within Tokyo itself. In 1919, both the Town Planning and Zoning Act (Toshi keikaku hō) and the Urban Building Act (Shigaichi kenchikubutsu hō) were enacted. In November of that year, the Ministry of Education also sponsored a Life Improvement Exhibition (Seikatsu kaizen tenrankai) at the Tokyo Museum of Education. This exhibition paid particular attention to the total environment of residences and gave serious consideration to garden cities. Given this background, Satō's choice of the "beautiful town" as a literary topic is not surprising, but he resorted to a far more idiosyncratic dream of a better life. With a regulatory approach no less dogmatic than that of the government, Kawasaki dictates that only about a hundred houses should be constructed. What is more, potential residents must fulfill very stringent requirements:

(a) People most satisfied with the houses I have built. (b) Married couples who have chosen each other. And both partners should still be in their first marriage and have children. (c) People who have chosen for their employment what they most desired to do, and who therefore have established themselves as most proficient in their work. (d) No merchants, no government officials, and no military. (e) People who promise never to carry out cash transactions in the town, and thus people who foresee a certain amount of inconvenience in the future. For this reason, I expect to build a separate place where money can be handled for the townspeople close to, but outside of, the envisaged town. (f) People living there must rear a dog with loving care. People who have no innate love of dogs may rear a cat. People who dislike both cats and dogs can look after a small bird, and so on.[33]

The stipulation of animals reflects Satō's particularly strong attachment to pets, also illustrated in the loving relationship between the narrator and his dogs in *Rural Melancholy*. And although the separation of living and business areas fits in with the garden city ideal of city workers who dwell in a separate rural environment, the banning of all money transactions takes it to an extreme. The exclusion of apparently undesirable elements—merchants, bureaucrats, soldiers—reveals the extent to which his vision differs from other versions of modern life in which such members of society were normally considered indispensable.

An article appearing in the *Yomiuri shinbun* on May 2, 1920, concerning the millionaire Nishimura Isaku, also from Satō's hometown, gives a clue to how the writer's ideal community differs from what was envisaged not only by the government but also by more "realistic" representatives of private enterprise:

[Nishimura] will purchase 2,000 *tsubo* near Odawara station and create a small-scale garden city. Ten so-called cosmopolitan homes will be constructed mainly to accommodate artists. He wishes to use this place as a center in which to make the kind of household objects produced by people like the Englishman Bernard Leach and other refined household implements and tools of general and practical use.[34]

The writer and the millionaire knew each other personally; while still living in Shingū, the young Satō had attended Nishimura's salon. Nishimura had an interest in ceramics and oil paintings as well as home construction, and he also founded the Bunka gakuin (Cultural academy) in 1921, which employed famous literary figures such as Yosano Akiko (1878–1942). This cultivated entrepreneur's plan to create a colony mostly for artists links him to Satō, who shared a desire—albeit in a more extreme and exclusive fashion— for a site in which artistic ideals might flourish. On the other hand, his more utilitarian bent is apparent in his goal of a center that will produce items "of general and practical use."

Nishimura's Odawara colony was never built, but Satō spelled out the nature of his own enterprise when he identified the "beautiful town" more as the product of a fantastic dream than an object of the everyday world. This miniature tabletop town, like the imagined city street of *Rural Melancholy*, provides the writer with another "model landscape in which the mind can wander." When the model town nears completion, however, Kawasaki reveals that, once he realized he did not have the necessary money to produce the design in reality, he "came to feel a desire to express it through art, so that it might exist securely at least in people's hearts."[35] The writer's purpose is to show that, by refusing to turn cardboard models into actual buildings, by keeping the town forever in a realm of fantasy, any compromising of artistic ideals can be avoided. The underlying message is that only a town devoid of people and their mundane concerns can manifest true beauty.

Satō rejected his real native place in favor of a potentially more productive "home" shaped by the imagination. His literary exercise in urban planning provided an opportunity to assert his own power in creating an aesthetic alternative. If only in model form, an ideal town has been built despite a lack of funds and without commercial interference. To a certain extent Satō's artistic fantasy succeeds, for every time the bitterly disappointed E. tries to forget the model

town, he "suddenly remembered the garden of the 'beautiful
town,'" and every Tokyo roof "recalled the roofs of the 'beautiful town.'"[36] In this sense, Tokyo's mundane architecture is rendered secondary, the feeble reflection of an aesthetically perfect
world. In fact, Satō designed and built a house in the Tokyo district
of Sekiguchidai in 1927. However, its fantastic appearance—it was
painted light pink and had a sun dial and fountain in the garden—
suggests that his interest in house building was less the commonplace Taishō aspiration for a better living space, than what has been
described as a "poetic task" (*shiteki jigyō*).[37] Satō's struggle to formulate a literary home was immensely productive but, as confirmed
by his actual involvement in construction, highly idiosyncratic. Indeed, it was this deliberate pursuit of private fantasy as a means to
link personal identity with the modern environment that separates
him from the earlier generation of writers.

Spectacular Transformations

Uncoupled from direct ties to the native place, Satō sought to rein-
sert himself into a broader national landscape through remarkable
and spectacular fantasies, an effort that was greatly helped by his
painter's eye. The play of light and darkness in his work is striking,
for example. In the first five sections of *Rural Melancholy*, the narrator's expectation that his move to the country will release him
from the pressures of city life is reflected in an atmosphere of almost excessive brightness, and the cottage, seen for the first time,
appears "surrounded by the restless dizzy light of a summer morning."[38] With the onset of the rainy season, however, his initial,
bright enthusiasm begins to cloud as fleas, recurring stomach problems, and a monotonous diet make him increasingly bored and depressed. His state of mind takes on the character of the gloomy
weather, and his life slips into a shadowy reality filled with fantasy
and paranoia. He fumbles, for instance, in the dark house of evening for the lamp, convinced that "it has suddenly disappeared
somewhere."[39] Within this twilight world, light itself sometimes
seems a source more of fear than of hope. When he finally manages
to light a fire for his evening meal, the enormous flickering shadows cast on the wall by himself and his dogs come closer and "ap-

pear to be about to swallow up the real bodies."[40] In the final section, the skies suddenly clear, and he momentarily attains the serene bliss he has been yearning for; as he observes sparrows eating grains of rice dropped at the well-side by his wife in the bright sunshine, his thoughts turn to St. Francis, the patron saint of animals. But this brief respite serves only to increase his eventual shattering when he realizes that the beloved roses he nurtured in the garden, cut by his wife to decorate the breakfast table, are rotten.

Yet precisely when he is lost in gloomiest depression, the impulse to anchor himself within a landscape entirely under his control comes to the fore through a spectacular fantasy. I suggest above that his imagination roams through increasingly smaller spaces within the enclosed garden. In a traditional garden, however, "the sense of enclosure never becomes confining or absolute. There is always some visual escape, a sense of promise."[41] This is also true for the narrator. His attention is drawn to a hill with a striped pattern at some distance from the cottage. He first noticed it after the monotonous rains begin, and he feels the whole world is rotting:

Looking from the verandah of his house, a dome-shaped space had been formed by the tangle of pine and cherry tree branches jutting toward each other in the garden: the arching curve produced by the branches and leaves of these trees was supported from below by the dead straight line of the bush's top. The result was what one might call a border of greenery (*midori no waku*). It was a picture frame. And in the very depths of the space formed by the picture frame, the hill could be seen far in the distance.[42]

An echo of "borrowed scenery" (*shakkei*) can be found here, a feature of the traditional garden. Distant scenery unrelated to the garden is "borrowed" as a background in order to give the garden greater depth. In a real garden, a careful selection of the background view would require that the trees be carefully trained to produce such an effect. In this fictional story, however, it is the writer's prerogative to dictate the views visible from the garden even if the plants grow wild, since he is its ultimate creator.

Isoda Kōichi places Satō's "picture frame" against changes in aesthetic consciousness in eighteenth-century Europe in a way that suggests parallel developments in the mind of the Taishō writer:

We should probably note here that the eighteenth-century western "land-scape garden" was also called the "picturesque garden." It was a parallel development to eighteenth-century painting, which placed "nature" in a "frame," and formed the source for Romantic landscape poetry. This ten-dency might be called an artistic movement, an attempt to give artificial support to nature, which was facing a critical decline with the develop-ment of the industrial revolution.[43]

Satō revealed his antagonism to elements of his own industrial age with his concern for natural beauty. It is not surprising that, with his interest in painting, the writer offered pictorial details in his lit-erary depictions. Satō perhaps also draws from an earlier Edo lite-rati (*bunjin*) tradition that delighted in the artificial representation of natural scenery, thus providing a further kind of distance or pic-torial perspective with which to "frame" his countryside.

But framed pictures also featured in the traditional Japanese gar-den. To create a distant scene in the right proportions, use was made not only of the eaves of buildings and large pruned trees within the garden but also of a special "picture window." This was generally formed from an opening carved into a wall and "presents the most obvious connection between gardening and landscape painting: It selects a view and presents it as if it were a painting."[44] In his disturbed state of mind, the "painting" perceived by the nar-rator of *Rural Melancholy* is of a particularly fantastic kind, appear-ing to him "like a fairy land. It was beautiful and small, and today it surely held something even more mysterious." Moreover, "bor-rowed scenery" generally consists of a static natural feature like a mountain in which change is due only to slow seasonal variation, but he witnesses a far more dynamic scene:

As if peering through the end of a marvelous telescope and observing the folk at work in fairy land, and with far from ordinary feelings toward this small hill, he gazed unblinkingly and with a sense of longing, just like a child who peeps into a kaleidoscope. He finally brought out his tobacco tray and cushion onto the verandah and devoted all his attention to watch-ing the purple color of the earth grow of its own accord. The purple earth appeared to well up. In wave after wave it grew. As he watched, the area of purple earth encroached relentlessly into the green space. The pale sun gradually brightened. Suddenly, through a narrow chink in the gradually clearing westering clouds, the evening rays gushed forth in one mass and struck the top of the hill. The hill became suddenly radiant among dancing light beams. As if colored footlights had been thrown onto the hill. On the hill itself, both fairies and assorted trees drew long, deep shadows across the earth, so that the fairy land scene stood in even sharper relief. The newly arisen purple earth emitted a sound like the lowest tone of an organ and seemed to cry out with one voice. The thatched roof among the woods on the top of the hill appeared smooth, and there rose from it a single thread of dense white smoke, unceasingly, like a plume from an incense burner. Spellbound, he had become the fairy king.[45]

Although one of the first things he noticed about the hill was its striped pattern, these stripes were nevertheless all green; the hill appeared to be a polished emerald in all its facets. Only when he puts on his glasses does he realize that what makes it "even more mysterious" this day is the way the green is gradually becoming purple. By straining his eyes, he can just make out that the tiny fairy folk creating the color change are in fact farmers harvesting some green produce that had been cultivated between the tree seedlings. The tone of the "organ," meanwhile, may be a synaesthetic substitution of color for sound or simply the noise of farm machinery. In any case, the whole strange spectacle diverts the narrator from the pressures of his daily life.

Wolfgang Schivelbusch notes that lighting has been an important indicator of the relationship between audience and performance in European theater in a way particularly relevant to this discussion of the hilltop scene. In the Renaissance and Baroque theater, both the stage and the auditorium were lit up because there was no clear division between audience and actors. This began to change in the eighteenth century:

The fact that the auditorium gradually got darker as the stage grew brighter throughout the eighteenth century signalled that a change was taking place in the social, aesthetic and moral role of the theatre. The audience that assembled in the auditorium now directed all its attention to the events on the stage. In essence, it was no longer "an audience," but a large number of individuals, each of whom followed the drama for him or herself. The new ideal was to achieve direct communication between the spectator and what was being presented, to the exclusion of all distracting, external factors. The idea of darkening the auditorium was to enhance this feeling of community between the viewer and the drama by shutting out the social phenomenon of the audience for the duration of the play.[46]

A similar transformation began in Japan during the Meiji period, becoming even more pronounced over time. As with so many other cultural activities, people started to view the theater with far greater seriousness. In the puppet (*bunraku*) theater, for example, the older, rather haphazard manner of watching—eating box lunches in a lighted auditorium during the performance, dozing, or trying to listen over the din of playing children—became increasingly rare. This point is made in Tanizaki's *Some Prefer Nettles* (*Tade kuu mushi*, 1928): Kaname has to travel far—from Tokyo to Shikoku, in fact—to experience the old atmosphere of *bunraku* in his attempt to recapture fading Japanese traditions.[47]

There are strong similarities to the new theatrical experience in Satō's hilltop scene. On his verandah, the "distracting, external factors" of the everyday world are pushed away, as the house, already gloomy because of the miserable weather, is enveloped in evening twilight. In the narrator's theater of illusion, even a natural phenomenon like the chance break in the clouds is invested with the role of artificial "colored footlights" that illuminate the activity on the distant "stage." But it is only when the shadows cast by the evening rays dramatically transform the picture into a magical three-dimensional world that the stage truly comes to life. What is more, in this case the "large number of individuals" who watched the eighteenth-century performance has been pared down to only one viewer; an even closer analogy might be the solitary viewer enclosed in darkness at the cinema—a popular pastime in Taishō. Certainly, the scene's existence depends entirely on the concentrated fantasy of the narrator, and for this reason the "reality" of farmers working the land becomes virtually meaningless. Independent farmers are transformed into minions, acting out their part for the single pleasure of the "fairy king." Through illusory techniques, Satō has allowed the narrator temporarily to regain power over an external "real" world and claim it as his own.

This tendency to view the outside world from an increasingly narrow perspective can be traced not only through changes in stagecraft but also through other forms of visual representation that first appeared in Meiji. For instance, the panorama displayed a 360-degree image inside a circular room, normally viewed from a central platform. It was invented in Britain in the late eighteenth century and became popular in Paris during the early nineteenth century, and it attracted a great deal of attention in Japan from 1890 when the first panorama opened in Ueno Park. The panorama was a spectacle "which aimed at restoring the 'scene' to its original state," so that "the spectator is totally enveloped by the exhibit. The exhibit is overwhelmingly dominant."[48] Such a device perfectly fit the open and enthusiastic mood of that age, when people were suddenly able to satisfy their curiosity about a world that, until recently, had been mostly unknown to them. For instance, the "Arts Panorama," which opened in Asakusa in 1891, offered a show in the form of a journey from Shanghai through the Suez canal to Europe and finally to New York.[49] Not strictly a panorama—it was a series of dioramas—it allowed people to view or, to put it another way, to be dominated by these representations of the external world. It must have been a source of huge pleasure to those who hungered for novel experiences.

In the Taishō period, on the other hand, writers like Satō moved away from that early enthusiasm for the external world and began to form an engagement with surroundings that depended on a more internalized, individual interpretation. For this reason, even the narrator's wife in *Rural Melancholy* is excluded from an appreciation of the hill's "true" magic by her prosaic attitude; the striped hill reminds her of a pretty kimono. In order to emphasize the hill's fantastic effect, Satō removed her entirely from the scene (she is sent off shopping in Tokyo for the day) and the narrator is left alone to fully savor the spectacle of "fairyland."

There are ways, then, of placing Satō's representation of spectacular art in the context of post-Meiji imported technology. Let me conclude, however, by returning to a more native-based genealogy and suggest that his fantastic depiction depends not only on a new set of attitudes specific to his own generation of writers, but also on a reappropriation of some features of earlier Edo culture.

In particular, the writer's concern with strange and unnatural events links him to the "frivolous" entertainments and spectacles of that earlier age. In the peaceful Tokugawa period, the practice of setting up temporary stalls in temple grounds and amusement quarters (*sakariba*) became a popular means of showing exhibits (*misemono*) of various skills and unusual objects. The new Meiji government put an immediate stop to certain shows deemed unsuitable to progressive tastes. Imaginative sexual performances, for instance, were banned in 1868. Other temporary stalls were restricted by government ordinance because of an increased concern with fire prevention and public hygiene. As more permanent structures were built to house the exhibits, the manner in which they were perceived by the viewer also underwent a transformation:

For instance, types of artistic exhibit, conjuring tricks, acrobatics, top-spinning, stunts, feats of strength, and so on were absorbed into the circus and variety hall (*yose*). And apart from human freaks, exhibits of oddities such as rare birds and animals, strange insects and fish, odd plants and rocks, were put into public institutions like the zoos, aquaria, botanical gardens, and museums.[50]

Just as the theater was now something to be appreciated with a greater degree of seriousness, the fun of gaping at odd things was pursued within in well-defined places like the circus. The viewing of unnatural phenomena came to be seen more as an educational "museum" experience; this "superior" knowledge of such things became one more way to gain an advantage over others.

By the time Satō was writing, the enclosure of oddities into strictly delineated areas of life had become the norm. And yet, it is precisely against this conformity and decidedly unfrivolous view of the world that the writer struggled in his works. In *Rural Melancholy*, by depicting the increasingly deranged narrator's terror at being haunted by the freakish ghost of a mad white dog, Satō sought to derationalize the seemingly fixed boundaries of stable reality. This is another reason why he had to shift the scene away from the urban environment, for he could impose his fantasies only on a rural landscape whose "reality" is open to greater interpretation by city-based writers and therefore more susceptible to his own imaginative interpretations. Reflecting the rebellious instincts of a Kumano man, Satō freed the freaks from their "proper" place to roam in a fantastic territory of his own making, although he could not avoid a serious compromise with the realities of modern life: despite the pleasure he might gain from his spectacular art and its promise of settled identity, it could be realized only through the illusion of imaginative texts. It is, however, precisely this imaginative function that distinguished him from Doppo and Tōson, and empowered him to anchor himself in a reconstituted national landscape.

Electric Utopia

Satō's obsession with the minutiae of life and his highly individualistic fantasies might be interpreted merely as the desire to escape social reality. On the other hand, in his pursuit of what Harootunian called an "authentic movement unaffected by history and change," he was giving voice to a distinctive turn in the national character during Taishō. But beyond that, the fragmentation of social reality into private experience, stimulated by technological developments, provided him with the means to articulate a utopian vision of communal reintegration.

Light functions as key to Satō's close relationship with place. Takahashi Seori suggests that the writer was particularly receptive to the quality of light because he grew up in a region with an especially sunny climate. The critic relates that one of Satō's earliest memories was of almost drowning in a river because, according to Satō, the bright sunlight on the water's surface had lured him into the water.[51] His continuing fascination as an adult with the effect of light—electric light in this case—is expressed in "Beautiful Town" when Kawasaki realizes that his list of residency qualifications may be too demanding. If suitable people cannot be found, he says, "I would just like to have someone keep the houses I have built swept clean. And at night time, I would have bright lamps lit inside the houses where no one is living so that the beauty of the lamps can be seen from the windows."[52] The reference to cleaning and the total absence of people with their possibly corrupting influence on the aesthetically perfect scene suggest that the author may be associating the traditional ablutionary role of water with light, since the two were inextricably linked together in his mind from childhood.

Another feature that makes light attractive to Satō is its role as a contact point between mundane and mysteriously beautiful worlds, what Takahashi calls "a fulcrum between light and dark" (*meian no shiten*).[53] This is seen in a particularly beautiful observation of the interaction between sunlight and flowing water in *Rural Melancholy*. Although he is describing an irrigation ditch next to the house, the pure water comes from the mountains and the ditch resembles a beautiful brook:

Sunlight pouring down through green leaves strengthened this impression. The red earth sludge had dried out so completely that no trace of muddiness was left. From time to time, something would cause the shallow running water to dam up, and it would sparkle with uncharacteristic brightness; then, before it could be fully appreciated, it gleamed delicately like wrinkled crepe or seemed suddenly struck by the flicker of tiny convulsions. Then again, the small glitterings might pile up like the scales of a fish. When a cool breeze moved low and smooth against the water's surface, there for a moment were thin slivers of silver foil.

The play of light serves as an entrance point for the writer to satisfy his hungry search for intricate details of beauty. Satō was concerned less with the straightforward depiction of a "real thing" that would interest a Naturalist writer than with the possibility of exploiting aesthetically pleasing patterns as a stimulus for his own poetic imagination.

The description of the ditch shows the value of light not only for its ability to serve as a kind of window into other worlds that the narrator can then claim for himself but also for its reflective powers; sometimes coming to a halt, it "mirrored the color of turquoise—turquoise like the afternoon summer sky."[54] The mirror, one of the three imperial regalia, has long been a potent Japanese symbol of power. The "eight-hand mirror," for example, was used to attract the moody sun goddess, Amaterasu, toward the bright beauty of her own reflection and draw her out from the Rock-Cave of Heaven in which she had hidden herself. Satō's equally deep fascination with mirrors is revealed in "Beautiful Town": not content with constructing just model houses, Kawasaki uses mirrors to increase the illusion of a totally self-enclosed environment. Trees are made from "wire and scraps of frayed woolen yarn," and he even creates a model river:

He laid out mirrors on the board in place of the rivers that would surround the whole area, so that the inverted image of rows of toylike houses was reflected within them. When the mirrors were too clear and failed to give the effect of the water's surface, he clouded the mirror surface by turning it into semi-transparent frosted glass.

The model town, already a replica of the "real" town to be built, is itself reproduced as an "inverted image." The model is consequently reformulated as a "real" thing capable of being reproduced as a second image in the mirror. The effect is to create an object of beauty existing by and for itself.

The purely aesthetic appeal of light and its playful representation as an illusive reality becomes clear when Kawasaki turns off the lights:

He must have set it all up beforehand without our knowledge, but now, inside each and every house in this tabletop "beautiful town" of paper, a faint light leaked out from those exceedingly minute windows: a night-time district, tiny by any measurement, had appeared before our eyes. The lamp light flowing out from all those windows was dimly reflected on the quiet water surface of the frosted glass mirrors. And even there, his fine attention was evident. It appeared that the mirrors had been laid at just the proper angle against the houses so that much of the lamp light cast long and narrow beams just as if it were brushing across the surface of water.[55]

Like Amaterasu, who was tempted from the cave by her own attractiveness, this miniature town, free of the real world's imperfections, can quite literally reflect upon its own beauty through mirrors—a narcissistic beauty multiplied, moreover, through its reflection.

In the case of *Rural Melancholy*, Takahashi points out that there are no mirrors, although the diseased rose might be seen as symbolically mirroring the troubled narrator's inner feelings.[56] But the well in the final scene functions in a similar manner to a mirror. The narrator seems to have regained his zest for life with the sudden arrival of beautifully clear weather, but when he asks his wife to cut some of his roses for the breakfast table, he discovers in horror that they are worm-eaten. Out of control once more, he involuntarily intones snatches of William Blake's poem "The Sick Rose" as he peers down, distraught, into the water: "His face was reflected in it. A single sickly persimmon leaf went fluttering down and came to a stop on its surface. From that insubstantial point, circular ripples spread quietly across the whole surface, and the well water flickered. And then it returned to its original stillness. It was quiet, so quiet. Quiet without end."[57] Standing in the real world of sunshine, the narrator finds one more peep hole, a dark tunnel leading into another bright realm that is actually the reflected sky in the water. This time, however, the "mirror" acts less as a reflection of perfect beauty than as a sign of his own desperation. For although the "ripples" draw attention to a border between real and fantastic spaces, the floating leaf cannot enter that perfect reflected world; it can go no further than the point where the two worlds meet. The mirror as unbreachable membrane is emphasized further when it returns to a state of pristine impassivity, coldly throwing back the isolated narrator's anguished image of himself. It now suggests a living nightmare "without end."

Another function identified by Satō, and already observed in the writer's interest in miniatures, is light as a source of magical power. This is especially true in his story "Okinu and Her Brothers." As in so much Meiji and Taishō "fiction," an author's experience often forms the basis of his writings, with the result that different stories often appear as a continuation of each other. In this case, Okinu is the village woman who guided the narrator and his wife to their cottage in the opening part of *Rural Melancholy*, and "Okinu and Her Brothers" is a description of her tumultuous life after her brother forcibly removed her as a young girl from the protective home of a kindly aunt and uncle. The narrator has written down Okinu's story as it was told piecemeal to his wife during Okinu's visits to their home.

In one of her adventures, the fourteen-year-old Okinu is forced to work as a maid in the pleasure quarters of Hachiōji. Badly treated, she runs out of town in the general direction in which she believes her uncle lives. When she becomes too exhausted to run any further, she "walked oblivious to herself, as if in a dream (*mugamuchū de*)."

She finally falls asleep, lost among the misty mountains. An old charcoal burner discovers her and is surprised to hear that she had come all the way from Hachiōji in a single night:

For a second time, the old man was surprised and drew back two or three paces from Okin, just as he had when he first discovered her. Then, in a voice loud enough to make Okin jump up in fright, he exclaimed: "You have been possessed by a fox! Good grief! look at those eyes!"

Like a child, the old man poked his fingers towards Okin's face. Okin was taken aback. The old man suddenly appeared calmer.

"That's better. The fox-spirit has now left you. But what terrible eyes those were . . ."

Throughout the story, Okinu is known by the shortened name Okin. It is only at the very end when she is reunited with her aunt and uncle that the full name is revealed in a way that speaks of Satō's skill as a storyteller. Her full name means "silk thread," and much of her work as a child revolved around silk spinning. In narrative terms, the revelation of her name is the final "thread" that draws the story to its conclusion.

When Satō describes Okinu's encounter with light, the image of threads recurs but this time as a "line of lamps." He also evokes light as a source of mysterious power. After the old man's outburst, Okinu is also convinced that she was indeed possessed and recalls some of the events of her escape:

Come to think of it, there was something that Okin remembered. After dashing off as fast as her legs would carry her, she glanced back from time to time. But whenever she looked—no matter how many times—two lines of lamps (*akari*) of the Hachiōji pleasure quarters appeared to twinkle right behind her as if very close. Although she walked on and on, they never once disappeared from sight. From beginning to end, they pursued her at the same close proximity. Okin had continued walking on with the sole desire that those lamps might retreat far, far into the distance. At the very moment that Okin was taken aback to be told by the old man that she was possessed by a fox, the creature must have left her. Okin believed it. The old man believed it too.[58]

Her exhaustion and dreamlike state might explain the hallucinatory effect of the lamps on her mind. The fact remains, however, that the great distance she traveled cannot be logically explained. The only conclusion is that those beautifully eerie lights that never left her were part of an unnatural, magic experience. As with the black lily discovered by the narrator as a child in *Rural Melancholy*, Satō portrays light here as a sign of mystery beyond rational human comprehension.

The mysterious mood in such passages is reminiscent of an Edo-period ghost story. Since the word translated as "lamps" (*akari*) gives no hint whether they are electrical or more traditional oil lamps, there is nothing to suggest a particularly modern setting. In *Rural Melancholy*, however, Satō presents a scene that can be more specifically placed in the new age of electricity. The sound of a distant evening train evokes memories of the narrator's past life:

At this moment the sound made him feel nostalgic. In moonlight as bright as daytime—no, rainy days were darker than this—he cast his eyes across the fields to the southern hills. . . . On the other side of the hills in the direction of the sound was a wonderful bustling city. . . . There, clusters of lamps (*akari*) were glittering in the windows of every house. . . . For no apparent reason, the simple reverberation of the distant train had suddenly evoked this idle fancy. Then, for a moment—just for a moment—the whole surface of the sky behind the hills seemed to blush with the afterglow of countless lamps. . . . It was a truly mysterious moment.[59]

Tokyo—the city where he felt "crushed under the weight of people"[60]—has become, with the softening effect of distance and time, a desirable place, a "wonderful bustling city." The use of electrical lighting had spread rapidly in early Taishō; the beautiful glow depicted here consists mostly of electrical lights.

In Satō's work, then, there appears what might almost be called a tug of war between the pleasures of the past and a fascination with modern developments. This attraction to modern lighting contrasts sharply with the manner in which the narrator first articulated his desire to escape the city:

"Ah! On such a night as this, I wish I could stretch out my limbs just as I please in the shade of a dark red lamp (*ranpu*) in some quiet thatched country cottage—anywhere would do—and slip into a deep sleep, oblivious to it all!" It was not at all uncommon for his heart to be oppressed by such painful feelings while, with steps like those of an utterly exhausted vagabond, he paced the stone pavement under the glare of incandescent electric lights.

"Oh! Deep sleep! How many years has it been since I last knew it? Deep sleep! It's another name for religious ecstasy. That is what I most desire now. The ecstasy of sound sleep. The ecstasy, that is, of someone whose body is truly alive. That is what I am looking for more than anything else. Let me go wherever it might be. Yes, let me go quickly!"[61]

In this passage, electrical lighting has ruthlessly dispelled all shadows in the Taishō city, and sensitive literary youths are afflicted by "modern mental illnesses such as nervous prostration (*shinkei suijaku*) and insomnia."[62] The words express nostalgia for some idealized rustic world of a quiet cottage with an old-fashioned oil lamp (*ranpu*); less ferociously bright and surrounded by a comforting shade in which the narrator can lose himself and forget his feelings of self-conscious isolation. For Satō, the "dark red lamp" was the remnant of an older age, which he conceived as a time when things were more peaceful, and people were at one with themselves.

The oil lamp evokes nostalgic desires that not only bring out Satō's yearning for a site of belonging but also align him with the earlier works of Tōson. Schivelbusch notes that, in nineteenth-century Europe, there was a disinclination to give up old forms of lighting entirely for the sake of more advanced technology. Surprisingly, it was the technologically backward paraffin lamp, rather than gaslight, that was considered most suitable for the French bourgeois living room of the time. He attributes this to a desire to keep an independent source of lighting in the most personal center of the home, separate from the gas supplied from a centralized location in the city.[63] In the same way, the use of oil lamps in a peasant's more lowly home had a special appeal that disappeared with the advent of modern electricity. For the oil lamp with its open flame carried memories of an even earlier age:

The open light succeeded to the place that had been occupied by the ancient hearth fire. Until the end of the nineteenth century, the peasant household would gather around the light in the living room every evening when the day's work was done. The light was mostly placed directly next to the stove or on the table—both positions relate to the original hearth. The fire that had disappeared into the stove underwent a sublimated resurrection in the open light, a stand-in for the fire that the eye obviously still needed.[64]

In *The Family*, Tōson showed a similar need to gather round the traditional sunken hearth (*irori*); it may have become a distant childhood memory by the time he grew up, but it was still retrievable in literary form. But Satō, less concerned with any real furusato and a further generation removed from the age when the open hearth was common, found equal solace in the symbolic presence of the hearth/furusato contained within the naked flame. The two writers also differ in another sense: whereas Tōson's fantasies of native place imply a site of shared intimacy with others, a more introverted Satō can enjoy the oil lamp's restful properties as an isolated activity.

But if Satō's preference for solitude might be explained as reflecting the rise of fragmented individuality in an increasingly commodified society, one such modern commodity, electricity, ironically provided the material for the imaginative reconstitution of a communal experience. In "Beautiful Town," Kawasaki explicitly rejects the suggestion to use old-fashioned oil lamps since this would amount to giving in to a tiresome nostalgia for the past. "I take no pleasure in an age that looks backward, in whatever shape or form. It offers a sense of nostalgia, but really nothing more than that. We should look only to the future so as not to get our eyes stuck on the past."[65] Since Satō appears to have suffered from the emotional stress of living in an overcrowded and ever-expanding city, the prospects for the future were none too promising. The wearying effect of electrical lighting contributed to his decision to flee to the cottage. And as if to confirm the impossibility that a private, protected space of one's own could be maintained in a modernizing capitalist society, Schivelbusch makes some further comments on the broader social significance of electrification in the West:

The period of electrification also witnessed changes in the economic structure of capitalism. The transformation of free competition into corporate monopoly capitalism confirmed in economic terms what electrification had anticipated technically: the end of individual enterprise and an autonomous energy supply. It is well known that the electrical industry was a significant factor in bringing about these changes. An analogy between electrical power and finance capital springs to mind. The concentration and centralisation of energy in high-capacity power stations corresponded to the concentration of economic power in the big banks. . . . To cling to entrepreneurial autonomy and energy independence in the new world of the second Industrial Revolution would have been a quixotic act. The new industries, electricity and chemicals, were the breeding ground of the new faith in technical, scientific and politico-economic planning that emerged after about 1900.[66]

In the Japanese context, centralized control was an important aspect of modernity from the earliest days of Meiji. And although Satō's individualism set him against the idea of a single national interest, centralization nevertheless remained one of its dominant markers. Just as in Europe, the development of power stations in Tokyo during the first great wave of electrification in early Taishō was paralleled by the new interest in urban planning discussed above. Meanwhile, technological changes like electrical power—passing from "high-capacity power stations" directly into individuals' homes—increasingly worked against the possibility of an autonomous existence as people were tied together quite literally by the unavoidable bonds of modern living.

In this context, to "look only to the future" seems a dubious exercise, and Satō's nostalgic recourse to the old-style oil lamp is what one might have expected of a writer with a "quixotic" interest in things like antiquated gardens. It is the same impulse that led the French bourgeoisie to cling to the paraffin lamp for their most personal room despite the offer of a more "progressive" alternative, an attitude that Kafū would probably have approved. However, Satō used those very obstructions to self-fulfillment in modern society in order to forge a utopian vision. Specifically, he attempted to resolve the conflict by means of those same central electrical generators Schivelbusch described as working against the possibility of personal autonomy. After rejecting the idea of simply looking backward, Kawasaki continues:

When science reaches its full development, we will no longer depend on large-scale electric light companies, which we now consider indispensable—and this is true of more than just electric lights. In order to obtain the illumination necessary for a single house, an age will undoubtedly come when people will turn on their own electric lights by their own simple machinery through exactly the same amount of effort and prepara-

tion spent on lighting a lamp. Just as if every household had the priceless
treasure of a sewing machine for its personal use. It will be the first time
ever that all forms of machinery will no longer be something to fear or
hate: instead, they will be something to love, a truly indispensable element of our daily lives. . . . Machines will become simple to handle, and
an ultimate tool to help each individual most incisively in the pleasure of
his preferred handicraft. So that, rather like a gentle wild beast that has
been domesticated through tender nurture—a horse or an ox—only its
beautiful abilities remain to aid mankind. So that people can approach it
with feelings of love. The age would be an essential stage for the raising of
mechanical work into art.[67]

The writer sets out an aesthetic alternative in order to challenge
the prevalent negative view of modern technology as an object of
"fear or hate" and the apparently relentless historical inevitability
of human degradation. Alien technology becomes domesticated to
produce a "natural" and well-loved companion, like the horse or
ox. Characteristically against the grain of his times, Satō privileged
self-autonomy over what he saw as excessively close human ties.
And yet his vision was theoretically available to all and, in that
sense, constituted the fantasy of a common future. Essentially, Satō
sought to reintegrate a nation of displaced individuals through a
shared aesthetic sensitivity.

Satō depicted a landscape of belonging that suggests a national
identity more complex than that of the earlier generation of writers.
In contrast to Doppo, his sense of cultural exclusion is countered by
the greater self-assurance with which he draws on native and
western influences. And the feeling for authenticity I noted in
relation to Tōson was reconfigured by Satō in a way that eliminates
even the necessity for an actual native place. Instead, his "home" is
authentic to the degree that it corresponds to the needs of an inner,
spiritual world articulated through fantasy. This imaginary space
appears to stand outside history and provided Satō with a means to
take on problems and contradictions beyond his immediate control.
In short, a sense of home may be projected onto a range of possible
sites in the Japanese landscape rather than onto a single fixed locality, when viewed through the aestheticizing gaze. This amounts to a
powerful reclamation of space, the articulation of a form of modernity claiming links to both past and future. On the other hand,

Satō's writing offers insights into the more general realm of possibilities and fantasies—for both good and bad—by which Japan was coming to imagine itself. In a negative sense, such a narrow approach presented the real danger that broader historical events and the writer's participation in them would be willfully ignored. The landscapes in Shiga's work may be more subdued, but they are equally dependent on fantasies. The deleterious implications of this tenuous relationship with broader circumstances are spelled out more clearly in the following chapters.

FIVE

Shiga Naoya:
Grounds for Authenticity

The Native Place of Literature

Reflecting on the enormous influence of Shiga Naoya (1883–1971) on many writers since the Taishō period, the novelist Takeda Rintarō (1904–46) captured a feeling shared by many writers and critics when he described Shiga as the "native place of literature" (*bungaku no kokyō*).[1] Shiga was born in the town of Ishinomaki in Miyagi prefecture in northern Honshū, but his parents took him to live with his grandparents in Tokyo before he was three years old, and it is difficult to make easy connections between Shiga and the furusato (*kokyō*). As Marilyn Ivy reminds us, the furusato is something that

resides in the memory, but is linked to tangible reminders of the past; when the material, palpable reminders of one's childhood home no longer exist, then the furusato is in danger of vanishing. Since the majority of Japanese until the post-war period had rural roots, furusato strongly connoted the rural countryside while the urban landscape implied its loss.[2]

In Tōson's case, a relationship exists between his literary works and his birth place, even if proving a direct correlation between the two is highly problematic. Doppo's stories, too, justify regarding rural parts of Yamaguchi prefecture as his literary furusato, although it was not strictly his place of birth. By contrast, Shiga had no substantial experience of a native place outside Tokyo and is, of all the writers examined in this book, the closest to what might be called a true child of the capital. At the very least, the chronology of meaningful engagement with areas normally associated with a native place is reversed, as shown in his only full-length novel, *A Dark Night's Passing* (*An'ya kōro*, 1921–37), which draws on a trip Shiga made in 1912 to the town of Onomichi on the Inland Sea. It is not until the hero, Tokitō Kensaku, reaches young adulthood that he feels driven to abandon what has become the deeply alienating urban landscape of Tokyo where he grew up and set off on his own journey of self-discovery through Japan. Clearly, then, making sense of Takeda's association of Shiga with the furusato requires a wider perspective.

My main argument in this and the following chapter is that the link emerged principally from Shiga's exceptional skill in tracing literary landscapes that convey an "authentic" Japanese identity based on powerful furusato associations. In this sense, his writings function in a similar way to Tōson's. The fact that Shiga had no real furusato of his own, however, gave him more license to invent. This is true of Doppo and Satō as well, but Shiga stands out for the self-confidence with which he carried out his project. The "authenticity" of Shiga's furusato owes more to his literary skills than to a greater insight into what it meant to be Japanese in the early part of the twentieth century: in other words, there is nothing unmediated or commonsensical in Shiga's authenticity.

Edward Fowler's discussion of Shiga's "sincerity" may help clarify this point. Fowler argues that Shiga's "sincerity in literature," which some have claimed to be a defining feature of the Japanese I-novel, depends on his skilful presentation of the image of sincerity, or what Fowler calls the "donning of a verbally well-wrought mask, the masterful *display* of honest emotion."[3] As for Shiga's acclaimed reluctance to write more than is absolutely required, Fowler considers this to be part of an equally deliberate construction, arising less from a desire to convey only the bare truth than from the writer's need to cover his own tracks:

Shiga continually felt the need to excise those experiences that would tarnish the image of author-sage, or at the very least to present them in such a way as to lessen their impact—even at the expense of a good story. Rather than contradict this scrupulously conceived literary image, Shiga would generally lay down his pen—hence the impression one gets of an impenetrable core of privacy in much of his writing.[4]

Shiga's aim of presenting himself as a "sage," with its associations of age and wisdom, suggests an anachronistic role harking back to an earlier, pre-Meiji age when (at least from his viewpoint) relative stability was prized, and before dramatic and continuing change became the fabric of everyday life. In writing, it amounted to a process of deliberate selection and omission in order to produce the desired self-image most effectively. Shiga's authentic literary landscapes similarly arose from a deliberate and systematic process of selecting those elements that best fitted his particular version of Japanese reality.

Before we examine the general background against which these apparently authentic landscapes were produced, other connections between writer and furusato are worth considering. One possibility is to think of Shiga as a literary figure of such fundamental importance to the creation of modern Japanese literature that he serves as a kind of national wellspring, a deeply self-confident source from which other writers have drawn inspirational nourishment. In a similar way, the native place was a source of comfort, albeit with varying results, for the main characters of both Koshoshi's and Doppo's furusato literature. The analogy may sound excessive, but Fowler has suggested that, probably because Shiga's father was so opposed to his becoming a writer of fiction, he chose for himself the serious and Confucian-inspired role of writer as author-sage. His literary aim was less to depict lived experience in a fictional manner than to demonstrate his moral integrity to an appreciative readership.[5] Such an ambition became conceivable only because of a particular characteristic of the I-novel (*shishōsetsu*)—the form in which Shiga excelled—namely, Shiga's personality is often thought to overlap with the narrating personae in his texts, creating a hybrid that William Sibley has designated the "Shiga hero."[6] Indeed, Shiga was not adverse to emphasizing this perception: his essays "A Digression on Creative Writing" ("Sōsaku yodan," 1928) and "A Digression on Creative Writing, Continued" ("Zoku sō-saku yodan," 1938) went out of their way to connect events and characters in his fictional stories with details of his personal life.[7]

This image of sage-hero was highly convincing to many of his generation, but there were dangers in equating writer and works too closely. For instance, Akutagawa Ryūnosuke (1892–1927) elevated Shiga to near-godlike status because of what he considered Shiga's remarkable clarity of vision; Akutagawa's sense of his own personal and literary inadequacy in comparison is believed to have contributed to his suicide.[8] By contrast, Dazai Osamu's (1909–48) initial admiration turned into disdain. In "Thus Have I Heard" ("Nyoze gamon," 1948), he depicted Shiga as an "amateur" distinguished only by his unbearable personal "vanity" (*unubore*).[9] And yet the strength of this reaction confirms Shiga's continuing status as a touchstone against which Dazai sought to define his own literary stance. In other words, Shiga is an essential marker in the landscape of modern Japanese writing that cannot be ignored, and many writers have felt obliged to acknowledge him before making their own mark in the literary world.

Another link to the furusato may be found in the way literary critics have sometimes praised Shiga for his ability to articulate aspects of everyday life with such extraordinary precision that he has become associated with certain fundamental qualities of Japanese lived experience. In "Shiga Naoya" (1929), Kobayashi Hideo (1902–83) even suggested that Shiga's work retained a remarkable degree of "primitivism" (*genshi-sei*), a term that needs some explanation. Kobayashi believed that physical faculties of the ancient Japanese (*kodaijin*), such as vision and hearing, were infinitely more refined than those of his contemporaries. Moderns experienced so many complex stimuli that their sensitivities had become completely fragmented, with the result that the "acute sensibility" available to the ancients was now largely lost. To Kobayashi, Shiga differed from other writers of his day in that his sensitivities remained perfectly acute and he had lost none of his receptivity (*kanju-sei*).[10] Building on this understanding of Shiga's extraordinary talents, Kobayashi suggested in a later article, "On Shiga Naoya" ("Shiga

Naoya ron," 1938), that the success of *A Dark Night's Passing* as a love story owed nothing to conventional romantic clichés. Instead, the novel is

rooted fundamentally in sexual desire. The way in which two people contribute to their own idealization through "action" is portrayed in a passionate style. Love boils down to action, to will. But it does not just simply exist; it is discovered, invented, and sustained by people. For this reason, the beauty and truth of a really great love novel is based without exception on an oath between a man and woman to bring about their own happiness.[11]

Kobayashi's concept of earlier Japanese as more "sensitive" is debatable, but not his general argument that Shiga possessed unusual insight into the unsentimental and willful nature of human relationships. Not a few critics have gone much further in admiring the writer's supposedly unrivaled ability to offer unmediated "reality" to his readers. One example is Tanikawa Tetsuzō, who thought Shiga's skill in writing with utter casualness (*nanige nai*) was so remarkable that he could not be considered in the same category as the ordinary novelist: "But the very act of looking natural in a casual fashion indicates someone who looks thoroughly. Shiga is someone in possession of such eyes. This is Shiga's rare quality. For this reason, the works he has completed are produced by following a completely different path from that of the professional (*shokugyō teki*) writer."[12] Tanikawa seems to imply that Shiga was following a higher path, perhaps closer to the scholar-sage's way that the writer himself was keen to promote, in opposition to the run-of-the-mill "professional" writer. This view is not restricted to Japanese critics. Roy Starrs has more recently identified Shiga as part of a seamless and unproblematized Japanese culture by linking him to a vague and rather ill-defined "Zen tradition." He is dismissive of Sibley's Freudian-inspired analysis of Shiga's first published piece of fiction, "One Morning" ("Aru asa," 1908), a brief story about the tension between a young man and his grandmother as she tries to get him up in the morning. Starrs sees the text as "perfectly transparent to anyone who is not too preoccupied with unearthing psychological profundities." Some of his suggestions—for instance, that it is precisely the seemingly insignificant, "small things" of the story that should be "appreciated in all their simple, immediate reality"—are well taken. But real problems arise when he arbitrarily likens these "small things" to the frog in Bashō's famous haiku or rocks in a Zen garden: "As soon as the reader begins to analyze, to intellectualize, to look for deep symbolic or psychological meaning, he has immediately 'lost it,' as the Zen masters say."[13] Apart from derogating from his own role as critic, the approach denies the possibility of other productive critical ways of seeing, and the reference to Zen, Starr's assertions to the contrary, amounts to pure essentialism with regard to Japanese culture.

As this glance at Shiga's critical reception suggests, there has been a tendency to describe him in somewhat hyperbolic terms. The danger is that critics fall into a *Nihonjinron*-like argument in which writer and works are equated with a distilled and unique essence of what it means to be "truly" Japanese or, conversely, in which the essence of Japaneseness can be surmised from Shiga's texts. Indeed, it is because similar associations are sometimes made in connection with the furusato that parallels have emerged between the two. In any case, such circular arguments fail to lead to greater clarity, and it is important to resist such essentialism by concentrating on the more concrete aspects of his literary work. Since Shiga was renowned above all for his concise literary style and content, it seems reasonable to seek for more text-based clues to how a link was made.[14]

In a rather negative sense, Shiga's literature and the furusato display common traits. For example, what Ivy suggests as the corollary to the native place—the urban landscape as a manifestation of loss—figures strongly in Shiga's novel. And Jennifer Robertson makes clear what is only implied in Ivy's understanding of the furusato when she acknowledges the paradox that its very existence depends on the fact that it "is, or is imagined as, distant, inaccessible, lost, forsaken, or disappearing."[15] Such associations readily fit the kind of native place depicted by both Doppo and Tōson. And indeed, a similar sense of abandonment and loss pervades a large part of *A Dark Night's Passing*, although it often finds expression in the unhappy restlessness permeating almost every aspect of young Kensaku's emotional life. This dissatisfaction is never stronger than

when his elder brother, Nobuyuki, reveals that Kensaku's real father is the man whom, until that time, he had considered to be his
distinctly unlikable grandfather. Devastated, he felt that

the only path available was to uproot himself and escape completely from
his present circumstances. Like someone with an unstable personality, he
wished that his character could transform itself all of a sudden into an entirely different person. Things would be so much better then! His wish was
to turn into someone with no knowledge of this man Tokitō Kensaku.[16]

In the course of the novel, Kensaku's understandable desire to
escape the unbearable reality of his sordid origins becomes a major
force driving him toward a complete emotional and spiritual upheaval. The impulse to distance himself from the negative aspects
of his life most closely parallels another characteristic identified by
Robertson: the furusato "names a place that exists in contrast with,
and therefore amplifies the aimlessness and malaise of, the present
moment."[17] Such words resonate with that fundamental reaction
against Meiji urban life first articulated by Koshoshi and by what
was then the new genre of "furusato literature." In Shiga's case, this
reaction was voiced initially through a desire to escape metaphorically by occupying the space of an entirely other person, but it
eventually found expression in the search for a more settled and
amenable landscape beyond Tokyo. He differed from the other
writers, however, in the way he confronted the "malaise" of everyday (urban) life; rather than revisiting compensatory (rural) sites of
childhood memories—after all, he had none to speak of—he traveled to discover such a place for the first time. In other words, far
from reclaiming what Ivy called the furusato's "tangible reminders
of the past," Shiga's only option is to create it anew.

Another more positive correlation between Shiga and the furusato can be found in his distinctive use of *kibun*, a difficult term to
translate (it means something like "mood" or "state of mind"). The
term has been described as pivotal to any understanding of Shiga's
work. According to Ted Goossen, *kibun* does not function in
Shiga's literature simply to express the mood of a subject's consciousness; rather, it "possesses its own discrete identity." More specifically, it is used to represent "that part of ourselves in which the
independent active principle of *ki* is located; the seat, as it were, of

all our moods and mental states."[18] Goosen draws on an early scene from Shiga's novella *Reconciliation* (*Wakai*, 1917) to demonstrate *kibun* at work. The story, loosely based on events in Shiga's own life, describes the reconciliation between a young man called Junkichi and his father. As the story opens, they are still estranged, and Junkichi is not welcome at the family house in the Azabu district of Tokyo, but he desperately wants to visit his elderly grandmother, who lives there. At a loss what to do, he visits the grave of his deceased grandfather to ask for advice: " 'That's fine. Go ahead and see her.' Grandfather's response was immediate. It emerged too clearly, too naturally, and too suddenly to be simply a figment of my imagination. There was an objective quality about it, like an encounter with someone in a dream, just like grandfather when he was still alive."[19] Granted that Shiga acknowledges the imaginary aspect of this experience, its "objective quality" is strong enough to be accepted as perfectly sound advice, and Junkichi does indeed visit the family home. Shiga used this scene to present *kibun* as an autonomous source of advice—wisdom even—that stands above and beyond the troubled young man's everyday capacity for thought.

Goossen's presentation of *kibun* as a concept that appears to function outside the material conditions of everyday life is problematic. By identifying the term as a discrete state rather than as a process subject to the specificities of its own time and place, he runs the risk of simplistic essentialism. Nevertheless, his analysis offers a means to identify certain parallels between Shiga's articulation of *kibun* and aspects of the furusato. For one thing, just as *kibun* is represented as an activity independent of the individual, so literary depictions of the furusato seem to have a considerable degree of autonomy, existing as enclosed and self-sufficient environments cut off from everyday (urban) experience. This point is emphasized, for example, by the elaborate journey Mineo must undertake when returning to his native place in "Let Me Return." In addition, both *kibun* and furusato hint at the potential for an extraordinary degree of unmediated reality. In *Reconciliation*, rational order (in which the dead cannot speak to the living) is suspended so that grandfather's message can be received directly through the irrational and intuitive channel of *kibun*, and the "dream" metaphor used to press home Junkichi's experience of "objectivity" enforces the view that everyday waking reality is a less effective medium for this uniquely "clear" and "natural" form of transmission. Likewise in Doppo's story, it is through the most vivid and direct physical sensations—hearing the shrill cicada cries and seeing the deep blue summer skies—that childhood furusato memories are reconstituted most effectively in compensation for the dull monotony of city life. Moreover, both *kibun* and furusato embody the yearning for a safe and dependable haven in a disturbed world. When Junkichi is unsure how to proceed, his willingness to trust his *kibun* produces an immediate and unambiguous solution in a way inaccessible to the troubled everyday mind: for Mineo, the bountiful furusato stands in opposition to an upsetting world, even if a harsh reality ultimately breaks through.

All these various attempts to link Shiga and furusato are valid to a degree, but as with the other writers under consideration here, it is in Shiga's construction of his literary landscapes that his engagement with the furusato concept and his articulation of a particular national identity become most apparent. Like any writer of fiction, Shiga had a certain amount of choice in the form and significance of the landscapes he presented, but such choices are also limited by historical context. The array of ostensibly authentic landscapes available to him, as well as the extent to which he is able to respond to the needs of his readers, can be understood only through the lens of the general social and intellectual environment from which he emerged as a Japanese subject. The distinctive form of his landscapes turns on the shift from Meiji to Taishō.

The State of Taishō

A Dark Night's Passing was completed in a long and rather complicated process. In 1912, Shiga started writing an autobiographical work tentatively entitled *Tokitō Kensaku*. He had promised Natsume Sōseki it would be ready for publication in the *Asahi* newspaper once the serialization of Sōseki's novel *Kokoro* came to an end, but in 1914 he was reluctantly forced to concede that he would be unable to finish the manuscript. Much of this early draft was incorporated into *A Dark Night's Passing*. The first part of the novel appeared in 1921, and the second part in 1922-28; the concluding chapters were added in 1937.[20] Chronologically, then, Shiga's work covered a time span almost identical to many of Tōson's writings—from *The Family* of 1910-11 to *Before the Dawn*, which was finished in 1935—and yet it differs markedly in terms of literary style and articulation of landscapes. A major reason for this is that Shiga was born just over ten years later than both Doppo and Tōson, and his *furusato* emerged through the eyes of a different generation.

If the Meiji period can (very simply) be characterized as a time of hard work and austerity driven by the Japanese desire to avoid China's fate at the hands of the western imperialist powers, dramatic changes had begun by Taishō. An emerging middle class found itself with more disposable income and the leisure to spend it. Between 1912 and 1925, there was a sixfold increase in advertisements placed in national newspapers. In 1916 nearly 60 percent of all advertisements were for books, cosmetics, and medicines. The appearance of the last two in particular reflects a fierce commercial battle among Japanese companies to meet domestic needs since many western products were unavailable during World War I, indirect confirmation of Japan's integration into the world economic system. The advertisements for books suggest a growing interest in reading materials of all kinds in Taishō. By late Meiji, special-interest publications such as *Youth* (*Shōnen*, est. 1903) and *Woman's World* (*Fujin sekai*, 1906) emerged in response to a perceived market, and the pace increased in Taishō when the Kōdansha publishing company started *Kōdan Club* (*Kōdan kurabu*, 1911), a popular magazine specializing in vaudeville and the theater. This was followed by *Youth Club* (*Shōnen kurabu*, 1914), *Woman's Club* (*Fujin kurabu*, 1920), and *Girls' Club* (*Shōjo kurabu*, 1923). "Highbrow" literature was represented by the Iwanami publishing company with its first collected works (*zenshū*) of Sōseki in 1917 and the general magazine *Thought* (*Shisō*) from 1921.[21] There was also an expansion of interest in many other topics, such as photography and the cinema.

At the end of Meiji when Naturalism was at its peak, specialized literary publications emerged around an alliance of anti-Naturalist groupings. For instance, *Pleiades* (*Subaru*), founded in January 1909 under the direction of Mori Ōgai, marked the beginning of the modern Aesthetic school (*tanbiha*). Ōgai's *Vita Sexualis* (1909), with its parodic treatment of Naturalism, first appeared there. *Mita Literature* (*Mita bungaku*) started in May 1910 under the auspices of Nagai Kafū, who had returned to Japan from the West in 1908 and obtained a position at Keiō University with Ōgai's backing. It was in 1909 that his critique of Japan's enlightenment culture, his own version of "furusato literature" centered around Tokyo's Shitamachi district, and his advocacy of hedonism attracted an enthusiastic readership to produce the first Kafū boom. September 1910 also saw a revival of the journal *New Currents* (*Shinshichō*). It had first emerged briefly in 1907 as an arts magazine focusing on the work of Osanai Kaoru (1881–1928), but the revival (which was also short-lived, running for only seven issues) was important in introducing writers like Tanizaki Jun'ichirō and Watsuji Tetsurō (1889–1960) to the reading public.[22] Clearly, this was a highly creative and energetic period of literary history when generational change engendered new modes of literary perception. However, it would be wrong to suggest that Naturalism was simply overwhelmed by newer schools of thought, since its influence remained strong and led to the growth of the I-novel and later in the rise of proletarian literature. Nevertheless, the anti-Naturalist reaction was real and productive, as witnessed by the emergence of yet another journal, *Shirakaba*, in April 1910.[23] Closely identified with Shiga, this journal came to represent an important aspect of the Taishō sensibility and is worth examining in some detail.

Individualism—a key theme of the age also taken up by Sōseki in his influential 1914 essay "My Individualism" ("Watakushi no kojinshugi")—was of particular concern to the loose band of sometimes talented but always self-confident young men who, by contributing to the journal, came to be identified as members of the "*Shirakaba* school" (*Shirakaba-ha*). Most of them discovered one another at the prestigious Peers' School (Gakushūin) or later at Tokyo University. Some of them like Shiga were children of successful families with ties to the Meiji government or business; others were of aristocratic origins, for example, his friend and the best-known representative of the group, Mushanokōji Saneatsu. Upper-class backgrounds linked them with urbane "traditionalists" such as

Kafū in their disdain for what they saw as the excessively crude realism of Naturalist writers like Tōson, but they differed markedly
in their attitude toward western influences in Japan. Whereas Kafū
grumbled that Japan was being destroyed by creeping westerniza-
tion, Donald Keene notes that *Shirakaba* played an invaluable role
as a forum of fine arts, particularly in its early years (it lasted until
1923), by introducing the paintings of numerous western artists
such as Cézanne, Renoir, van Gogh, and Gaugin. The school was
also highly enthusiastic in its reception of Tolstoy's humanistic
ideals as well as Maeterlinck with his declaration that "mankind
must come to a better appreciation of the human condition."[24] The
quality of the journal's articles varied widely, but all were infused
with a new mood of "self-assertiveness" (*jiga shuchō*), based on the
assumption that people could legitimately "devote themselves to
literature in the search for maximum fulfillment of the self."[25] In
the context of a literary culture in which, only twenty-five years
earlier, Tsubouchi Shōyō's decision to attach his own name to a
piece of fiction had shocked his contemporaries and been greeted
with considerable disdain, the boldness of this declaration in favor
of literature as a worthwhile pursuit should not be underestimated.

Shiga's belief in the innate value of writing and in himself as a
worthwhile object of literary study properly locates him as a *Shirakaba* member, but Honda Shūgo is perhaps stretching the point to
identify his "sensitive" hesitancy and Mushanokōji's ebullient but
"insensitive" enthusiasm as together forming the "indivisible and
indispensable kernel" of this "school."[26] On the other hand, mention of Shiga's "sensitive" side draws attention to an introspective
aspect in his work that resonated closely with others of his generation. Yasuoka Shōtarō saw strong similarities between Shiga and
Daisuke, the fictional hero of Sōseki's *And Then* (*Sore kara*, 1909),
who has been taken to represent a particular kind of Taishō youth.
Like Daisuke, Shiga left university but, thanks to a guaranteed
income from his family, he felt no pressing financial need to find
employment. Both rebelled against fathers whose experience of life
was entirely different from their own, shaped in the case of Daisuke by war during the Restoration upheavals and for Shiga by
successful business ventures in the heady days of early

Meiji capitalism.[27] In fact, Shiga was already twenty-seven in 1910 and could hardly be counted a green youth. Moreover, if Daisuke had only one father figure to confront, Shiga's experience of generational conflict is complicated by the fact that he shared a home with both his father and his grandfather, whom he greatly admired. The powerful theme of father-son conflict, which runs through much of Shiga's work, made him a spokesperson for many of his generation. Not surprisingly, his literary production dropped off remarkably after a reconciliation with his father in 1917.

Beyond the set of experiences shared with others of his generation, it is the willfully narrow manner in which he interpreted conflict that helps identify Shiga, like Satō, as a distinctive kind of Taishō personality. His fictional depiction of two real incidents that affected him as a young man drives this point home. In 1901, the first case of large-scale modern industrial pollution occurred when waste products from the Ashio Copper Mine, which were being poured into the Watarase River, caused severe copper poisoning among the local inhabitants. Like other concerned individuals, Shiga wanted to visit the site to show his sympathy for the locals. He was unaware at the time of a family connection—his grandfather had once had financial dealings with the mine—but in any case he backed down in the face of his father's strong opposition. These experiences were fictionalized in "A Certain Man and the Death of His Sister" ("Aru otoko, sono ane no shi," 1920).[28] The second incident was more personal. In 1907 he fell in love with a family maid and determined to marry her, but his father's vehement disapproval again led him to give up the idea. The theme is taken up in his story "Ōtsu Junkichi" (1912).[29]

Remarkably, in both cases Shiga did not seem at all moved to a wider social concern with the evils of capitalist pollution, inequality between the classes, or, more generally, the struggle against an overbearing patriarchal society. Rather, he identified the two stories together with *Reconciliation* as a trilogy, or what he called "branches of one and the same tree," whose aim is to "depict as accurately as possible the psychology of my father and myself."[30] In other words, he argued that they should be interpreted entirely at an individual level as a study of family conflict. Sōseki's Daisuke is also largely unconcerned with wider interests, but at least the author made him defend his nonparticipation in social issues in a heated discussion with his erstwhile friend Hiraoka. In any case, his love for Hiraoka's wife, Michiyo, gradually forces some sort of engagement with the world. Shiga, by comparison, evinced a total disregard for social issues and brings to mind Harootunian's concern that the period may have been rich in new currents of thought, but it also contained seeds of potential danger. Associating Meiji with civilization (*bunmei*), self-sacrifice, and state-centered nationalism, Harootunian sees Taishō culture (*bunka*), which was dominated by individualism and consumerism, as prefiguring a growing middle-class disengagement with political and social affairs that had serious consequences in the future.[31]

This view undeniably addresses a highly significant trend of the age, which informed the work of both Shiga and Satō, but other contemporary movements did aim at far greater social participation. The Great Treason Trial, which resulted in the execution of Kōtoku Shūshui (1871–1911) and eleven other socialists and anarchists for allegedly plotting to assassinate the Meiji emperor, signified the state's unwillingness to tolerate political opposition. At this time, Ōgai stood out as one of the few literary figures to address the issues of state censorship raised by the case in his story "Tower of Silence" ("Chinmoku no tō," 1910), whereas Kafū's later reflections on the trial in his essay "Fireworks" ("Hanabi," 1919) are often taken as symbolic of the more general intellectual retreat suggested by Harootunian.[32] Yet the very fact that the government felt obliged to crack down indicates that this was, conversely, a time of considerable political and social turbulence. Tokyo was being transformed by intense migration from the countryside in early Taishō, and rural areas were experiencing increasingly widespread tenancy disturbances. Especially following World War I, tenancy disputes increased "from a reported total of 256 in 1918 to over 2,700 in 1926,"[33] and this general mood of social upheaval was exacerbated by the 1917–18 Russian Revolution and Japan's own rice riots of 1918. In the literary field, *Bluestockings* (*Seitō*), founded in 1911 by Hiratsuka Raichō (1886–1971), marked the rise of Japan's foremost feminist group, which helped pave the way for future

generations of female writers. The improvement of women's position was also linked with radical, progressive politics in the mind
of some male writers. In *Rough Living (Arakure,* 1915), Tokuda
Shūsei describes a seamstress, Oshima, who is determined to
remain economically independent from the men who surround her.
And Arishima Takeo, another writer associated with the *Shirakaba*
magazine, created a very different literary landscape from Shiga as
he traced the vicissitudes of his strong-willed heroine, Yōko, in *A
Certain Woman (Aru onna,* 1919).[34] Many expressions of social concern, which often translated into Marxism and proletarian literature in the 1920s, clearly have their roots in early Taishō.

Given this range of contemporary Japanese "realities," Shiga was
obliged to make choices when he came to interpret his own relationship with the wider world. On this point, Alan Tansman identifies him as one of a group of writers, emerging in Taishō but
most active in the 1920s and 1930s, who preferred to speak a language of loss: "As a balm for the wounds of modernity, literary
works evoked moments of repose in scenes where the agitated
movement of modern, linear time temporarily ceased, and senses
fractured by modern stimuli could rest in a moment of simultane-
ity."[35] Shiga's choice was to shape his literary landscapes in accordance with introspection, the mood of many writers and thinkers
as Taishō began. Indeed, although the period proper started in 1912,
key cultural and intellectual shifts appeared from the time of the
1904–5 Russo-Japanese war that would affect the way many came
to perceive themselves and their relationship with society; in other
words, what was later identified as a distinctive Taishō sensibility
first started in the final decade of Meiji. Earl Kinmonth describes
how a new group of youths—the "anguished youth" (*hanmon
seinen*) or "decadent youth" (*tandeki seinen*)—arose to voice opposition to their classmates who, as "success youths" (*seikō seinen*), remained committed to the search for financial success first articulated during Meiji. He locates this rejection of worldly ambition
less in a vague loss of purpose after the war or a breakdown in the
traditional family than in the practical difficulty of finding meaningful and satisfying employment that led many educated youths,
turning inward in search of satisfaction, to redefine *risshin shusse* in

terms of a "romantic pursuit of self-fulfillment." This anguish was exacerbated by the increasing difficulties in obtaining a higher education and the corresponding fear of failure. By 1902, only one in ten applicants was accepted, and this soon increased to one in twenty.[36]

Thomas Rimer remarks an equally dramatic shift in the intellectual life of those coming to maturity between the turn of the century and World War I:

In one sense, young intellectuals believed they required some kind of basic understanding of the functions of society; on the other hand, they found themselves encouraged to respond to a growing sense of a need to search out the authenticity of their own interior selves. If any synthesis was to be created between the sometimes congruent, sometimes conflicting demands of civilization, self and society, each element would have to be examined and defined before any genuine relationship among them might be posited. Many during the period decided to begin with an examination of the self, that realm of the personality that heretofore had been relegated, indeed conceptualized, as an adjunct to the primacy of social relationships and obligations. The search for that self was often to prove a painful one.[37]

Shiga may be an extreme example of a Taishō writer drawn to explore his own sense of authenticity above any obvious engagement with society, but in fact *A Dark Night's Passing* was only one of several influential books that displayed a preoccupation with the details of an inner self (*naimen*). Naitō Arō's (1883–1977) *The Renewal of Life and the New Arts* (*Sei no kōkai to shingeijutsu*) came out in 1914, and Nomura Waihan's (1884–1921) *A Study of the Self* (*Jiga no kenkyū*) appeared in 1915. One of the books that best represents the mood of the generation was *Santarō's Diary* (*Santarō no nikki*, 1914) by Abe Jirō (1883–1959). The first part of it appeared in 1914, and it has been compared to Shiga's novel for its amalgam of literature, thought, and philosophy.[38] Shiga's work, however, does not engage in formal philosophical debate; at most, it may be seen as an indirect exposition of the writer's philosophy of life through what has been called a "literature of experience."[39] What these books do share, however, is the determination to probe the big questions of who we are and where we come from.

Such questions were certainly fundamental to the distinctive mood of the time, but they could not be described as exclusive to Taishō; they were, for example, instrumental in the creation of Doppo's furusato. As they did the earlier writer, they pushed Shiga to respond to the problematic relationship between the "interior self" and the external environment through the formulation of a series of literary landscapes. *A Dark Night's Passing* is typical of much "furusato literature" in that it begins with urban problems. Part I shows Kensaku to be a young man who cannot relate to his father, who seems remarkably unproductive in his chosen profession of writer, and who is driven by a sexual desire so powerful that it frightens him. He even dreams that his friend Sakaguchi has died from an unspecified but highly dangerous sexual practice called *harima* which he fears may prove irresistible.[40] Much of his life revolves around shallow encounters with young women in the pleasure quarters. Eventually deciding he must leave Tokyo, he is happy to take Nobuyuki up on his suggestion that he visit Onomichi. But his feelings toward the city in which he grew up are not entirely antagonistic. In a way reminiscent of Tōson's equally complex response, Kensaku's attitude becomes apparent just before his departure when he agrees to meet his elder brother outside his workplace:

Just before four o'clock the following afternoon, he was on the corner of Mitsukoshi's, waiting for Nobuyuki to come out from the nearby fire insurance company. It was near the end of the year, and Muromachi Street was bustling that evening. An endless succession of streetcars from both north and south came by, pausing in front of the building: the conductors would say the same thing, and then the trains would move off again. There were rickshaws, cars, carts, and bicycles, through which people wove in every direction just as they pleased. Dogs, too, passed by. His face sensed the breeze of men's shoulders as they went by, almost brushing his nose. I will soon be going to a far-off tranquil place with a view of the sea, he thought. He felt pleased, but also a little sad.[41]

Although keen to escape Tokyo and its wearying frivolities, the prospect of losing the more general ambience of city life—presented here as a lyrical confusion of collisions and near-misses between humans, dogs, and vehicles—produces a mixture of pleasure and regret. Even if the street scene with its cacophonous dramas seems so cramped that strangers intrude into his private space, Kensaku's "far-off tranquil place" will offer neither the possibility of such new encounters nor the urban landscape's capacity to surprise.

Notwithstanding his mixed feelings, there are very practical reasons why Kensaku is in a position to contemplate an extended journey around the country. As he waits, the clock strikes 4:00, and people begin to emerge from work:

Suddenly, large numbers of people seemed to be spewed out from the Mitsui building which formed a square on three sides. Some tucked their walking sticks under their arms while they lit a cigarette. Others ran quickly after colleagues who had gone ahead. Wherever one looked, the square was packed with these people. They came from the Bank of Japan, the Specie Bank, among other places. And they passed by in an endless succession of little groups. He soon spotted Nobuyuki among them.[42]

Kensaku's departure from Tokyo is partly a reaction to these major economic institutions of modern Japan—Mitsui, the Bank of Japan, and so on—that suck human beings into offices each morning in large and anonymous groups and spew them out every night, these masses that constitute a source of the city's delightful unpredictability as well as its unbearable weight. But the reaction itself is not new. This passage evokes the opening scene of Futabatei's earlier *Floating Clouds*, in which Bunzō and his companions likewise swarm from offices like worker bees caught up in a bureaucratic system far more powerful than themselves. In Shiga's novel, the scene serves mainly to underline the relentless pressures of city life Kensaku hopes to leave behind on his highly idiosyncratic passage to self-understanding. At the same time, it inadvertently highlights his privileged position in a market economy that has enriched his own family and given him the financial freedom and leisure to undertake that journey.

It is through Nobuyuki that Shiga clarifies why Kensaku needs to leave. In the process, and more fundamentally, he also sets up a spatial dynamic in the novel whereby the impetus to explore literary landscapes beyond the city is tied to a search for greater authenticity. As the two figures stop to watch some construction workers, Nobuyuki surprises his younger brother by revealing a deep dissatisfaction with his own job. The laborers, by contrast, appear fortunate to him:

"It's not bad how they work, working day by day just to eat. The work I do totally lacks such a sense of necessity." Nobuyuki suddenly continued, "I cannot help sometimes feeling strangely uneasy about it."[43]

By working at an insurance company, Nobuyuki has found a secure niche in precisely the kind of finance-related work that oils the wheels of Japan's industry. On the other hand, the nature of his work means that he lacks an immediate correlation—a "sense of necessity," as he describes it—between physical action and emotional need. His enthusiasm for laborers motivated (as he sees it) by the simple objective of the next meal reveals his naïveté; no shades of gray corresponding to those identified by Tōson in his more perceptive depiction of country farmers. But the main point in terms of the novel's narrative dynamic is that for Nobuyuki the laborers appear so integrated into their environment that their physical efforts promise to satisfy their albeit limited needs. By contrast, both brothers experience daily life in Tokyo as lacking the immediacy they crave. Nobuyuki finally decides to tackle his problem through religion, and he gives up his job to study Zen in Kamakura. Kensaku, meanwhile, had already sought to address his own "sense of necessity" through the pursuit of sexual partners in the city; indeed, for a brief moment he even seems to attain a wondrous sense of physical completion as he holds the "rich harvest" of a woman's breasts in his hand.[44] But the moment passes, leaving him once more with an unresolved inner "uneasiness." In the end, Kensaku has no choice but to move beyond Tokyo in search of a compensatory, more settled landscape.

In this exploration of a seemingly more unmediated, authentic experience, Shiga portrays Kensaku as a character struggling to locate a place of unquestionable belonging, where "necessity" can be realized without difficulty. But questions remain: What choices were available to Shiga when he came to articulate such landscapes in his literature? What were the general circumstances that shaped his choices? And what do such choices say about the writer's articulation of a distinctive national identity? *A Dark Night's Passing* strongly suggests an internalized and very personal metaphorical landscape, a site of narrative movement structured specifically to set out the depth of Kensaku's mental anguish and the breadth of his search for peace of mind. This impression is strengthened by the novel's title in Japanese, *An'ya kōro*, with its echoes of the human journey through life (*jinsei kōro*). To belabor a point made above, such a choice also involves the rejection of other more socially engaged and potentially disruptive landscapes, such as politics and feminism; after all, no text can possibly be expected to embody every aspiration of its age. But in Shiga's case the point does need emphasis precisely because his work—not to mention his very personality—has been invested over time with the excessive burden of standing for a *uniquely* authentic representation of Japanese experience, with the implication that other interpretations are less valid. My point is not to deny Shiga's significance as a Japanese writer who fleshed out an important relationship between people and place; indeed, the following chapter examines the specific ways in which his texts skillfully trace a literary topography that tapped into his readership's equally pressing need to identify themselves with a settled home. However, as I argue in the next section, Shiga was only one player among many in the struggle over the "reading" of a single national space that intensified during the Taishō period, when the very concept of stable literary landscapes was becoming increasingly tenuous.

Malleable Landscapes

Yoshida Seiichi is surely right to attribute the *Shirakaba* journal's lasting influence to its introduction of new and exciting western artwork, Mushanokōji's infectious enthusiasm, and the high quality of Shiga's short stories.[45] Beyond that, the variety of its members makes a simple definition of the group difficult. Nevertheless, the "*Shirakaba* school" is a useful shorthand term for a shared understanding of the world that first manifested itself in Taishō. Although the term originated in a specific response among the elite, to which Shiga belonged, it became part of a more widespread generational transformation in the Japanese perception of what it now meant to be Japanese. In short, the school made a quintessential contribution to the intellectual mood by which early Taishō would later be defined, primarily by articulating ways of reinventing "Japan" within a western-dominated global order.

From early Meiji, social and political upheavals had forced the Japanese to become particularly sensitive to their own culture vis-à-vis the outside world, but, as Satō's writings indicate, by Taishō aspects of western culture—from food and clothing to the things people read—were so familiar that they seemed almost a natural part of the native environment to younger Japanese. The perception of these elements as alien had constituted part of the underlying problem for the older generation, which included Tōson, and it remained a matter of deep concern for some major writers in Taishō like Akutagawa, whose posthumously published "Cogwheels" ("Haguruma," 1927) features a character completely overwhelmed by a frightening whirlpool of diverse cultural effects. By contrast, many *Shirakaba* writers were notable for their enthusiasm for western art and literature; they not only easily and willingly accepted "foreign" things but even celebrated a newly discovered international consciousness.

This is understandable, given the privileged background of members of the *Shirakaba* school, who enjoyed direct contacts with a worldwide community of fellow artists denied to other groups in Japanese society. The Naturalists in particular were so short of funds that they often could not afford to buy the books they were desperate to read; Tayama Katai, for instance, gained access to his favorite Japanese and Russian authors by spending two or three days a week in Ueno Library.[46] By contrast, some of the *Shirakaba* members were on close personal terms with resident foreigners such as the English potter Bernard Leach (1887–1979), and they carried on a correspondence with the French sculptor Auguste Rodin, who sent them a small collection of his bronzes.[47] Their willing reception of this free exchange of ideas and artifacts is reflected in Abe's comment in *Santarō's Diary* that they lived in an exciting new world without boundaries:

I am a "citizen of the world" determined not only by the history of my race but also by the history of the world; educated not only by the history of my race but also by the history of the world. The fact that we are

"Japanese" does not mean that we can neglect the "fact" that I am also just "I" as well as a "citizen of the world."[48]

The easy grandeur of the phrase "citizen of the world" echoes Mushanokōji's exclamation: "Spiritually we are children of the world."[49] It can well be imagined that the ideas of a personal individuality greater than any national identity and membership in a world family must have had an intoxicating effect on those whose forebears had lived in a high degree of isolation from the outside world.

In their enthusiasm, however, they forgot the "fact" of a world order in which not all "children" are born equal. The *Shirakaba* school's position as a small group of elite youths within Japan was a mirror image of their position in an international citizenship dictated by the West. Sōseki in particular demonstrated a sensitivity to national racial ranking when he compared his "dwarf"-like physical self unfavorably to the "tall and good-looking" people he encountered during his altogether distressing stay in England.[50] Moreover, Mushanokōji's use of the western calendar to signal his forward-looking modernity and his rejection of the strictures of old Japan[51] reveals his acceptance of an international pecking order in which western paradigms have come to predominate. It was a worldview shared even by Kafū, who lamented in 1908 that his travels through America and Europe were about to end and he would soon return to a Japan, in the "distant extremity of the East."[52] He implicitly accepted his own country's distance from the world's center. For many of his countrymen, Tokyo, the nucleus of modern Japan, was similarly distant.

Even in Shiga's largely introspective writing, these wider issues find indirect expression. For instance, the description of Kensaku's boat ride from Yokohama to Onomichi hints that Japan's integration into a hierarchy of other nations has led to a situation in which distinctions between "Japanese" and "foreign" views of Japan have become less clear-cut. Kensaku is in a listless mood, thrown together rather against his will over lunch with another passenger, a young Australian who is passing through Japan on his way home from America. After taking a long nap in his room, Kensaku comes out on the deck to witness a splendid sight:

In the dull, ash-gray sky of evening, Mount Fuji stood out clearly. With the sea before it, and soaring high above the hills of Izu, it appeared very much like a neatly composed picture, reminiscent of the Mount Fuji depicted by Hokusai.

In the smoking room, someone was playing a piano poorly. It stopped, and the young foreigner came out. "I have seen Mount Fuji for the first time." He seemed pleased.[53]

Of all "composed pictures" that might represent Japan to a foreign eye, Mount Fuji perhaps most readily comes to mind. It is not surprising, then, that the young Australian, who had earlier expressed concern that the cloudy weather might obstruct his view, should be delighted with his good luck. More remarkable, however, is the complex manner in which the view is experienced by Kensaku. Growing up in Tokyo, he would have had ample opportunity to see the real mountain from time to time, and this present sighting may be counted as just another "real" experience, albeit from a different angle. And yet, for that brief moment when they stand side by side on deck, Kensaku finds himself compelled by the Australian's enthusiasm to at least contemplate the concept of viewing Mount Fuji for the first time. In other words, Kensaku's gaze momentarily overlaps with the foreigner's. Moreover, reference to the woodblock artist Katsushika Hokusai (1760–1849) reconfigures the physical mountain into a wider cultural context that removes any exclusive claim of authenticity Kensaku might have as a native Japanese in relationship to this most Japanese of mountains. There is no reason to assume that this print or some similar "Mount Fuji" was not as familiar to the Australian as to Kensaku. Indeed, it is quite likely that the foreigner's exited anticipation of the real experience was fueled precisely by prior knowledge of such a print. In short, Shiga's artistic reference lifts Mount Fuji out of its local origins and transforms it into an exchangeable image, a piece of global art accessible to all spiritual "children of the world."

It would be wrong to read too much into this passage. Shiga is not presenting his main character as a foreigner (*gaijin*). Kensaku did not relish trying to speak English with the Australian at lunch, and he was unwilling to play a game of cards according to foreign rules.[54] Nevertheless, as Kensaku departs from Yokohama harbor, the "land became gradually more enveloped in mist as the ship advanced,"[55] a process that suggests he does adopt an outsider's (*gaijin*) viewpoint by going beyond the physical boundaries of his country. This separation from the Japanese mainland might also be taken symbolically to imply the loss of a stable cultural grounding, rather as Yōko's journey across the Pacific in *A Certain Woman* has been seen to represent her temporary escape from Japanese convention.[56] In any case, Shiga certainly raises a question that became important in the Taishō period and was now applied to Japanese and foreigner alike: What constitutes an authentic experience of Japan? Tōson's writings reveal the anxiety he felt as he confronted the loss of an older, more familiar Japan, which he then tried to recapture through his work; Akutagawa lost track of Japan in his fractured world and simply fell to pieces. Shiga, however, takes the blend of "Japanese" and "foreign" elements so entirely for granted that—in this scene at least—it requires no special comment on his part.

This likening of Mount Fuji to an artistic representation further illuminates Honda Shūgo's suggestion that the numerous photographs in *Shirakaba* created a habit of appreciating western fine art only through imitations.[57] Honda's observation is limited to Japanese perceptions of western artifacts, but it may equally be applicable to a radical change in the way the Japanese were coming to appreciate their own native culture. It was a process already under way in "Let Me Return," when young Mineo's appreciation of his native place is colored through a reading of Johnson's *Rasselas*, and this more complex configuration of "home" became more and more pervasive with time. As western perspectives became increasingly naturalized during Taishō, a distance inevitably opened up in the relationship with what came to be perceived as an earlier and inaccessible "original" Japan. Consequently, Mount Fuji was viewed as a visual image with as much—but no more—sense of reality than any other artistic representation, foreign or Japanese, that might appear in the pages of the magazine. Put another way, the emerging Japanese re-evaluation of Japan might be compared to the new arrangement of disparate literary schools that made up the intellectual "villages" (*bundan*) of Tokyo—an uneasy coexistence of

so-called traditional and western paradigms, equally valid but unable alone to explain the whole picture, interacting in complex and
sometimes contradictory ways.

Even Kafū's literary representations of "traditional" Japan turn
out to possess a more complex lineage than might appear at first.
He used a technique similar to Shiga's by viewing Japan from the
external perspective of a boat in his 1911 essay "Pierre Loti and the
Japanese Landscape" ("Pierre Loti to Nihon no fūkei"), but his
complicated interplay between Japanese and western elements
makes an illuminating comparison with the other's work. Kafū
imagined what Loti's thoughts might be on his return to Japan after a fifteen-year absence, especially his distress upon entering Nagasaki harbor to find how features of the new Japan have blighted
the old beauty he once knew and loved:

The picturesque sailing vessels and rowing boats had become fewer, while
the steamships, tugboats, and metal freighters had increased in number.
Nagasaki was coming to resemble France's Le Havre and England's
Portsmouth. The verdant seacoast had been cleared and factories built.
On the beautiful mountaintop, which stretched as far as the eye could see
outside the city, large American-style billboard writing was to be seen describing the existence of foodstuffs factories. With every feeling he possessed, Loti brandished a scornful pen against such sights.[58]

Kafū's lamentation for a Japan whose distinct characteristics are being swamped by intrusive Western influences is ironically expressed—in literary terms, at least—through the pen of a French-
man. The ease with which he adopted this "foreign" role far
outstrips the more opaque ambiguities of Shiga's text. It was facilitated by Kafū's greater sophistication; according to Miyoshi Yukio,
a French fin-de-siècle aesthetic sense stimulated Kafū's love of Edo
arts and "led him to dream of his old country as if it were a foreign
country."[59] The extent of Kafū's exposure to foreign culture should
not be overestimated. Apart from the few years' travel abroad as a
young man, his long life was spent entirely in Japan. His literary
references to overseas culture largely served the purpose of casting
a critical light on Japan. Nevertheless, Kafū's upbringing—he ate
and dressed in western style as a child, for example—as well as his

limited travels set him apart from writers like Shiga with their more domestic backgrounds and their consequent unease with foreigners.

But precisely because personal experience made Kafū better acquainted than Shiga with both "Japanese" and "foreign" ways, he differentiated the two more sharply in his writing. In particular, he pinpointed the unfair nature of the struggle by which, as he saw it, the softer and more vulnerable culture of Japan, with its handpowered "rowing boats" and traditional sailing ships propelled by wind, had been pushed aside by the mechanical power of "steamships" and the "metal freighters" produced by a culturally alien Industrial Revolution. In this knowledge, he rose above Mushanokōji's naïve aspirations for membership in a world family and more closely resembled Sōseki in his dispassionate awareness that Japan belonged to an unequal hierarchy of nations. Always a great Francophile, Kafū berated not so much the West as its incongruous imposition on Japan's landscape, literal as well as figurative. This translated into an attack on the signs of western capitalism that have scarred a once "verdant seacoast" with ugly factories and substituted "American-style billboard writing" for the beautiful view of a mountain. In its stubborn maintenance of the illusion of two distinct and separate spheres, one "Japanese" and the other "foreign," Kafū's work suffers from his inability to conceive of a more complex Japan beyond the orbit of his own literary needs. Nevertheless even this writer had no option but to express his desire to recover an authentic Japan through a literary medium that, in its very composition, demonstrates the inextricable blending of diverse cultural traditions.

Fundamentally, Kafū's anxiety centered on his perception that authenticity had been lost; his writing was driven by an impractical and unrealizable impulse to satisfy his yearning for an "original" Japan. Indeed, a large number of writers from the Meiji period on shared this fascination with authenticity—the concern over its loss and an insistent urge to recover it. One intellectual who gave eloquent expression to this matter was Kobayashi Hideo, whose seminal essay "Literature Without a Native Place" ("Kokyō o ushinatta bungaku") considers the troubling concept of the native place. Although written in 1933, it embodies his reflections on the increasingly tenuous links between people and place that he experienced as he grew up. For instance, he recalls his discomfort whenever he was addressed as a true child of Edo (*Edokko*), even though he was born and raised in Tokyo. Perhaps echoing Akutagawa's famous mention of a "vague uneasiness" (*bonyari shita fuan*) in his suicide note only a few years earlier, Kobayashi laments that "I have a kind of uneasy feeling (*fuan na kanjō*) that I possess no home." It was a familiar phrase; Nobuyuki used a similar locution to express his own "uneasy feeling" (*fuan na kimochi*) in the city. Kobayashi compares his bereft frame of mind to that of Takii Kōsaku, a friend who originated from outside Tokyo. While taking a train together back from Kyoto, Kobayashi is startled how the sudden sight of mountain roads as the train emerges from a tunnel moves Takii deeply:

> While I listened as he related how the sight of the mountain path brought forth a host of childhood memories that made him choke with emotion, I felt strongly that I did not understand what the "countryside" (*inaka*) meant. Or rather, I had a deep sense that the "first home" and the "second home"—indeed, the very meaning of the "native place" (*kokyō*)—were alien to me. Where there are no memories, there is no native place. If a person does not possess powerful memories that are the product of an accumulation of numerous immutable impressions provided by an immutable environment, then the healthy emotion that fills out the word "native place" will mean nothing to him.[60]

Place itself means nothing without accumulated associations. Doppo had learned this lesson long before when he experienced utter desolation during the autumn rains on his trip along the Sorachi River. For Kobayashi, the physical reconstruction of Edo into Tokyo that had begun in early Meiji had never stopped; particularly after the earthquake of 1923, even less of the old city remained. The result was that, unlike Takii, whose recollection of childhood experiences is set off by specific visual sensations, Kobayashi's upbringing in a constantly changing urban landscape denied him the ability to link his personal history with fixed physical details of the city. To his mind, moreover, *inaka* and *native place* had become virtually interchangeable terms as sites of belonging. A somewhat similar rupture between youthful memories and place was described by Tanizaki in his postwar memoirs. He advised readers against trying to locate his home in the old Minami Kayaba-chō district of Tokyo, since names in the area, and even the location of nearby bridges, had changed so completely that he was unable "to clarify things through particular landmarks."[61]

In Tanizaki's expert hand, these very uncertainties of place and memory became the material of aesthetic play; for instance, in *Portrait of Shunkin* (*Shunkin shō*, 1933) or *The Floating Bridge of Dreams* (*Yume no ukihashi*, 1959). For Kobayashi, however, they amounted to the loss of a vital sense of "healthy emotion." Of course, the critic had his own bank of personal childhood memories that helped define his self-identity, but he differed fundamentally from Takii in that physical surroundings had so changed over time that they no longer had the power to touch his emotional core. Or, more precisely, the only effect of his present environment was to compound his mood of "uneasiness." In any case, his memories floated unanchored in a rapidly expanding city among the equally fluid memories of countless other inhabitants, many of whom had moved there only in recent times and were still emotionally attached, if anywhere, to their native place. This, of course, merely describes the general state of uprootedness frequently identified as a major symptom of the modern experience in Japan as elsewhere, but a writer like Tōson was at least able to make a conceptual distinction between an alienating Tokyo and his own native place. Kobayashi, by contrast, was a native of the rootless city itself and so lacked any "immutable" (*kakko taru*) base to counterbalance his daily experience of loss.

Kobayashi outlined modern life as a kind of tragedy and presented himself as an orphan cut off from the source of his own origins. In fact, it was precisely this sense of loss and his search for compensation that, in his own words, produced deep feelings of "respect and affection" (*keiai*) toward Shiga Naoya and his works.[62] In the following section, I examine in greater detail how writings on the furusato by various literary figures, including Kobayashi, may be related to Shiga's work. However, in order to throw the constructed nature of Shiga's literary landscapes into sharper relief, I conclude this section by considering positive conceptions of the uncoupling of place and association.

Some writers showed through their work that malleability could serve as a source of considerable empowerment. Kobayashi may claim that "where there is no memory, there is no home," but Uno Kōji's (1891–1961) "The Dreaming Room" ("Yume miru heya," 1922) hints that both memory and home may be open to a more positive interpretation and, indeed, more manipulation than the critic allowed. The story depicts the increasing isolation of the narrator from family and friends, as he gradually comes to center his life around a separate room that he has secretly rented—the "dreaming room"—in which he can fully indulge his fantasies. In one scene, he is walking through Ueno Park, where construction work is under way on a forthcoming "great exhibition," a reference to the real-life Peace Exhibition (Heiwa hakurankai), which opened on March 10, 1922. He walks on Ueno hill above Shinobazu Pond and glances through a break in a line of cherry trees:

Through that tiny gap, one can catch an unobstructed view from the low-lying Shinobazu Pond below all the way to the heights of Hongō. Looking in that direction, I gave a start, rooted to the spot: through the break in the cherry trees the distant Hongō heights could be seen against the setting of the evening sky, and below it the leaden Shinobazu Pond gave off a faintly white gleam from its surface so that it looked like a lake. I stood there staring with utter amazement that Shinobazu Pond should appear so much bigger than I had remembered. Standing in the park, in what might be called the foothills of the heights, and looking toward the base of the distant Hongō heights—it may have been because it was twilight, a time when things are most likely to appear slightly larger—it looked as large as the mountain lake in my beloved Shinano prefecture.

After standing there for "at least a minute," it becomes apparent to the narrator that the "lake" is an illusion. He is really seeing the gleam of the newly constructed exhibition hall's "large, barrel-shaped roof." Most remarkable, though, is the fact that, having realized the source of his mistake, the narrator consciously and repeatedly attempts to recreate the same illusion:

Once I realized the real situation, I felt slightly silly, but I immediately felt the urge to go back and think of it again as a lake. Once I knew it to be the roof, however, although I tried screwing up my eyes, took a few steps backward and walked past it again, moved to a place a little further away from the original spot, and tried moving closer, it was impossible now for me to see it as anything else but a roof.[63]

Whereas Kobayashi deplored the constant change in the Tokyo landscape as a sign that links to the native place have been severed, Uno used the very ambiguity of such links to his own advantage. For him the cityscape becomes a space on which to impose his own native-place fantasies. It may be that Tokyo is best understood as a deeply fragmented city, saturated by individuals with memories unattached to place. This leaves the non-native narrator of "The Dreaming Room" (and everyone else) free to anchor recollections of his own "beloved Shinano prefecture" to the epiphenomena of Tokyo. In this sense, Uno was at one with Satō in demonstrating that the concept of authenticity related to an "original" landscape had become virtually meaningless. Kobayashi was mortified to discover that "I had memories but they lacked any substantial content. I even felt there was something fictitious about them."[64] For Uno, it was precisely this insubstantial relationship between people and place—its very unreality—that became the source of creativity.

These different responses to environment offer a clue as to how Shiga produced his own literary furusato. He may not have been a third-generation inhabitant of the Shitamachi, which would have entitled him to the status of *Edokko*, but like Kobayashi he felt detached from the urban area in which he had grown up. Uno's narrator tries to overcome similar feelings of isolation by "discovering" his lost native home in the very center of modern Tokyo. But this option was not open to Shiga, since, as seems true of Kobayashi, the city evoked too strong a sense of failed opportunities for him to feel comfortably at home in it. Instead, he sought an outlet for disappointments by projecting his expectations and needs onto a phantasmagorical landscape beyond the boundaries of Tokyo. Given Kobayashi's equally strong associations of the urban center

with loss, his eagerness in latching onto Shiga's imaginary landscapes and their promise of a reconstituted home is not surprising.
Of course, Shiga made up his literary furusato as he went along—
he had twenty-five years to work out its shape—but this is not to
say that it emerged from nowhere. Even his feeling of emptiness
was culturally rooted.

Talking of Home

Far from being a sagelike individual who stood outside history,
Shiga was an important participant in the intellectual currents of
his time. This comes into sharper focus if we survey the views of
two of his important contemporaries, the critic and novelist
Sakaguchi Ango (1906–55) and the poet Hagiwara Sakutarō (1886–
1942), who, together with Kobayashi, were also articulating their
sense of home, of native place, and ultimately what it meant to be
Japanese. Although their texts range in date from the late 1920s to
early 1940s, all reflect the particularly high level of interest in the
native place characteristic of the 1930s, that is, just as Shiga was
writing the final part of *A Dark Night's Passing*.

Sakaguchi Ango's interesting views on the subject of the furusato take it beyond a simple desire to reclaim the old or return to
one's origins. His insights provide a useful comparison for unpack-
ing Shiga's literary impulses. For instance, Ango identified the native place with a fundamental human attraction toward unembel-
lished necessity. His essay "A Personal View of Japanese Culture"
("Nihon bunka shikan," 1942) pursues this argument through an
examination of nostalgia (*natsukashisa*), a notion frequently associated with the furusato. He recalls feeling sad as a junior high-school
student when the splendid wooden bridge spanning the river of his
native city of Niigata was replaced by a metal one. From his adult
perspective, however, he has come to realize that not only is the
loss of the old nothing to worry about but, like most other Japanese, he enjoys watching the furusato being transformed by the introduction of more practical western constructions. This view sets
him entirely at odds with the likes of Kafū, whose literary language
obtains its nostalgic lyricism precisely through its tenacious clinging to every outward sign of earlier times. As far as Ango is con-

cerned, it would make no difference if all the ancient objects in Kyoto and Nara disappeared, but the disappearance of trains would be unbearable. In short, only the basic necessities of life (*seikatsu no hitsuyō*) are important.[65]

Ango's depiction of things that evoked his sense of nostalgia make his understanding of the furusato clearer. Three sights struck him as irresistibly beautiful; the Kosuge Prison on the outskirts of Tokyo, which he often saw from his commuter train; a dry ice factory on Tsukudajima Island in Tokyo Bay, only a short boat ride from Tsukiji; and a Japanese warship he came across during a trip to a port. His description of the ship illustrates his general attraction to huge structures of concrete and metal seldom associated with a feeling for home:

Not a single pole or sheet of metal was added for the sake of beauty, and nothing was taken away because it failed to look beautiful. It was just necessary objects located in necessary places. As a result, a distinctive shape was formed in which all unnecessary objects were excluded and only necessity was demanded. It was a shape that had no resemblance to anything except itself. The poles were unceremoniously bent, the metal sheets were stretched into every contortion, and the rails suddenly protruded about the head, all according to necessity. It was all nothing but necessity.[66]

Ango appears to have isolated that "sense of necessity" which evaded Nobuyuki when he stood with his brother on Nihonbashi Bridge. The ship's beauty lies not in some extraneous quality but in its perfect realization—everything comes together, nothing is amiss. It is no coincidence that Ango's objects of nostalgia are human constructions. For just as Nobuyuki considered manual labor a means to effect a harmonious relationship between emotional and physical needs, Ango was drawn to these highly specialized, painstakingly crafted structures because they represent the aesthetic ideal of an exact fit between the two sets of needs. Ango's nostalgia is also triggered by the enclosed and highly regulated human communities signified by all three structures; namely, prison routine, factory monotony, and naval discipline. These are worlds in which everything has its place, and every moment is invested with full significance. As an intellectual cut loose in the modern world and left to his own devices, Ango must have been drawn to such tantalizingly contained and knowable sites. None of these structures could possibly have attracted him as a place of everyday experience, but they speak of security and a fullness of the moment reminiscent of distant childhood that suggest common ties with the furusato landscapes of Doppo and Tōson. It is the yearning for a similar experience of totality that drives the lonely Kensaku throughout the course of Shiga's novel.

Ango also related the furusato to an experience of complete integration. Although this aspect has often been viewed in a positive light, as for example, in Kobayashi's somewhat envious depiction of his friend's lingering ties to his native place, Ango interpreted it in terms of a particularly raw and poignant reality stripped of all niceties. His article "The Native Place of Literature" ("Bungaku no furusato," 1941) discusses three stories that capture the feeling for him; a brief *kyōgen* comedy piece in which a *daimyō* bursts into tears after seeing an ugly temple gargoyle that reminds him of his wife; an episode from the tenth-century *Tales of Ise (Ise monogatari)* in which a young couple elope and the man, having taken great care to hide his beloved in a ruined storehouse for the night, discovers the next morning that a demon has eaten her;[67] and "Little Red Riding Hood." One example of such rawness is found in the fairy tale, a disconcerting story of an innocent and sweet girl, who visits her sick grandmother and ends up being deceived and gobbled up by a wicked wolf (in the Grimm brothers' version). Ango saw no redeeming moral, nothing to make her death bearable, and yet the story conveyed to him something of the furusato, with its "painful sadness and beauty, like holding ice close to one's heart."[68] This mood emerges because, fundamentally, all three stories concern themselves with feelings of the "absolute isolation" arising at moments of utter cruelty and helplessness.[69] A comparable scene takes place in Shiga's story "The Kidnapping" ("Ko o nusumu hanashi," 1914), based on the author's trip to Onomichi, which tells of an unhappy young man who leaves Tokyo to stay in a small city on the Inland Sea coast, where he intends to work on his novel. Deeply troubled, he walks to the coast on the outskirts of town one blustery evening:

Several tile-baking kilns illuminated the surrounding dusk with their powerful light. Burning oil sizzled on pinewood under the pressure of a fierce wind. I stood facing the sea. In my present mood, I could find no song to sing. I simply cried out, but my voice seemed feeble and unpleasant. I could find no voice: when forced, its tone was strangely pathetic. The cold north wind howled down from behind. Black smoke from the tile kilns, driven by the wind, brushed the surface of the churning sea and flew on in tatters. I began to feel sad, like a child caught in its sobs.[70]

The story opens with the harsh fact that the young man has been expelled by a father who despises him; from the beginning this is a "child" without a home. The insignificant figure he cuts in the face of equally cold and indifferent nature seems even more pathetic. No wonder he can barely raise a voice to affirm his presence in the world. But it is precisely his state of homelessness, the fact that no place will have him, that heightens the raw intensity of this experience to an unparalleled degree. As with "Little Red Riding Hood" and the other examples cited by Ango, this scene contains no pocket of ambiguity, no trace of sentimentality, to soften the impact. The result is that, for this brief instant, his emotions appear to crackle in the wind and the sea itself sobs.

Ango's reflections on the act of writing provide another means to re-evaluate the relationship between Shiga and native place. By pushing a conventional reading of the furusato as a compensatory site to its most painful extreme, Ango anticipated Said's observation on Conrad that "the chasm between words saying and words meaning was widened, not lessened, by a talent for words written." In "The Kidnapping," although Shiga's aim was to convey through words a young man's inability to communicate by depicting him as speechless in the full and unforgiving glare of the moment, the literary medium inevitably fails to deliver completely. Writing implies a painful realization: "To have chosen to write, then, is to have chosen in a particular way neither to say directly nor to mean exactly in the way he had hoped to say or to mean."[71] However, Ango understood this harsh reality to be not only an essential element in the process of writing itself but the very source of its beauty:

A line created with the purpose of displaying beauty cannot exist. Beauty does not emerge from a special place where beauty has been consciously formed. You just have to do your very best to write what you really must write, what needs to be written, as necessity dictates. It is just "necessity," be it one line or two lines or a hundred, it is "necessity" from beginning to end. And the distinctive form in which the essence of necessity is sought gives birth to beauty.[72]

The warship's beauty emerges from its perfect embodiment of necessity: literature and the furusato may also be seen as part of a common practice. Shiga's seaside scene attains its bleak attraction precisely because no gap appears between basic need and its representation. Likewise, although the scene speaks of a young man's complete isolation from his environment, it may also be read as a moment of sheer beauty in the sense that the barriers between man and his environment have completely dissolved.

Kobayashi identified several qualities in Shiga's works that overlapped with Ango's understanding of the native place. For instance, Kobayashi's argument that thought (or cogitation, *shisaku*) and action basically amount to the same thing in the writings of his favorite author comes close to Ango's concept of necessity:

He is not conscious of the gap between thought and action. Even if he were conscious of such a gap, it would mean that, at that moment, his thoughts were still unripened, and that before long his sensual passion would suddenly forge an unmistakable bridge across it. Truly, for Shiga to think is to act, to act is to think. For such a temperament, doubts are foolish and regrets are foolish.[73]

The exceedingly reverential tone of these words almost invites a contradictory reaction, and one can well imagine Dazai's glee in trying to knock Shiga from his pedestal. It is nevertheless useful to read "The Kidnapping" in light of Kobayashi's argument. Soon after the young man arrives in the seaside town, his literary powers dry up, and he falls into a depressed state in which dreams and fantasies relating to kidnapping young girls occupy an increasing part of his time. The shift from thought to action occurs almost casually in the text. Having almost given up on the idea, he happens to catch sight of his masseur's five-year-old daughter in the street and quietly leads her away while the mother's attention is diverted.

Shiga's remarkable narrative barely acknowledges what would be considered, from any conventional viewpoint, a highly reprehensible act. This is not to say that the moral issue is ignored, although the young man concludes that "kidnapping other people's children may be a bad deed, but this does not mean that it is bad in an absolute sense."[74] In fact, a concern with morality holds the story together, but less in terms of human relationships than in the privileging of a union between thought and action. In the first part of the story, the young man's thoughts are still "unripened," and he cannot act. After seizing the girl, however, his language suggests his feelings have undergone an almost purifying transformation:

I've finally done it. I've done something really frightening. And now that I've done it, I'm pleased. I can't go back now: my only choice is to go forward. Right now I have no idea what I should do. But the point is that everything I have done until now, every failed attempt to act, has now been put right. I've been too feeble in myself, but those thoughts have been conquered now.[75]

This moment of celebratory self-reflection should be seen as the story's high point, when Shiga articulates the highly desirable unity of thought and action in "an absolute sense." Put another way, Shiga identifies conditions in which *kibun* arises, at least temporarily, to cut through the imperfections and indecisions of everyday life. True, at the end of the story, the man's nerves fail and he feels regret for his actions, but by then the narrative climax— and his status as a "Shiga hero"—have passed. In conventional terms, the man's actions are selfish and deeply disturbing, but the story's driving force is to acknowledge and respond to the overriding *necessity* of answering fundamental emotional needs.

Another theme integral to both Ango's and Kobayashi's understanding of the furusato is the sense of continuity. Indeed, it was precisely Kobayashi's failure to experience this on a daily basis that informed his high regard for Shiga as a writer who appears to have closed the gap between action and thought. The theme is pursued in "Literature of the Lost Home," which opens with an extended quotation from Tanizaki's article "On 'Art'" ("'Gei' ni tsuite"), first published in the journal *Reconstruction* (*Kaizō*, April 1933). Tanizaki complained that writers of "pure" literature were so

caught up in the narrow universe of the *bundan* that they completely failed to provide works that offered "consolation and a life-
time of untiring companionship" to adult readers. The result is
that people over thirty read only Chinese literature or else Japanese classics and popular fiction. Kobayashi was particularly struck
by Tanizaki's condemnation of modern writers so incapable of
stepping beyond their small worlds of personal experience that
they have become "cooped up in a cramped universe."[76] Tanizaki
was referring specifically to the I-novel form, but his own literature might equally be characterized as frequently concerned with
highly specialized worlds, notably erotic fetishism. His gloomy as-
sessment nevertheless contrasts strongly with a scene from Uno's
"Dreaming Room" in which one particularly "cramped universe"
is represented in positive terms. The narrator remembers that he
used to hide in a closet at home in order to enjoy his own magic
lantern show alone:

In the cramped closet smelling of something weird and unknown, I
would be bent almost double over my magic lantern apparatus with its
lamp inside the small tin box, and devote all my attention to the projection I had made for myself: the surrounding air was hot, damp, and stuffy
like the inside of a cauldron, and the flame from the lamp of my apparatus gradually heated me up from my stomach to my chest, so that my
whole body became soaked in sweat. In these conditions, what pleasure,
what peace of mind, what a sense of mystery I was able to enjoy![77]

For Uno, the very claustrophobic nature of this environment, utterly cut off from the wider world, proved a source rich in imaginative possibilities. Kobayashi, on the other hand, was more troubled that his own experiences of life did not amount to a
continuous whole; looking back over his past, he saw only a series
of fragmented memories with no unifying element that—according
to the logic of his own essay—might be equated with a stable sense
of furusato. It was for this reason that he was so keen to mythologize Shiga as a writer still in touch with "primitivism," since such
instincts promise to uncover an enduring and pervasive sense of being that can be traced back unbroken into prehistorical times and
far excels the discontinuities of modernity.

Kobayashi associated home with consolation, and he viewed Shiga as its most successful exponent, but Ango's perspective on the significance of home points to a different evaluation. In "The Kidnapping," it is the young man's hopelessness that draws comparison with the furusato, not so much as a site of comfort but as a place where pretence is unnecessary and inappropriate. Seen in this light, the idea of the native place merely as a pleasant retreat from undesirable circumstances is insufficient; rather, feelings of sadness, loss, and regret are absolutely integral to a sense of home. Ango made the point through an analogy. Living alone, he had no wife or children to share his feelings when, as happened frequently, he returned home in a sad mood. Yet the very act of returning involved an unavoidable confrontation with this strange "demon" (*mamono*):

In other words, in order to escape this regret and sadness, you must return. And it is always right to go forward. Napoleon always advanced and did not retreat until Russia, and Hitler has never retreated. But I believe it is inconceivable that even such geniuses as these can avoid home. The fact that home exists means that they must inevitably return. And as they return, they will most certainly be unable to escape the same strange regret and sadness that I felt.[78]

Although subsequent events gave the lie to Ango's assertions, his point that "going home" is an inescapable event that inevitably involves pain remains valid. In this sense, the seaside scene in "The Kidnapping" may be read as a moment in which the young man has no choice but to acknowledge an utterly desolate but nevertheless necessary component of his true "home."

But if a return home is inevitable, one final note by the poet Hagiwara Sakutarō offers a useful corrective to those who were too literal in their desire to revisit the native place. His article "Return to Japan" ("Nihon e no kaiki," 1937) suggests that the West has figured as the furusato of modern Japan since Meiji times. In particular, he compared the experience of modern Japanese to the legend of Urashima Tarō. The most common version of the story recounts how Tarō rescues a turtle from mistreatment by some children by the seashore. The grateful turtle turns into a woman and invites him to stay with her in the sea-god's palace under the waves. There he spends three delightful years. When he finally returns to his village, no one recognizes him. At a loss, he opens the box given by the woman, even though he was forbidden to do so. Immediately white smoke billows forth, and he changes into an old man. It turns out he had been away from the village for three hundred years.

Hagiwara believed that the Japanese of his own day were similarly bewitched by the sea-god's palace of the West and had only recently awakened from their fantasy. However, when they returned to the "real native place" in the 1930s, they found themselves shockingly aged, a sad but inevitable consequence of the fact that they had remained on their alien travels for too long:

Now that we have returned to our native home, traces of the past have already disappeared; the eaves are rotten, the garden is wasted, not a single memento of things Japanese remains. We are amazed to find that everything has been lost. We are an unrivaled band of sorrowful drifters, wandering aimlessly in our desolation as we recall old memories with the hope of extracting from the corners of this blighted land something real of those "things Japanese" that once existed.[79]

This lament—that the knowable past has been tragically lost—is a well-worn cliché found in most cultures and most times. But especially in the Japanese case, a sense of identity has always involved a constant negotiation with other cultures, particularly that of China.[80] The poet nevertheless raised the important point that the attempt to return to a "real" Japan is no more than an impossible fantasy. The reference to his fellow countrymen as sad *drifters* merely underlines the blurring of the lines of demarcation between Japanese and foreign elements, as noted above with regard to the *Shirakaba* group. But it is in the context of this far from settled understanding of what it meant to be Japanese that Shiga's talent for presenting a seemingly fixed and authentic Japanese landscape gains significance. The very year in which Hagiwara's troubled article about an unstable Japanese identity appeared, Shiga completed his own novel, which closes with a scene in which all conflict appears banished by the spiritual serenity of Mount Daisen.

This chapter has been concerned with a broad examination of how Shiga's writings, and even the personality of the writer himself, became linked to the notion of the furusato, especially in connection with the theme of "authentic" Japanese identity. During the late 1920s and 1930s, native place discourse attracted particularly close scrutiny from a variety of sources. The very variety demonstrates that the furusato is best viewed as a site of multiple interpretations dependent on the conflicting needs and motives of its various literary creators. Perversely, any attempt to pin the furusato down through simple definitions highlights its contentious status as a site where the arguments surrounding "authentic" culture and national identity were played out. In the final chapter, I examine the links between Shiga, identity, and the native place by considering four important themes drawn mainly from *A Dark Night's Passing*—harmony, nature, mother/mountain, and history—in order to investigate how the writer so effectively generated the impression of a calm and unproblematic furusato in his texts and how his personal approach overlapped with wider historical developments. In other words, how did his furusato work, and at what cost?

SIX

Shiga Naoya:
A Dark Night's Making

Harmony by Force

In an essay on images of "repose and violence" among Japanese writers of the late 1920s and 1930s, Alan Tansman warns against the temptation to equate literary works with an increasingly authoritarian and repressive political environment. Unlike Germany, Japan had no mass fascist movement that attempted to subject the population to "a totalizing, unified aesthetic experience." Rather, he argues, "the fascist aesthetic characterizing the language of certain writers can function on a level apart from their identities as citizens, their political commitments or antipolitical postures, or even the semantic content of their work."[1] To be sure, the political slant of certain writers is not hard to determine. Hagiwara Sakutarō's complaint about Japan's excessive earlier infatuation with the West merely reflected the bias of his times. By contrast, the opening stanza of Satō Haruo's poem "Song of the Dawn of Asia" ("Ajia no yoake o utau," 1942) in which he commemorated the seizure of Singapore from the British, suggests a more overt and particularly bloodthirsty celebration of the wartime spirit.[2] However, a subtly turned phrase tends to have a more pervasive influence than propaganda precisely because the reader (and often the writer) is unaware of the full ideological implications. Ango may have been drawn to the warship because it embodied aesthetic beauty in its pure utilitarianism, but he neglected to note that such vessels were designed specifically to threaten and kill. Likewise, at the time he was writing "A Personal View of Japanese Culture," the Kosuge Prison housed political prisoners, and factories provided the economic backbone for imperialist adventures. Moreover, Ango's attraction to these various forms of human community reflects not only individual nostalgia for a lost communal identity but also his daily experience of a general atmosphere increasingly regulated by authoritarian control.

In Shiga's case, it is certainly less easy to attach a political label. Indeed, a seminal essay of 1919 by the author and critic Hirotsu Kazuo (1891–1968) highlighted the inability to pin Shiga down easily as one of his most commendable characteristics. Shiga's famously bare literary style turns out to be more complicated than it first appears, because "it cannot be grasped through any handle (*tegakari*) or hook (*hikkakari*), and the slightest inattention allows it to immediately slip away through one's hands." Writers like Mushanokōji and Arishima Takeo reveal a clear view of life through their works, but such clarity is missing in Shiga, whose wholehearted concentration on personal detail makes him an unusually profound realist (*riari-suto*): "He relates to us what he himself has seen, heard, touched, and felt just as (*sono mama*) he saw it, heard it, touched it, felt it, as far as possible avoiding affectation or exaggeration."[3] Such words set the tone for later praise of Shiga's writing style; they also hint at inherent shortcomings. Shiga's deliberate refusal to acknowledge any reality beyond his own experience effectively naturalizes the events recorded in his texts by depriving the reader of a contextual "handle" with which to grasp them: in other words, the reader is invited to ignore the broader picture. This does not, however, entirely negate the possibility of placing Shiga in a wider historical frame. The element of cruelty in all three stories chosen by Ango to exemplify his nostalgic mood echoes the harshness of his age. Similarly, certain stories by Shiga such as "The Kidnapping," in which the emotional violence done to the little girl counts for little, may be seen as prefiguring that heartlessness. In *A Dark Night's Passing*, the far from condemnatory manner in which Shiga portrayed several eruptions of violence might be interpreted as indirectly complementing the increasingly intolerant and single-minded Japanese identity of the 1930s. It is in this wider context that Shiga's overwhelming concern in his literature to establish a harmonious mood should be read.

The concept of harmony (*wa*) is sometimes evoked in Japan and elsewhere as a historically transcendent cultural trait indicative of a high degree of collectivism in Japanese society; it is often cited, for instance, in company management policies. Itō Kimio has attempted to place the term in a historical context by linking it to the formation of national consciousness from the Meiji period. He examines how especially from 1903—supposedly the 1,300th anniversary of the Seventeen-Article Constitution—school textbooks were used by the Meiji authorities to promote Prince Shōtoku (572–621) as a symbol for officially sanctioned virtues, which changed with the times. Shōtoku was identified as enlightened cultural reformer in Meiji, as a major political figure in the 1920s when political parties were active, and as an embodiment of social and political harmony from the latter half of the 1930s when a more enforced consensus became the norm. It was particularly this last role that informed government thinking in the 1937 Basic Principles of the National Polity (Kokutai no hongi), edited by the Educational Bureau of the Ministry of Education. This document noted that harmony is "not merely peace achieved on the surface. It is inner and spiritual harmony and peace. This ideal brings about a unity of communal spirit by maintaining not only hierarchical distinctions but also the essential equality of an ethical order."[4] Itō's interest in this text arises from his concern with currents in modern intellectual history, but it presents interesting parallels with literature. *A Dark Night's Passing*, which reached its conclusion in the same year, might be characterized as articulating similar aspirations, especially in the final section, in which Kensaku attains "spiritual harmony and peace" on Mount Daisen. On the other hand, the "communal spirit" so highly prized by government authorities was purchased through sustained and increasingly repressive actions against social groups antagonistic to their own point of view, as witnessed, for example, in the hounding of proletarian writers. A similarly enforced harmony operates in Shiga's texts. His literary landscapes outside Tokyo aim to represent the kind of relaxed tranquility to which Doppo and Tōson aspired in their furusato works, but this calm is achieved only at the expense of considerable struggle with an extraordinary level of the barely repressed violence that pervades his writing. An examination of how Shiga negotiated these conflicting impulses will illuminate his high literary skill in producing the image of native place as a site of unruffled harmony.

If the furusato partly evokes the pleasure of "coming home," Kensaku's determination to go elsewhere in search of a tranquil furusato-like landscape is not surprising, since his memories of his home, particularly those relating to his mother and father, are tainted with violence and confrontation. The Prologue to *A Dark Night's Passing* consists of memories from Kensaku's life as a young boy, and their inclusion suggests the indelible imprint they left on his mind. One scene describes him as a four- or five-year-old who has mischievously climbed on top of the main roof of the house. Horrified, his mother can only watch until a servant manages to fetch him down, at which point she gives him a severe beating: "After my mother passed away, my memory of this became etched in my mind. In later years whenever I thought about it, I came close to tears. At least mother really loved me, I thought."[5] Kensaku's recollection is strongly colored by the fact that his mother died in childbirth only two years later. But another incident—this time with his father half a year after his mother's death—indicates that violence was not always equated with love. Kensaku has been forced to move in with his unpleasant "grandfather" and returns to the old house only occasionally. On one such visit, he is delighted when his normally distant father invites him to a game of sumo wrestling. Things turn sour, however, when the father appears determined to beat his son and ends up ruthlessly pinning him down to the floor with his knees. Even worse, he uses his sash to tie the boy's hands and ankles together behind his back and demands that his son admit defeat. Kensaku describes his father at that point, and his feelings toward him:

Due to the unexpectedly strenuous activity, father's face appeared pale and menacing. He left me there and turned toward his desk.

A hatred toward father welled up in me, while the sight of his broad heaving shoulders filled me with loathing. Before long I was unable to focus clearly on him any more. It was too much for me, and I burst into tears. Father turned round in surprise.

"Don't be silly. It's nothing to cry about. All you had to do was ask me to untie you."[6]

In this scene, the father's affectation of innocence belies an extraordinary level of sadistic intent, and his bodily fatigue reflects the seriousness of his psychological engagement. Under the circumstances, the boy's hatred is understandable.

Georges Bataille postulates a link between violence and eroticism that may explain why such memories remain so deeply etched in Kensaku's mind. He suggests that people are "discontinuous beings" who find true shared continuity only in the final reality of death. Eroticism is an attempt to temporarily overcome that state of isolation by breaking down mutual barriers. Through such an effort there develops a feeling of "elemental violence. In essence, the domain of eroticism is the domain of violence, of violation."[7] The implications of the game between Kensaku and his father are clearly erotic in that such rare moments of naked aggression are the only times that a shared intimacy—an opportunity to violate personal space and enter into each other's minds—is at all possible, even if it takes on a sadomasochistic edge. At other times, their feelings of mutual antagonism are so strong that they hardly know how to talk to each other. Kensaku's relationship with his mother, meanwhile, may be marred by constant scoldings, but their mutual love finds immediate, physical expression through a spontaneous and violent smack of flesh.

This interpretation helps explain Shiga's obvious fascination with violence. For instance, neither of Kensaku's experiences can be described as desirable, yet these highly charged exchanges are portrayed as moments of great intimacy with his parents before—one way or another—he loses them both. He ends up profoundly estranged from his father, but at least reconciliation remains possible. By contrast, his memories of his mother carry greater significance since they are colored by foreknowledge of their irreversible separation through death. In addition, both incidents serve as keys to Kensaku's complex emotional responses in later years; the violence of such scenes may be recalled in some pain, but it also evokes a certain pleasure by confirming that at times he stood at the undisputed center of his parents' attention. Indeed, it may well be that the use of a first-, rather than a third-person narrator in the Prologue—a technique that distinguishes it from the rest of the book—was appropriate precisely because it is only here that Kensaku's separate ego-consciousness is marked out so clearly. Some critics have noted that the story is written entirely from Kensaku's point of view, and that it is only in the final scene, in which his wife, Naoko, joins him on Mount Daisen that the narrative shifts to her perspective.[8] Having reached the conclusion of his journey of self-discovery, he can return to his origin, where he can be viewed once more from an external point as a separate and fully knowable human being.

Shiga articulated violence as an eroticized medium even more clearly in some of his short stories. "Seibei and His Gourds" ("Seibei to hyōtan," 1912) describes a twelve-year-old boy (that is, one on the point of sexual maturity) with an unusually strong interest in collecting gourds, an activity that infuriates his father. One day he buys a gourd so attractive that he cannot resist taking it to school, and "he even ended up polishing it under his desk during class."[9] Seibei is discovered by the teacher, who informs his parents. The father takes a hammer to his son's collection of polished gourds and "smashed them to pieces, every one of them. Seibei simply stood there, pale and silent."[10] Sibley notes that the gourd is nowhere identified in this story as pertaining exclusively to one sex or the other, but a direct link to males is found in another short story, "An Accident" ("Dekigoto," 1913), which describes the rescued boy in terms of his "perfect little penis, like a tiny gourd."[11] One way to interpret gourds in the Seibei story, with its father-son rivalry, is obviously in terms of phallic substitution.

Eroticized violence is even more marked in "The Razor" ("Kamisori," 1910), where powerful sexual feelings erupt with deadly consequence. Yoshisaburō, the proprietor of a barber shop, is feverish with a cold and regrets having dismissed his two assistants for stealing from him to finance visits to the pleasure quarters. Various circumstances conspire to increase his irritability as his sickness worsens. His mood is foul by the time a laborer, who enters the shop for a quick shave, intimates he will visit a brothel that night. The barber is revolted by this "disgusting little man," and the thought of his planned activities "brought a sequence of sickening scenes" to his debilitated mind.[12] Yoshisaburō is a master of his trade, but his illness causes him to nick the young man's throat accidentally with his blade. He finds this small scratch utterly compelling: "At first the shallow cut turned a milky white, but a pale crimson spread over it, followed by a rapid accumulation of blood."[13] Although not at all horrific, this image is comparable to a nightmare recounted in "The Kidnapping," in which the young man encounters an aging hag with an unpleasant mouth, formed by "an unpleasantly red lower lip dangling down as if her tongue was hanging out."[14] According to Sibley, the sexual details here are "uncomfortably blatant—not because they are sexual, of course, but because the eroticism seems so malignant and clearly reflects childish fears."[15] In Yoshisaburō's case, he demonstrates a violent reaction related to equally fundamental fears:

Never having cut the face of a customer before, Yoshisaburō was overcome by an extremely powerful emotion. His breathing became shallow, and his whole mind and body seemed drawn into the cut. It was completely unstoppable now. Grasping the razor so that it pointed downward, he plunged it as far as it would go into the young man's throat. The man did not even shudder.[16]

The young man is asleep in the chair, probably lost in reveries of pleasure to come. He therefore remains unaware that the barber's febrile imagination, seized by a mixture of fascination and disgust, has inscribed him with barely concealed forms of sexual desire. The result is a spectacular denouement where the laborer's body, penetrated to the hilt by the barber's savage blade, becomes the recipient of irrepressible and infantile rage or, to return to Bataille's words, an eroticized "domain of violence, of violation."

Shiga's literary works are strongly driven by the attempt to control such destructive impulses, which threaten to take on a life of their own. In *A Dark Night's Passing*, for example, intrusive sexuality is represented by a pet goat Kensaku keeps at home; what began as a cute kid has turned into a fierce young goat with "three-inch horns" and an offensive smell that cannot be ignored. It is no coincidence that just at this point Kensaku announces his intention to take a trip out of Tokyo, thus implying the need to take charge of his own insistent desires.[17] Meanwhile, in *Reconciliation* Shiga confronted his aggressive side, specifically in terms of the father-son relationship. In line with the introspective viewpoint outlined in the previous chapter, Junkichi reveals considerable antagonism toward his father, but in highly personalized terms: "Granted that this [antagonism] involved various twisted and complicated feelings unavoidable in any parent-child relationship, I felt that it was based mainly on a hatred arising from an additional level of discord."[18] To suggest that a lack of harmony (*wa*) has arisen from discord (*fuwa*) is only to state the obvious, and such language had led several critics, including Francis Mathy, to complain that the causes of discord "are never adequately explained."[19] But this is to ignore an important point. Shiga explicitly rejected the possibility of reconciliation through anything so obvious as logical argument, and this is demonstrated when Junkichi visits the Azabu family home after hearing that his grandmother has suffered a dislocated jaw. Her condition turns out to be not particularly serious, but his stepmother asks him to leave quickly to avoid any encounter with his father. By this time in the story, Junkichi's attitude toward his aging parent has become more sympathetic, to the extent that he determines to write him a letter explaining his resentment. In the end he does not send it, partly because he feels that any cheap appeal to his father's emotions (*kanjō*) would be degrading to both of them, but also because an excessively logical (*rikutsu*) argument would not solve their antagonism anyway. As it happens, the decision to forgo the letter and meet his father face-to-face leads to long-term resolution. What is most remarkable in this story is the way that Shiga identified discord not with some specific, logically explainable problem but with a general lack of equilibrium. Consequently, a proper reconciliation can emerge only by somehow readdressing this imbalance.

Attempting to interpret how Shiga articulates the process of reconciliation is a frustrating business. If we conclude that Shiga failed to uncover the practical causes of discord, as Mathy claims, then that is the end of the matter, but we are left none the wiser as to his underlying motivation. If, on the other hand, credence is given to Shiga's line of thought—with its supposed rejection of logical argument—then the critic has little choice but to confirm it through use of an equally vague and insubstantial language. A clearer approach might be found through Shiga's article "Recollections of Uchimura Kanzō" ("Uchimura Kanzō sensei no omoide," 1941), in which he discussed three figures who had the greatest influence on his life: the Christian preacher Uchimura Kanzō (1861–1930), under whom he studied from 1900 to 1908; Mushanokōji; and his grandfather. What attracted him so much to these characters was less a particular word or deed than a "sympathetic resonance" (*kyōmei*).[20] Again, this less than crystal-clear explanation hints that—at least as far as Shiga understands it—there exists a shared form of communication beyond the level of verbal articulation. As such, it inevitably invites comparisons with *kibun*. Karatani argues that the main protagonist in Shiga's literature is never the "self" (*watakushi*) or the "other" (*tasha*)—both are lacking in his work—but *kibun* itself.[21] If, as Shiga implied, "sympathetic resonance" operates in a similar manner, then it might be defined as the mutual recognition of *kibun* in others, which suggests an equal capacity for communication outside human subjectivity.

In the previous chapter, I acknowledged real problems in considering *kibun* as an autonomous concept standing outside the contextualizing exigencies of time and place; the same criticism might be leveled at the mystifying and intangible features of a "sympathetic resonance." It is useful nevertheless to consider the expression as Shiga himself presented it, since it helps clarify the extent to which he was willing to disclose his own literary motivation. In *Reconciliation*, Shiga tried to demonstrate this kind of "sympathetic" recognition between father and son not through spoken language but through an exchange of looks. The gaze as a negative power is established early in the story during one of Junkichi's visits to the Azabu house when his father returns home unexpectedly soon. After first failing to recognize his son after a space of two years, the father confirms the depth of their estrangement through such an "unspeakably disagreeable expression" on his face that Junkichi ends up confined to bed with a physical ailment for two days.[22] In contrast, a shared look seals the re-establishment of harmony at the story's conclusion. Junkichi has already made his tearful, rather formal apology at the family home, but they experience an unspoken and deeper level of communication a few days later when he sees off his father at the railway station. Junkichi first feels aggrieved that his father, who is sitting in the train awaiting its departure, hardly reacts to his own heartfelt bow from the station platform. His mood is immediately transformed, however, by a "sympathetic resonance" arising from a change in the older man's countenance: "At which point a certain expression suddenly appeared in father's eyes. It was what I had been looking for, what I had been seeking unconsciously. With the pleasure and excitement of two hearts meeting, my expression was even more caught somewhere between a frown and tears." The earlier reconciliation had necessarily involved a public exchange of words witnessed by other family members in order to confirm Junkichi's return to the family fold. This second event suggests a far more direct and intimate contact, a meeting of "two hearts" that seems to negate the need for spoken language. Both Junkichi and his father would be hard-pressed to explain in logical terms the exact nature of this exchange, but the son is so certain a harmonious equilibrium has been re-established that he feels able to declare that "this time, my reconciliation with father would never be broken."[23]

Such a reading, however, leaves questions unanswered. In particular, problems arise with the suggestion that it is possible to represent a form of communication in literature outside the language of the text itself. However spontaneous or unplanned Shiga may present these tenuous feelings as being, they can find expression only through language; in the end, they are a fruit of human subjectivity. Fowler, who reacted strongly against Shiga's self-proclaimed virtue of "sincerity" and the way critics have often accepted it at face value, sought to expose the literary techniques by which the author conveyed this impression. I am not so convinced that Shiga was as consciously *deceptive* as Fowler seemed to imply, but the point remains that qualities like sincerity never exist in free-floating isolation. Instead, they depend on an author's skill in literary production. This understanding helps clarify how apparently intangible elements such as *kibun* also rely on linguistic skill in order to guarantee their material presence within a text. An acknowledgment of this aspect of artifice presents itself in *Reconciliation*. Junkichi's relationship with father is at its lowest ebb following the tragic death of his new-born child and his father's refusal to allow the baby burial in the family grave. The son is moved to recall the plot of a story he began writing three years earlier during a stay in Matsue when he tried to give literary shape to his problematic relationship. His story began with a visit from a miserable youth:

The youth brings along a serial story he had been writing at the time for a Matsue newspaper. I read it. The story is about discord with his father. Before long the newspaper suddenly ceases publication of the serial in the middle of its run. In a state, the youth comes to see me. It turns out that the youth's father had found out about it, despite the fact that it was writ-ten under a pseudonym, and sent someone from Tokyo to pay off the newspaper in order to stop it being published.

The complex layers used by Shiga to distance himself from the father-son conflict reveal his huge difficulty in discussing it; his fic-tional character Junkichi writes about his own story of a youth who is writing a story about a character who uses a pseudonym for the real character of his father, with whom (just like Shiga) he is having problems. In fact, Junkichi notes his own reluctance to publish any work relating to father-son discord because of the shadow it might cast over his good relationship with his grandmother. The fact that he decides not to publish the Matsue story is tacit acknowledgment that his actual conflict with father would have been revealed; in-deed, a fantasy of how his father might have reacted is played out in the passage quoted above. On the other hand, the story's recapitula-tion within the *Reconciliation* text implies that harmony has been restored, since the present act of storytelling presumably still needs to meet the criterion not to harm the ongoing relationship with grandmother (who, in real life, did not die until 1921).

Clearly, the shape of Shiga's text was far from haphazard and emerged only after a great deal of deliberation. But it is at the point where Junkichi considers how to conclude his Matsue story that the constructed nature of an apparent spontaneity comes into sharpest focus. After recounting how the unhappy youth (like Junkichi himself) is expelled from the family home, Junkichi describes the story's final tragic scene. Grandmother is about to pass away, and two rival fantasies present themselves as possible resolutions to the conflict:

In my imagination, I pondered the scene where the unstoppable, excited youth storms in and has a fight with his father, perhaps a wild fight that goes beyond blows: Would the father kill him? Would he kill his father? But unexpectedly another scene came to me: just as the fight was reaching its peak, the two suddenly grasp each other and passionately burst into tears. This scene, which had sprung out from nowhere, was totally outside my expectation.

This passage cleverly provides expression for elements of both harmony and violence. As Junkichi himself suggests, the setting out of worse-case scenarios is in part a form of therapy: "By writing about them openly, I thought I might prevent them happening in reality."[24] In other words, violence with the father is voiced as a means of negating it. At the same time, Junkichi is taking the opportunity to vent a real and visceral hatred, by which, as it were, the boy who lost at sumo finally gets his revenge. On the other hand, the passage also allows previously untapped conciliatory emotions to emerge, and it presages the formal reconciliation between Junkichi and his father. However, its apparently spontaneous appearance in the son's mind is disingenuous; after all, every thought can be considered to have appeared spontaneously. Rather, Shiga sets out to convey the illusory sense that harmony has naturally reasserted itself. For this reason, the narrator's professed surprise at its "unexpected" emergence creates the sense of a gulf between thought and thinker, as if they were entirely discrete entities. The aim is to emphasize a process that seems beyond mere logic and supersedes any personal motivation on Junkichi's part. In short, Shiga downplayed human intervention in order to privilege the effortless and "natural" function of *kibun*. The reality, however, is that apparently spontaneous impulses emerge from pre-existing conditions that inform Junkichi's character and can find shape only through the author's skillful manipulation of language.

Shiga's exceptional talent and intelligence as a writer enabled him to shape a calm and settled furusato landscape in his literature. It has been suggested that in *A Dark Night's Passing* the quietly ecstatic mood that pervades the final scene on Mount Daisen reflects not so much Shiga's actual visit to the place in 1914 but the gradual process of reconciliation between a fifty-four-year-old author and the tormented youthful version of himself from twenty-four years earlier.[25] Such a reading would confirm a deeply reflective and intuitive quality in the author. Already in the earlier *Reconciliation*, Shiga depicted a newfound inner calm specifically in terms of a return home. Junkichi, after a tearful reconciliation with his father, visits the home of his painter friend S.K. in Yotsuya. He feels tired, but the mood is not unpleasant: "It was a weariness laced with light-headed tranquility, reminiscent of a small lake deep in the mountains and enveloped in thick mist. The weariness of a traveler, worn out by an extremely long and unpleasant journey, who has finally returned home."[26] After the huge emotional effort required to reach this point, this moment of escape into a "light-headed tranquility" is well deserved. On the other hand, the process of tempestuous social interaction, no matter how "unpleasant," was itself an integral element of this journey.

I began this section by suggesting that a government document of the mid-1930s praising the ideal of harmony should be set in the context of an increasingly oppressive social environment. Shiga's desire to delineate a harmonious furusato in his literature should carry a similar caveat. Such landscapes expunged of conflict emerged at a time of growing social tension and underlying violence, when less "acceptable" versions—literary or otherwise—of what it meant to be Japanese increasingly had no voice both at home and abroad.

Natural Instincts

In earlier chapters, I discussed how furusato literature arose in Meiji as a means to critique the perceived shortcomings of modern life. In a similar fashion, the city/countryside binary emerged to imply a set of values in which the countryside generally embodied a closer, more authentic relationship with the world no longer accessible to city-based people. This is not to say that the task of integrating human needs with the natural environment was an easy one; the difficulties are clear in some of Doppo's texts. Even in Meiji the furusato ideal was not necessarily tied to the writer's actual place of birth, and this tendency became more pronounced during Taishō, when writers such as Satō reasserted their sense of belonging through more imaginative means. Moreover, Uno Kōji's story demonstrates how some writers even found it possible to project fantasies of the furusato onto urban landscapes. During the same period, Yanagita and other writers further explained rural sites as the generic "home" of Japanese authenticity. Such developments led Kobayashi Hideo, whose urban experience left him with feelings of homelessness, to view the furusato and the countryside (*inaka*) as virtually inter-changeable terms denoting sites of belonging to which he had no access. In this section, I discuss how Shiga inherited and further re-fined this range of views and to a certain extent answered the needs of his displaced urban readers by incorporating into his texts an un-derstanding of nature that was highly personal and exclusive. In the end, he outlined what it meant to be Japanese in a way that silenced the expression of other potential versions of national identity.

Certainly, Shiga implied that city life deprives people of natural rhythms. In the first part of *A Dark Night's Passing*, Kensaku is still unable to sleep at three in the morning and rises from bed the fol-lowing afternoon only because some friends have arrived. One of the first changes he notices upon leaving Tokyo on the boat to Onomichi is the relaxed quality of his sleep. He takes a magazine to bed as is his custom but soon feels drowsy: "He was sinking pleas-antly into sleep. But something still lingered in his mind: after these distasteful, bewildering three months of my life, a vast and peaceful sleep has finally come."[27] Kensaku's hope is that, through his re-moval to a more relaxed environment, he will find answers to ques-tions first raised in Tokyo, by letting loose his natural instincts in the expanded dream world of a non-urban landscape.

Another characteristic of the more "natural" environment out-side the city is the scarcity of people, in contrast to large crowds as-sociated with the urban experience. In Shiga's novel, the hubbub of pedestrians and vehicles that Kensaku witnesses in the city's commercial center is replaced by rural landscapes largely emptied of people. His major journeys outside Tokyo are almost always soli-tary, and other figures tend to appear only if they are related to the main character's fortunes. The early, happy days of marriage promise that his time of suffering as an alienated young man is over, but Naoko's sexual indiscretion with a cousin leads to deep tensions between the couple. Kensaku rejects her suggestion that they talk through the state of their marriage together, insisting that "from my own point of view it is purely and simply a matter for myself alone." This attitude reveals an extraordinary degree of selfishness, although, to give him credit, Kensaku admits to "an egoistical way of thinking."[28] Its narrative effect, however, is to propel him once more on a solitary journey, this time to Mount Daisen in his search for answers.

But if literary depictions of nature frequently involve a rejection of urban crowds, they tend to be concerned with greater attention to local flora and fauna. When young Mineo came back to his native place in "Let Me Return," the first thing he notices are the lush paddy fields and the promise of a rich harvest: similarly, *Broken Commandment* devotes considerable space to activities in surrounding fields and mountains. In Shiga's novel, a vibrant vegetable world takes center stage as Kensaku approaches the sacred mountain, as if to emphasize his earnest desire to rise above human imperfections. The scene is midsummer, and he gazes from a train window onto fields of rice, "the color of burning green," as they sway in the heat:

The rice, directly absorbing the powerful heat and light, was rich with color. Kensaku felt almost overwhelmed by the sight of the stalks struggling and jostling to raise their voices in jubilation. For the first time he realized that such a world existed. People may live like bickering cats in a hole, but this other life had been here all along. Today the powerful sunlight did not hurt his eyes in the slightest.[29]

Plant life not only presents Kensaku with a picture of harmony, unlike the less than satisfying human world he has known so far, but also hints at a sustained sensuality that he has found hard to attain in his relations with people. It is surely the attraction of entering further into such a world that pushed Shiga to write a number of short works devoted to animals and plant life. His best known of these, "At Kinosaki" ("Kinosaki nite," 1917), details the narrator's reflections on three creatures—a bee, a rat, and a lizard—during his convalescence at a hot spring after an accident with a tram, but there are many others.[30]

Such encounters provided Shiga with the opportunity to produce understated and quiet appreciations of natural phenomena—Starrs's reading of "At Kinosaki" as a "state of mind" novel (*shinkyō shōsetsu*) makes this point nicely[31]—but at other times, human interactions with nature are more like confrontations, depicting a raw intensity closer to Ango's vision of the furusato. Still on his boat trip, Kensaku stands on deck during a nighttime storm, an experience described as riding the back of a "great monster" as it plunges into pitch darkness against a powerful wind:

He stood wrapped in his overcoat with his legs set slightly apart. Even so, as the ship rolled on a great swell and the wind blew against him, there were times when he almost lost his footing. He wore no hat, but the wind pressed his hair down so tightly that he seemed to be wearing a cap. The battering of his eyelashes made his eyes smart. At that moment he felt enveloped by something extraordinarily huge. Above and below, in front and behind, to the left and the right; darkness without end, and he stood in the center of it.

This is a world from which all other people have been banished, leaving the hero not simply alone but, as Nakamura Mitsuo once described it, "bordering on an animal isolation."[32] Already adrift from a stable mainland, he is forced to face something much greater than himself as rough weather intensifies his sense of vulnerability. Natural elements seem to intrude even more powerfully here than they do on Doppo's train journey across Hokkaidō. Kensaku's hair is pushed down by the wind to his skull, the barest bone of his physical body. The wind threatens to obliterate every distinguishing trace of individuality, or perhaps quite literally pummel him out of existence. And yet there is a certain resistance, a willingness to look back. Although driven by nervous anxiety, his mind actively presses outward on an equally forceful impulse to describe and define this surrounding darkness "without end."

Here Shiga was experimenting with boundaries between self and other. What seemed so settled, so obvious in the city becomes blurred in a more dream-inspiring territory contained by nothing more than an indeterminate fringe of darkness, like a solitary eye that sees and is seen at the same time. Not surprisingly, this space engenders ambiguous responses in Kensaku. Just as his attitude to violence involves a complicated mix of pain and pleasure, the confrontation here with the imminent loss of self creates not only the obvious anxiety—the fear of death—but also a vaguely articulated pleasure. He presents himself as "mankind's chosen representative" face to face with nature:

He was seized by an exaggerated sense of standing there as the representative of all mankind. Yet he could not overcome the feeling that he was about to be swallowed up by something unbelievably huge. The feeling was not necessarily bad, but his mood contained a sense of forlorn hopelessness. He tightened his belly and took deep breaths of air into his lungs as a way of confirming the certainty of his own existence. The moment he relaxed, however, he was almost swallowed again by that huge entity.[33]

This portrait of a man examining himself at a fundamental physiological level brings to mind the "primitive" instincts Kobayashi claimed for Shiga. Reference to muscular activity identifies the body not so much as fixed structure than as flexible process, a continual flirting with the shifting lines by which self and external world are traced. Pleasure, meanwhile, is connected to the attraction of self-annihilation; to be "swallowed" by a greater entity has the appeal of eliminating all life's problems in a stroke. In Doppo's "River Mist," the emotional appeal of the distant ocean proves irresistible, but Shiga presents a more finely balanced conundrum: how to remain aware at the point of one's own obliteration? Unsolvable, the process is doomed to repeat itself like an eroticized pulse, a tantalizing game in which the narrator's consciousness alternately fades and rediscovers itself. This is, in short, a meditation on life and death.

By contrast, the final dramatic conclusion on Mount Daisen reveals a profound shift in Kensaku's frame of mind, specifically in terms of a more positive relationship with nature; indeed, this scene may be read as a long-considered answer to the threatening experience depicted earlier on the boat. A common complaint leveled at Shiga's novel is its "tenuousness of plot";[34] that is, despite its length and the time it took to complete, very little character development takes place. In terms of narrative action, it is true that not much happens. If, however, the work is seen as a kind of spiritual progress, then there clearly is a transformation, although the criticism that

Kensaku's enlightenment is too abrupt has some validity. The final path to sagelike awakening begins at midnight, when he sets out to climb to the mountain's summit with a group of pilgrims. He is weak from a bout of diarrhea, and the others leave him behind on the mountainside while they continue with their journey. Lying alone throughout the night, a semidelirious state induces in him a heightened awareness of the surrounding natural world:

Nature here was something undetectable to the eye, a body of air that enveloped him (insignificant as a tiny poppy seed) in its vast greatness. To dissolve into it, and thereby be restored: this was a feeling of pleasure inexpressible in words. It was rather like being tired and drifting into sleep without a care in the world.[35]

Once again, sleep emerges as an image of pleasurable self-oblivion. Earlier the boat is described as a "great monster"; Kensaku's human frailty in the face of great nature is again emphasized through the mountain ridge, which appears to him to be "the back of some enormous beast."[36] The fundamental change, however, is that his earlier anxiety has now given way to a pleasant anticipation of absorption into nature, which is perceived not as malevolent annihilation but the source of full emotional restoration.

Sudō Matsuo points out that Shiga's use of natural imagery here to imply the existence of a great cosmos may be unusual in a Japanese literary tradition that tends to confine itself to small details of beauty, but in general the author adheres to a conventional view by creating in Kensaku a character whose instinct is to harmonize himself with a benevolent force of nature.[37] Certainly, this willful surrendering of the self is a reading Shiga himself seemed keen to spell out. As the boundaries between self and other appear to melt away, Kensaku reflects that this is not the first time he has experienced such rapture:

Until now he had felt less a sense of blending into nature than of being absorbed. He had experienced some pleasure in this, although an urge to oppose it had also naturally arisen, while the very difficulty of opposing it had made him uneasy. This time, however, it was completely different. He had not the slightest urge to resist. There was no sense of unease, only the pleasurable anticipation of blending into nature wholeheartedly.[38]

Although interesting for the light it sheds on how the writer would like his work to be read, this interpretation need not be accepted at face value. Indeed, Shiga's explanation hides as much as it reveals. Sudō also suggests that Shiga experienced nature "intuitively (*chok-kaku*) through his instinct as a writer,"[39] but this is to ignore the importance of authorial subjectivity. After all, Shiga emerged from the *Shirakaba* group, for whom "self-assertiveness" was a major concern, and the early Taishō interest in the inner self—very much shared by Shiga himself—had evolved toward a more general interest in the relationship between an external, "natural" world and the self. The frequent use of the term "self-consciousness" (*ji-ishiki*) during the 1930s—it first appeared in Kobayashi's 1929 essay "Shiga Naoya"[40]— encapsulated such a concern. In this broader context, it is hard to accept that Shiga was simply replicating a vague and historically anachronistic notion of self-extinction in the face of nature.

It may be that, from the viewpoint of narrative closure, the final scene on Mount Daisen provides a reasonable conclusion, even if doubts linger whether Kensaku will survive, but it fails to address with any rigor the relationship between self and nature. This question is more central to Shiga's short piece "The House by the Moat" ("Horibata no sumai," 1924). As in *Reconciliation*, the story touches on life in Matsue, but this time the narrator's attraction to local plants and animals is privileged. The hierarchy of his relationships is established near the beginning: "Here I lived as simple a life as possible. Coming from life in the city and its exhausting dealings with people, people, people, I was now much calmer. My life now consisted of relationships with insects, birds, fish, water, grass, and sky, and last of all with people."[41] With little to do, he takes an interest in the neighbor's chickens and is upset one morning to hear that during the night a cat killed the mother hen, who was defending her chicks. At first happy to hear that the neighbor will trap and kill the cat, his feelings change that night when he hears its cries as it struggles to escape. In full knowledge that the creature will be drowned next morning, he considers how its instinctive killing of the chicken "was only to be expected (*atarimae*)," just as all parties involved— the cat, the mother hen, even the neighbor—have only followed their instincts throughout. Shiga's aim here was to articulate an idealized world shaped by "natural" drives, an environment in which no distinction is made between human actions and those of other animals. Yet the narrator himself accepts the inherent contradictions in such a world when, finally dismissing an initial impulse to release the cat, he acknowledges that his decision might be misinterpreted as mercilessness:

If this was mercilessness, then God's mercilessness was probably the same. It might be understandable to criticize a human being who is not God and who possesses free will for watching on the side without mercy as if he is God. But for me, the turn of events felt like irresistible fate, and I could not bring myself to lift a finger.[42]

Despite the narrator's earlier desire to place human beings at the bottom of his list of priorities, this later reflection indicates the paramountcy of human intervention in his world, no matter how "natural" it may appear. It also asks fundamental questions: What is the "natural" way for humans to act? Do volition or impulse have a legitimate part to play? And is it conceivable for things simply to take their course? Shiga concluded that nonintervention is the more natural choice but, unable to substantiate his reason with anything more than "destiny," calls on God as his ally. Yet the tortuous argument required to reach such a conclusion indicates that, however much things may appear to be "irresistible fate," the will to intercede in the flow of events always remains. Just as when Junkichi claimed his thoughts emerged "spontaneously," the presentation of the narrator's decision not "to lift a finger" as a natural choice fails to convince.

Shiga's understanding of nature was further complicated by the fact that it changed over time, inevitable perhaps in a novel written over such a long period. This change reveals itself in several instances in which Kensaku discusses the appearance of airplanes.[43] Near the book's beginning, he views them largely in positive terms. Reflecting on the strength of human will to attain a kind of immortality through scientific endeavor, he recalls how his sighting of the first airplane flight in Japan moved him "close to tears."[44] By the novel's end, however, Kensaku has undergone a dramatic change of heart. Adjusting to life at the temple on Mount Daisen, he reflects on the world around him and compares himself to when he was younger:

He looked up at a kite as it soared high above in the blue sky and considered the unattractiveness of the airplane conceived by man. Three or four years ago when he was totally engrossed in his work, he had praised the human will that sought to conquer the sea—its surface and its depths—and the air. Now, however, his feelings had completely reversed. Was the human will a natural one that sought to fly like a bird and pass through water like a fish? Would not these unlimited human desires eventually lead in some way to human misfortune?[45]

Shiga's negative criticism of modern man's desire to emulate the bird or the fish and his intimation that man will somehow have to pay for his "unlimited desires" is as old as the project of modernity itself—in Japan or elsewhere—and almost too hackneyed to merit serious attention. More noteworthy is the distinction he sets up between a young Kensaku with an ambition that leads him to work against nature and Kensaku as an older man who has abandoned unwholesome desires to follow his instincts. The implication is that man should not interfere in the workings of the natural world.

This view fails to acknowledge that the older Kensaku is equally engaged with his environment, albeit from a more "spiritual" angle. In a way reminiscent of the scene in *Broken Commandment* in which Ushimatsu watches the peasants worked, Kensaku also continues to "work" the land in a distinctive manner. This is shown when Kensaku, stopping to rest at a teashop on his way to the Daisen temple, is fascinated by a serene old man, almost eighty years old, who looks toward the distant bay and beyond:

What could the old man possibly be thinking about? Of course he was not thinking about the future. And very likely he did not have his thoughts on the present. Might not the old man be pondering his long life, the various events in the long span of his past? No, he had probably forgotten even that by now. The old man was simply situated before this scenery as if he were an ancient tree or a moss-covered rock. Kensaku felt that if he were thinking about anything at all, his thoughts were merely of the kind shared by trees or rocks. He envied him his feeling of tranquility.[46]

If the final section of the novel may be seen as the moment when Kensaku comes to terms with earlier conflicts, then the positive image of this old figure suggests a reconciliation with the negative memory of his "grandfather" introduced in the Prologue. But just as important is the manner in which landscape and personality become utterly interchangeable—the old man *is* the rock, the tree *is* the old man. For these physical features, acting as signposts to the way "home," are succinct representations of what Shiga understands the furusato to be. What is more, they redirect a sense of the furusato back onto the personality of Kensaku himself, since the old man clearly stands for what he aspires to become. Moreover, he appears to have attained this state by the novel's end.

How, then, did Shiga's representation of nature fit into the broader picture of his times, and what kind of national identity did he advance? In a way reminiscent of Shiga Shigetaka's work, there are dangers in Shiga's articulation of a subjectivity depicted in terms of a national landscape in which man, nature, and landscape appear to have merged. Through Kensaku's ultimate realization of "authentic" links between people and place, Shiga may provide an attractively authoritative voice able to speak on behalf of the land and confirming a sense of communal belonging, but the individualistic quality of the experience also implies an insistently singular and undifferentiated Japanese identity. By suggesting the ideal of submitting to reality rather than questioning its material conditions, he precludes any potential for change. Because of this, Tansman identifies Shiga as one of several writers whose literary interest in aesthetics during the 1930s gave shape to what he has called "fascist moments," by which he means "images of self-obliteration through the beauty of violence in the name of an idealized Japan anchored in ancient myth and transcendent of the strictures of time."[47] At a personal level, Kensaku's eroticized encounters with violent parents and his experience of elemental forces seem to confirm such images. More generally, the historical moment when Shiga concluded the novel was characterized by a high degree of coercion and mythical interpretations of national identity. This is not to suggest that the author actively condoned ultra-nationalist aggression. At a cultural level, however, the effect of his literary celebration of self-obliteration through violent outbursts and awe-inspiring natural phenomena was to downplay the potential for significant human intervention (other than his own kind) and the possibility of alternative subjectivities.

Mother and Mountains

Alternative understandings of what it might mean to be Japanese in the modern world were certainly available. One important example was the feminist vision of transforming society through greater gender equality, as articulated through the work of female writers. Thanks to the Meiji educational reforms, young women writers emerged who were keen to question a society that accepted prostitution as normal, although (male) critics tended to praise female writers who espoused gentle, "feminine" sentiments in a way that separated them from their supposedly less emotional male counterparts. In late Meiji, Naturalism provided women with a particularly useful tool for describing their real lives and speaking against the patriarchal family system. The increasingly liberal Taishō atmosphere, as well as the activities of western suffragettes, stimulated Japanese female writers to engage in a deeper questioning of social structures, and their works appeared in a wide range of venues. One important book was Nogami Yaeko's (1885-1985) *The Neptune* (*Kaiji maru*, 1922), which addressed general questions of morality and the human condition rather than domestic matters or the sad fate of women.[48] A typical literary magazine was *Women and Art* (*Nyojin geijutsu*), which was launched in 1928 and had a radical and highly political content. Its contributors included Hayashi Fumiko (1904-51), Sata Ineko (1904-98), and Uno Chiyo (1897-1996), and it focused on stories about prostitutes and the working class.[49]

Shiga addressed feminist issues only indirectly. Following the 1923 earthquake, the authorities increasingly cracked down on dissent, including that of feminist writers. Instead it promoted the more conservative ideal of "good wives, wise mothers" (*ryōsai kenbo*), and Shiga's writing reflected this attitude. It is against this general background that Shiga's distinctly traditional articulation of the feminine should be viewed, as he set out a gendered landscape and its furusato associations in a way that left no room for social conflict.

Doreen Massey has recently discussed how concepts of space and place might be understood in terms of social relations, with particular attention to gender. In an interesting parallel to Edward Soja's work, she argues that time is usually coded as masculine, relating to "history, progress, civilization, politics and transcendence," whereas the spatial dimension is formulated as feminine to suggest "stasis, passivity and depoliticization."[50] She suggests that place is particularly associated with a constructed version of "woman" in terms of home and nostalgia: "Woman stands as metaphor for Nature (in another characteristic dualism), for what has been lost (left behind), and that place called home is frequently personified by, and partakes of the same characteristics as those assigned to, Woman/Mother/lover."[51] Massey is at pains to point out that her study is limited to western culture, but such ideas are relevant to notions of the furusato, which also has strong associations with the feminine. Doppo's "Let Me Return" tied together native place and motherhood by presenting the valley where Mineo was born as his nurturing "cradle." Koshoshi's male narrator revisits the native place not only to reestablish contact with the feminine source but also to locate a suitable spouse—that is, one with traditional values and capable of carrying the seed of "authenticity" into the next generation.

Shiga's writings articulate a set of complex relationships with women; for the most part, these are linked to unresolved issues related to the mother. *Reconciliation*, for instance, concentrates on the narrator's difficult interaction with his father, but there is a telling moment when Junkichi tries to express the depth of his anguish following his newborn child's death: "I cried. I cried like the time my real mother died."[52] Another story, "My Mother's Death and My New Mother" ("Haha no shi to atarashii haha," 1912), gives a more detailed account of heartfelt grief at the loss of a parent. A boy watches his mother's corpse being laid out before burial, and he notices bubbles in the corner of her mouth. He rushes to inform his grandmother, only to be told that it is simply trapped air escaping from the body. His sense of desperate finality is compounded later by the heavy earth shoveled onto his mother's coffin, a sound that forces him to conclude that "even if she came back to life, she wouldn't be able to get out now."[53] Shiga's upbringing in Tokyo may have been largely in the hands of his grandparents, who blamed his parents for their first grandson's death from dysentery the year before Shiga's birth, but the writer's recollections show how feelings toward his mother retained their urgency even into adulthood.

Massey is surely right to speak of the generalized female image of "woman/mother/lover," since these terms indeed blur in Shiga's writing. A good example can be found in an episode involving Kensaku as a four- or five-year-old child in the Prologue to *A Dark Night's Passing*. His father brings home a piece of bean jelly (*yōkan*), and Kensaku pesters his mother to give him some even though he had just eaten his afternoon snack. When she adamantly refuses, he throws a tantrum and almost knocks her to the floor by tugging on her sash from behind:

Now mother really was angry. She grabbed my wrist and dragged me in front of the cupboard. Despite my struggling, she held my head tight with one arm and forced thick slices of bean cake into my mouth. With the feel of thin strips of cake being pressed through my clenched milk teeth, I was so terrified I could not even cry. With the excitement, mother suddenly started crying. I, too, soon burst into tears.[54]

Even if Shiga portrays the small child here as a less than willing participant, from his adult vantage point he is recreating a deeply erotic infantile memory in which the mouth is forcibly crammed with the sweet and the pleasurable; the reference to *misoppa* (literally, "decayed milk teeth") suggests the mother's breast. Indeed, the image is strong enough to stay with Kensaku into adult life. While still in Tokyo, he becomes romantically involved with a young woman called Tokiko from the Yoshiwara pleasure quarters. After paying her a visit, he is traveling home by streetcar and watches in fascination as a young mother plays with her baby:

Suddenly she covered her baby in an indiscriminate succession of kisses all over its cheeks and neck. The baby squirmed with delight as if being tickled. The woman tilted her coiffured head forward to concentrate on the baby's throat, revealing the beautiful nape of her neck. As he watched,

Kensaku felt strange: it was too cloyingly sweet (*amattarui*). Unable to bear watching any more of it, he nonchalantly turned his head to gaze out the window.

The affair with Tokiko has not been going well, and Kensaku's imaginative response to this scene may partly reflect his desire for an equally unabashed exploration of the flesh. But the orally erotic nature of something "cloyingly sweet" is underlined through its juxtaposition with the back of the woman's neck (*eriashi*, a traditional object of erotic desire) and even the kissing of the baby's throat. Shiga himself drew attention to the link by noting Kensaku's unease as he realizes that the scene probably mimics "the cloyingly sweet relationship between the woman and her husband unconsciously reenacted through the baby."[55]

The author's eroticized interest in the mother figure is perhaps understandable since his own mother died when he was thirteen; the boy Seibei is only one year younger when depicted in a similarly charged conflict with father. Shiga was by no means the first writer to reveal such concerns. The search for a lost mother through the medium of other women is a literary theme that can be traced back at least as far as the *Tale of Genji*. And in Shiga's time, a fixation on "mother love" (*haha-koi*) was a defining characteristic of Tanizaki's literature that sometimes spilt over into incestuous fantasy.[56] These more obviously transgressive desires also find expression in *A Dark Night's Passing*, when Kensaku somewhat shamefully recalls an incident that took place many years earlier:

Taking advantage of the fact that mother seemed to be fast asleep, he remembered how he dived right under the covers. Immediately he felt himself in the tight grasp of mother's hand—she must have been awake—and she dragged him unceremoniously back up to the pillow. Mother said nothing, and her eyes remained shut, as if she were deep in sleep. He was ashamed of his action, and he was conscious of what he had done just as if he were an adult.[57]

Yasuoka Shōtarō notes that Shiga was barely out of infancy when he lived with his mother. Even if based on a true incident, this memory probably overlaps with a similar experience with his grandmother later on, when he would have been more aware of sexual urges and an accompanying sense of shame.[58] If so, this follows a traditional pattern of using other female characters to compensate for a cherished lost mother. In "My Mother's Death and My New Mother," bereavement is alleviated by the introduction of the father's new wife—the boy's substitute mother—who is even younger and more beautiful than the first.[59] And in the longer novel, one reason why Kensaku proposes marriage to the young Aiko—unsuccessfully, as it turns out—is that her mother had been a close friend of his own, and in her mother he "looked for traces of his own dead mother."[60]

But it is around the character of Kensaku's personal maid, Oei, that the incestuous impulse most clearly manifests itself. Her central role in his life is shown by the fact that soon after Aiko's rejection, he proposes to Oei. This rather extraordinary action is rooted in their long-standing relationship. According to the Prologue, Oei was the live-in mistress of his "grandfather" when Kensaku first moved in their house. Despite the ill-will he harbored toward his "grandfather," he always felt ecstatic when held in her "powerful thick arms," and "gradually came to like her."[61] Consequently, at a point when Aiko's decision has inflicted a huge blow to Kensaku's self-esteem, Oei promises comforting familiarity in an uncertain and changing world. Moreover, although Oei is the closest Kensaku comes to a mother figure, since she is not his biological parent, no formal barriers exist to their potential union. On the other hand, as we learn later, Kensaku is the child of his mother and "grandfather." Since both Oei and his mother had been sexually intimate with his true father, Kensaku could get no closer than Oei to his initial maternal object of desire. In practical terms, Kensaku is not drawn to his maid because of this sexual history since he only discovers his true origins later. But this is a question less of strict narrative chronology than of Shiga's interest in incest as a literary theme. In other words, he structures the novel so that Kensaku proposes to the woman who has functioned through most of his life as a surrogate mother.

Similar incestuous motives observed by Hagiwara Takao deserve attention because they relate to Shiga's overlapping interest in mountains. He sees *A Dark Night's Passing* as a series of painful journeys sandwiched between two childhoods: the first, outlined in the Prologue, is real; the second involves a metaphorical return to the womb on the slopes of Mount Daisen. Hagiwara suggests that Kensaku's resemblance to a "poppy seed" enveloped in nature should be read as a semenlike insemination of female space. This "incestuous merger" with the mountain parallels the bed-cover incident with the mother.[62] What separates these two scenes, however, is Kensaku's newfound sense of independence from his long-dead mother obtained during an unusually positive period while courting Naoko. Visiting his mother's birthplace in Kameyama, he wanders round the old castle grounds in the hope of finding some link to his family past. He speaks briefly to a woman sweeping the castle grounds, but it is clear she has no concrete memory of his mother or her family. Kensaku's initial gloom soon dispels: " 'But that's fine. That's even better. Everything begins with me. I am the ancestor (*senzo*).' With these thoughts, he clambered down the steep and tortuous mountain path toward the pristine lake already with a look of autumn about it."[63] This response suggests a rediscovery of patriarchal authority just at the point when Kensaku expects to establish his own family. It also prefigures his later reconciliatory engagement with the more general maternal presence of Mount Daisen, and hints that the mountain will function as a site of restoration. As he is resting at the mountain temple, he observes a small shrub next to a temple called Amida's Shrine "which carried fruit like a dark-red bean at the center of each leaf. The individual fruits were borne like precious gifts in the palm of someone's hand."[64] And later, he writes to his wife that he had rediscovered a deep joy in observing the little details of life: "the little birds, the insects, the trees, the grass, the water, the rocks."[65] Kensaku's stay provides for a spiritual awakening conveyed through attention to minute aspects of nature usually associated with the child's all-embracing eye.

Religious implications tied to gender also underline Shiga's attraction to the mountain as a fitting site for the novel's denouement. Until just over a century ago, ritual ascents of mountains by religious pilgrims were practiced throughout Japan, although recently they have become restricted to two areas, Ōmine (linking Yoshino and Kumano) and Haguro (in Yamagata). Related austerities, identified with the practice of mountain asceticism (*shugendō*) and known as "entering the mountain" (*nyūbu* or *mineiri*), were considered effective precisely because of a belief in the mountain as a nurturing "maternal" space:

In the course of the ascent and subsequent sojourn in the mountain, austere exercises are enacted, which by symbolic action are intended to rouse the disciple's Buddha nature from its hidden state and bring about his transformation into a Buddha. Concurrently enacted is a second series of symbolic actions of an unmistakably initiatory kind, in which the mountain is seen as the mother's womb and the disciple as an embryo growing from conception to birth. These austerities are at the same time believed to endow the disciple with various magic powers, notably the power to subdue the spiritual entities, witch animals, and discontented ghosts responsible for sickness and possession.[66]

Kensaku specifically acknowledges the spiritual aspect of his trip: parting from his wife, he is convinced that "his departure today felt like someone renouncing the world for a religious life (*shukke*)."[67] Moreover, if a pilgrim's journey up the mountain amounts to a symbolic progression toward higher stages of enlightenment, parallels may be drawn with Kensaku's gradual ascent of Mount Daisen. In the first stage, ties to the mundane world are gently cut as a kindly rickshaw puller delivers him from Daisen railway station to a temple compound halfway up the mountain; stage two is a period of rest at the temple, where he contemplates nature and reads the scriptures; and the third stage involves his final walk toward enlightenment on the mountaintop. In this final stage, illness forces him to separate from the other pilgrims; he leaves "the path" and finds "a tranquil spot in the grass."[68] This acknowledges that at some point on the ascetic's spiritual ascent, he must break away from the mundane world and continue alone on his journey.

The significance of the mountain as a gendered site—particularly the way concepts of religious practice and the womb overlap—is taken further by Helen Hardacre. Her main concern is pilgrimages to the womb-shaped Oku no in cave in the Ōmine range, but many of her points clarify why mountains featured so prominently in Shiga's writings. In esoteric Buddhist thought, the Ōmine range is divided into two mandalas (that is, symbolic religious representations): mountains in the Yoshino region constitute the Diamond World mandala, and the Kumano area is identified with the Womb World mandala. The latter is explained through the double metaphor of a lotus and a womb. Much as the womb nurtures the fetus, meditation on the Womb World mandala causes aspiration for enlightenment to arise; just as a lotus proceeds from seed to full bloom, gestation in the womb eventually results in the birth of a human embryo. In both cases, the desired result is attainment of Buddhahood in this life. Hardacre suggests that the quality of a spiritual rebirth through the symbolic womb is probably experienced differently according to gender. For women, it amounts to a return to the source, the fullest expression of one's sexual being: men, however, re-emerge anew after uniting with the very heart of the opposite sexual principle.[69]

Shiga's story "Night Fires" ("Takibi," 1920) encapsulates this second approach, presenting the mountain as a site of the harmonious blending of male and female principles, like the relationship between K-san and his wife immediately following their marriage. Narrative development is less important than the evocation of a pleasant mood as the young couple and some close friends play cards, tell stories, and take a boat ride on the nearby lake. The idyllic nature of their carefree existence is caught in a striking image near the story's end after the group builds a bonfire by the lakeside at dusk. Just before they leave for their cottage, K-san plucks some glowing sticks from the fire and flings them across the lake: "The stick went flying through the air, red sparks scattering. Its reflection was cast on the water so that another stick went flying, red sparks scattering. Above and below they described identical arcs, meeting at the water's surface, where they were immediately extinguished. All around was suddenly dark."[70] Real and ideal images mirror each other until they disappear, dissolving entirely into each other at the point of the water's surface. Shiga uses this aesthetic image of two perfectly balanced arcs to suggests a sense of contentment and completeness, reflecting the newly married couple's happy union. It is a scene that strongly evokes the tranquil metaphor near the end of *Reconciliation* when Junkichi described his sense of homecoming in terms of a mist-shrouded lake deep in the mountains.

Home, cradle, native place, mother, mountain—Shiga marshaled these overlapping images to depict Kensaku's contentment as he awakens at dawn after his solitary watch on the mountain. It constitutes a vision of the feminine at once powerful and utterly oblivious to alternative views. He looks out over the distant bay to see Daisen's shadow cast before him by the rising sun:

Kensaku suddenly realized that he was observing a scene in which the shadow of Mount Daisen where he now lay was clearly reflected. As the shadow's outline moved from the bay toward him on the mountain, he noticed the town of Yonago for the first time as it suddenly emerged into brightness. The shadow continued to advance, like a dragnet being hauled in, like the shadow of clouds exploring every detail (*namete sugiru*) of the earth. Kensaku was deeply moved to witness this rare spectacle, the shadow of the highest mountain of central Japan, with its strong bold lines, passing across the land.[71]

From the depths of a long despair, the dragnet hauls teeming shoals of reawakened life. Shiga provides Kensaku access—an umbilical cord, if you will—to the long-lost maternal space from which he originated, in a way that echoes the erotic orality of the time when his mother crammed his mouth with sweets. For across the body of this land, which constitutes the only "mother" that Shiga can now hope to identify as his own, the mountain's shadow "licks" (*namete*) the mountainside. At this pivotal moment of emotional transformation, Shiga makes the landscape his own in a sublime rediscovery of the furusato replete with tradition and desire, yet unmovable and apparently bereft of political import. But in his reconstitution of a patriarchal Japanese identity at one with the landscape, there is no place for alternative visions, no discordant female voice, no distant sound of gunfire on the Asian mainland. Such a position begs the questions Where is his sense of history? and What is his place in it?

A Feel for History

When the narrator of "Banks of the Sorachi River" gazes through his train window at the bleak and forbidding Hokkaido plains, his overwhelming impression is isolation from an unfamiliar landscape with which he shares no history. *A Dark Night's Passing*, by contrast, presents an entirely different prospect: Kensaku boards a train at Kobe on the last stage of his journey to Onomichi:

The coast around Shioya and Maiko was beautiful. On a small boat gently rocking close to the shore of the becalmed sea under the evening sunset, a fisherman sat cross-legged fixing his nets. Long ropes extended from the roots of pine trees on the white sandy beach; a fishing boat had already settled there for the night. Kensaku looked on with feelings of pleasure. Night approached as the train advanced.[72]

If Hokkaido was a disturbingly new and uncharted territory for most Japanese near the end of the nineteenth century, the pleasure Kensaku obtains from this view of the Inland Sea arises from its long cultural familiarity, particularly in terms of literary associations. Fishermen with nets, pine trees against a background of white sand: these are clichés of harmony between man and nature backed up by centuries of poetic practice. After his disconnected experiences in Tokyo, the scene encapsulates Kensaku's expectation that his stay in Onomichi will provide the stable familiarity he craves. Yet the reality is different; Shiga portrays a provincial town identifiable not so much through the certainty of historical rootedness than through a far vaguer and more intangible historical mood.

The first impression of Onomichi is deceptive. In strong contrast to the previous images of city life in which Kensaku was mostly observed drifting between places of temporary pleasure such as the gay quarters or restaurants, this town appears anchored by a sense of unmistakable historical verisimilitude. Visiting the local masseur, for example, he is advised of numerous landmarks he ought to visit:

He heard about all sorts of places: Saikokuji, Senkōji, Jōdoji, as well as "Fistfight" temple associated with the priest Motsugai as mentioned in the story book; close to Onomichi there were the island of Sensuitō in Tomonotsu and the Kannon statue in Abuto; on Shikoku, there were the Dōgo hot springs, the shrine of Sanuki in Kotohira, the town of Takamatsu, Yashima, and Shidoji temple that appeared in the puppet play.[73]

This listing strongly conveys the feel of tapestry of place and human activity through which the region's authentic history reveals itself. A similar technique is effectively used to highlight Onomichi's indigenous population as a well-established community of people engaged in settled professions: "antiques dealer, secondhand dealer, grocer, general merchant, confectioner, watchmaker, foreign goods importer," and so on.[74] The reality, however, is that these never amount to anything more than lists, disparate fragments of reality that offer no way to uncover the deeper processes through which people and place interact.

This reduction of place to a cluster of historical associations invites comparison with the premodern literary practice of poetic place-names (*utamakura*) in which the names of certain places appeared in poetry to evoke not so much the details of a specific locality as conventional responses associated with the site. It also echoes the panoramic view in Tōson's *Broken Commandment* in which Ushimatsu presents his mountain home to Rentarō as a list of its salient features. But this naming of things may also be related to social changes, particularly tourism, at the time Shiga was writing. He starts from the perspective of a modern tourist, and his portrayal of Onomichi is not unlike the kind of material to be found in a travel brochure. Of course, visits to historic sites were not a new development, but tourism as a modern phenomenon became associated with a growing Japanese middle class only from early Taishō. The Japan Travel Bureau (Nihon kōtsū kōsha) was founded in 1912— the year Shiga undertook his journey to Onomichi—and built on the role of the Japan Tourist Bureau (originally a service for foreign tourists during Meiji) by responding to a growing domestic market. In this connection, some general comments by Yi-Fu Tuan on the distinction between visitor and native are relevant since they help clarify Kensaku's perception of Onomichi and its inhabitants:

Generally speaking, we may say that only the visitor (and particularly the tourist) has a viewpoint; his perception is often a matter of using his eyes to compose pictures. The native, by contrast, has a complex attitude derived from his immersion in the totality of his environment. The visitor's viewpoint, being simple, is easily stated. Confrontation with novelty may also prompt him to express himself. The complex attitude of the native, on the other hand, can be expressed by him only with difficulty and indirectly through behavior, local tradition, lore, and myth.[75]

The visitor's "viewpoint" reveals the importance of visual perspective in the discovery of the modern landscape, already noted with regard to the other three writers I examine here. The masseur's mention of a temple nicknamed "Fistfight" confirms how the residents know their own locality through local "lore"; Kensaku's engagement is, in contrast, guided mainly by a touristic point of view. During a boat trip around the nearby islands, he responds to his environment through a series of particularly beautiful "composed pictures":

The boat wove its way through the islands. Each of the barley fields created on the slopes of the various islands was clearly marked out from the others by the fact that some were light-green and other were darker. Under the cloudy sky, they appeared smoothly beautiful like velvet. The islands formed rows of peaks that appeared truly powerful and stunning, and set against a cloudy sky their outlines were particularly sharp. Reminded of the cracked lines on broken gourds he had seen in the Onomichi shops, Kensaku was impressed that lines made by nature seem to share a common strength and beauty.[76]

Like Satō's vision of the hill in "Rural Melancholy," a real landscape has been transformed into a beautiful tapestry. And what a different landscape to the one he left behind in Tokyo. There, Kensaku was so engrossed in the "totality of his environment" that he found it virtually impossible to comprehend the detailed nature of his relationship with people and place. As a visitor to the Inland Sea, however, he gains an "easily stated" confidence and can give play to those imaginative and pleasurable faculties that remained unfulfilled in the city.

The passage suggests an appreciation of the environment that is visual and primarily directed at landscapes rather than people. Moreover, the mode of expression is an aesthetic one, whereby islands appear to take on the shape of colorful pattered quilts. However, as David Pollack notes, the aesthetic impulse entails not only an articulation of beauty but also a less obvious set of cultural assumptions:

In much the same way that a particularly economical (or impressive, or convincing) mathematical or scientific narrative can be called "elegant" or "beautiful," so may a bowl, a painting, a piece of music, a novel, a dancer's movement, a mode of dress. These things are understood by conventional agreement (and maintained by education) to embody the truth of a particular group's proprietary construction of reality in tangible, sensual, and even ideational form.[77]

In other words, a shared aesthetic sense hints at a common ideological approach, a mutual recognition that certain events—in music, dance, a novel—perfectly match the expectation of that moment. In this sense, Shiga's depiction of the Inland Sea in its jewel-like simplicity merely confirms a common appreciation of beauty that can be traced back through centuries of Japanese literary endeavor.

The corollary to Pollack's assertion is that a particular ideological position involves the rejection of other possible constructions of reality. For example, there is a scene in Onomichi in which a site of human labor is completely reworked into an aesthetic experience. Kensaku has rented a hillside room, from which he enjoys the pleasant view of Mukaijima island, separated from the mainland only by a narrow channel of the Inland Sea:

There was a shipyard on the island opposite. The clanging of hammers could be heard there from morning on. And there was a stone quarry in the center of the hills on the left-hand side of the same island; the stonecutters endlessly cut stone while singing their songs among the pine woods. The sounds carried high above the town and entered his home directly.[78]

Kafū's description of a port involved a bitter attack on intrusive billboards and the evils of capitalism, but Shiga reconfigured hammering and the sound of singing—both connected to human labor—into a pleasing experience that leaves no space for a consideration of working conditions (an approach that would certainly have been taken by Proletarian writers). Rather, he created a scene to appeal to the emotions and celebrated a blend of human vigor and natural beauty unencumbered with the tensions of modern urban life. And this conscious avoidance of historical detail engenders a sense of timelessness; it is unclear whether the shipyard is hammering into shape the modern "metal freighters" Kafū decried or something more traditional. The stone quarry, too, was a familiar part of the landscape long before the West arrived, and so offers no chronological clue. This representation of Onomichi leaves the reader less with the impression of historical certainty than with a site of indefinite chronology, a mood of "tradition," which appears to have always existed in more or less the same form.

To be sure, Shiga was not alone in his search for a more historically rooted experience beyond the city; indeed, a craving for historical authenticity was symptomatic of the period. Whereas the 1920s were characterized by a cosmopolitan attitude that aimed to demonstrate that Japan's "unique" contribution to global culture was equivalent to anything the West had to offer, the 1930s saw a shift toward "culturalism" (*bunkashugi*). This term is sometimes equated with aggressive anti-western attitudes of the radical right, but it also covers more considered attempts to identify native cultural ideals. It was a search already prefigured in works like Yanagita's *Tales of Tōno*, an anthology of local stories intended to demonstrate the continuing existence of a communal rural life rooted in indigenous and customary beliefs, and Watsuji Tetsurō's *Pilgrimages to Ancient Temples* (*Koji junrei*, 1919), which was highly influential for its thesis that Buddhist art and architecture represented the "purest" expression of Japanese creativity. In the same vein, Shiga's association with the *Shirakaba* group stimulated an interest in his own artistic roots. The group's magazine introduced Impressionist and Post-Impressionist painting to Japan, but artworks from ancient Greece and Rome as well as from the Nara and Heian periods began to appear with increasing frequency in later years.

Thomas Rimer's discussion of cultural developments in Taishō in terms of the art world helps put Shiga's antiquarian interest in perspective. Rimer proposes that we view the growing interest in past cultures from late Meiji not as an attempt to recover some ideal former age but as a phenomenon related to the historical circumstances of the period. Classical Japanese and Chinese art had traditionally been available only to a limited number of wealthy connoisseurs, and it was not until the opening of museums from Meiji on that art collections became known to the general public. For a new generation of artists, coming of age in Taishō and overwhelmed by this sudden revelation of cultural richness, classical art "often helped stimulate the latest artistic fashions."[79] Rimer cites Watsuji's book as an example of how attempts were made to incorporate the newly discovered Japanese past into contemporary experience. Watsuji is a typically complex intellectual of his age: a western-educated Japanese philosopher seeking to uncover the ancient qualities of Japanese temples yet armed with an excellent knowledge of European art and culture:

> In its richness this influential book possessed a complex significance. Watsuji's basic methodology (seek out, observe, then chart the authenticity of one's own response) provided a model for engagement not only with European culture but with what often seemed to have become the "foreign culture" of Japan's own past. Traditionally, the arts had sought to portray the inner essence of the visible world. Watsuji validated his sense of the necessity to go and observe nature and history directly.[80]

Rimer's words point to the fact that it was only in Taishō that ancient treasures were brought out of storerooms, dusted, and presented to the wider public as representative of the nation itself. Although the process of modern nation-building began only in Meiji, such treasures became tangible proof of historical depth—a chronological continuity called "Japan"—that many people, now sensing its fragmentation, suddenly felt a need to reconstitute. Shiga's literary depictions of sites equally endowed with depth are part of the same response. Indeed, Shiga spelled out the beneficial aspects of an older, more settled native culture through Kensaku's attempt to overcome the break with his wife by revisiting places associated with a knowable past:

> He decided it was time to make pilgrimages to the ancient temples and shrines, with their works of art, that he had neglected for so long. He began traveling to places like Kōyasan and Murōji on two- or three-day trips. It was late autumn, a season of beautiful scenery, and gradually over time he regained a sense of equilibrium.[81]

The past, or at least its evocation, offers a panacea for present difficulties and the possibility of a restored subjectivity connected to historical verisimilitude.

But if history turns out to be more mood than reality in Shiga's writing, how does the past function in his literary landscapes, and what is the relationship between the past and his representations of the furusato? It might be useful to address these points by considering some comments by Robert Morris on the technique of Paul Cézanne (1839–1906), whose work often appeared in the *Shirakaba* magazine and was therefore familiar to Shiga. Morris poses the question: In what sense do the Mont Sainte-Victoire paintings that Cézanne's completed in the last four years of his life attempt to present the world? His answer is that, fundamentally, these landscapes offer a "furious animation of surface." By this, he implies that Cézanne works at an entirely superficial level, not in a derogatory sense but with the consciousness that it was at the surface that things are realized at the point of creation. Most obviously, these paintings relate to Cézanne's childhood memories of certain localities near Aix, but the relationship between painter and native place becomes clearer if we pay attention to the technique itself. His pictures of woods, mountains, and ponds are saturated with childhood memory:

But what was sought was not a primitive or edenic return to the innocence of nostalgia but a confrontation with the loss that memory, history, and change inscribe on the psyche. The issue of memory for Cézanne becomes the challenge of transfiguration forged in those confrontations with his charged sites. How is this loss to be redeemed through art—that mode which possesses the possibility of defeating loss? By, I want to say, representing memory's loss. And I do not mean the loss of memory, but the representation of memory's ravages of the psyche by means of metaphor.[82]

This resort to collage—the conscious concern with surface and technique—not only points to an important element in the modernist project but also reveals itself in Shiga's historical representations, which never quite stand up to scrutiny. For example, an inhabitant of Onomichi tells Kensaku a local story. A great rock at the Senkōji temple once had a huge jewel embedded in it, so bright that it functioned as a lantern at night. One day, a foreigner asked if he could buy the rock. Thinking him foolish since the rock was too heavy to carry, the locals agreed. He cut out the jewel and took it away.[83] On one hand, this story confirms Onomichi as a place with a real history, but its content suggests that the very heart of the place, represented by the jewel, was ripped out long ago. In this sense, Onomichi presents an interesting dichotomy and a metaphor for "memory's loss": its significance as an authentic site of history is "proved" by a story that also confirms its lack of historical continuity.

My argument is that Shiga failed to engage with historical realities, a failure very much rooted in the age. Just when modern technology and "foreign" attitudes were being incorporated into the increasingly complex experience of daily life by ordinary Japanese, he presented a skillfully crafted landscape that seems to stand outside history; in effect he offered the compensation of a simplified pseudo-history. It is fitting that Onomichi has served over the years as a popular "historical" location for Japanese movies—Ozu's *Tōkyō monogatari* immediately comes to mind—since it so neatly encapsulates the image of a traditional, provincial furusato environment. And it may well be that the place Shiga described was as charming and "untouched" as he suggested—I can personally vouch for its scenic beauty—but more noteworthy is the fact that he chose this place, rather than a location where the intrusions of modern life would be unavoidable.

It is at this point—where the writer makes conscious selections and omissions in the creation of a distinctive version of the native place and his subject position within it—that individual choices may be seen as part of wider social and economic conditions. I have argued that Japan's integration into a world order dominated by the West meant that it was no longer possible to differentiate the "Japanese" and "foreign" spheres. This is the broader context of Shiga's attempt to turn back the clock and form a mythical space that serves as a repository for "traditional Japan." And no less than Tōson's, Shiga's carefully constructed furusato mood is a response to the literary market of his day. At a time when life was becoming increasingly saturated with social conflict and war, Shiga gave his readers the opportunity to step temporarily out of everyday life and lay claim to a furusato environment superficially at ease with itself. However, his work is ultimately tied to the social order it seeks to escape because its creative impulse lies in the very need to formulate an area of "true Japaneseness" that compensates for an urban life— the actual basis of his everyday experience—incapable of offering such certainty. In other words, it is only with the loss of the "real thing" that the desperate search for an earlier authenticity and an established sense of identity begins.

Furusato literature serves as a useful tool for identifying how a sense of national identity was being worked, and reworked, between mid-Meiji and early Shōwa. The writings of both Doppo and Tōson reflect experiences of a transitional period when conflicting needs remained unresolved, as exemplified by the highly fragmented nature of their native landscapes. Doppo was keen to reinterpret place in terms of western literary allusion, but such attempts jarred with memories of home related to his own childhood or, more metaphorically, what he now saw as the "childhood" of Japan before the intrusion of western ways of seeing. Tōson appeared to draw on a greater sense of authenticity, but in fact he had undergone a similar fracture of lived experience, most obviously in his removal from the native place and his coming of age in an urban environment. The result is a rawness in their work, a touchingly open expression of both excitement and disappointment as they articulate areas of conflict but never entirely resolved them. Indeed, it is this impulse to experiment coupled with bewilderment and unease that represents the national mood of their generation.

Satō and Shiga were equally experimental but in a different way, as they learned to paste over these fractured realities through a greater imaginary engagement with the furusato and a willful forgetfulness of the broader picture. Satō's work represents a turning away from the pressures of everyday life as he explored the furusato less as a place-specific reality than a metaphorical space of belonging. Ironically, his own peripheral position within Japanese society gave him greater imaginative license to reinvent himself as a national subject dependent more on myth than history. Shiga, too, took full advantage of his lack of actual furusato to reinvent it in ways more amenable to his own needs. He was keener than Satō to equate his furusato landscapes with authentic Japanese experience, but this proved to be a narrow and overly exclusive interpretation lacking historical grounding. Given the events of the 1930s, his failure to acknowledge conflicting versions of Japanese identity make his articulation of a literary furusato emptied of conflict problematic, and, in this sense, he may be seen to have colluded indirectly with the oppressive cultural environment of his day. In this, both he and Satō reflected a dominant national characteristic that would be the object of much questioning following defeat in World War II.

Reference Matter

Notes

Introduction

1. Anthony Smith, *National Identity*, p. 14.
2. Hobsbawm, *Nations and Nationalism*, p. 103. Benedict Anderson (*Imagined Communities*, p. 43) sees the gradual replacement of Latin by local European languages from the sixteenth century on, facilitated by the rise of print technology, as an important early factor. The large number of foreign-language dictionaries produced in the nineteenth century also contributed to a growing sense of national identity (idem, p. 71).
3. Hobsbawm, *Nations and Nationalism*, p. 83.
4. Gellner, *Nations and Nationalism*, p. 55.
5. Anthony Smith, *National Identity*, pp. 91–92.
6. The word "nationalism" was coined specifically to describe the emergence of this rightwing shift in thought first in France, then in Italy (Hobsbawm, *Nations and Nationalism*, p. 121).
7. Pyle, "Some Recent Approaches to Japanese Nationalism," p. 15. The four other approaches he discusses are pure intellectual history, the functional or social communications approach, interest theory, and strain theory. The internal quotation is from Geertz, "Ideology as a Cultural System," p. 65, in David E. Apter, ed., *Ideology and Discontent* (New York, 1964).
8. Hobsbawm, *Nations and Nationalism*, p. 11.
9. Tansman, "Images of Repose and Violence," p. 114.
10. Gluck, *Japan's Modern Myths*, pp. 6–7, quoting Geertz, "Ideology as a Cultural System"; Berger and Luckmann, *The Social Construction of Reality*, pp. 123–28; Gramsci, *Selections from the Prison Notebooks*, pp. 12–13.
11. Harootunian, *Overcome by Modernity*, pp. 214–15.
12. Mitchell, *Landscape and Power*, p. 1.
13. Soja, *Postmodern Geographies*, p. 25.

14. Foucault, "Of Other Spaces," p. 22.

15. Anderson, *Imagined Communities*, p. 26.

16. Lefebvre, *The Production of Space*.

17. Massey, *Space, Place and Gender*.

18. Keirstead, "Gardens and Estates," p. 290.

19. Ibid., p. 292.

20. For the former, see Henry Smith, "The Edo-Tokyo Transition"; for the latter, see idem, "Tokyo and London."

21. Ivy, *Discourses of the Vanishing*. For a representative work by Robertson, see *Native and Newcomer*.

22. Vlastos, *Mirror of Modernity*.

23. Anderer, *Other Worlds*, p. 6.

24. Okuno, *Bungaku ni okeru genfūkei*.

25. Karatani, *Nihon kindai bungaku no kigen*.

26. See especially Maeda's *Toshi kūkan no naka no bungaku*.

27. Williams, *The Country and the City*, p. 12.

28. Around the time of the Napoleonic wars, it was realized that the Swiss were not alone in experiencing this mood, although some medics still held to the view that it arose from the incessant clanging of cowbells in the rarefied Alpine atmosphere! (Davis, *Yearning for Yesterday*, pp. 1–4).

29. Robertson, "It Takes a Village," p. 115.

30. Katagiri, *Utamakura*, p. 359.

31. Grosz, *Volatile Bodies*, p. vii.

32. Cranston, *A Waka Anthology*, pp. 382–84.

33. Ivy, *Discourses of the Vanishing*, pp. 107–8.

34. Shirane, *Traces of Dreams*, p. 185.

35. Ibid., pp. 188–89.

36. Ibid., p. 193.

37. Ibid., p. 22.

38. Pyle, *The New Generation in Meiji*, p. 57.

39. For a detailed analysis of this work, see Gavin, "*Nihon Fūkeiron*."

40. Ivy, *Discourses of the Vanishing*, p. 72.

41. Yamada, "Koshoshi to Doppo," p. 19.

42. Maeda, *Tekusuto no yūtopia*, p. 215.

43. *Pillow Book of Sei Shōnagon*, p. 244.

44. "Nagatsuka Takashi no shōsetsu 'tsuchi,'" in [*Natsume*] *Sōseki zenshū*, 11: 237–39.

45. Ivy, *Discourses of the Vanishing*, p. 72.

46. Morris-Suzuki, *Re-inventing Japan*, p. 38. This outline of nature is drawn extensively from her chapter on the subject; see ibid., pp. 35–59.

47. Ibid., p. 47.

48. Ibid., pp. 51–52.

49. Narita, *"Kokyō" to iu monogatari*, p. 23.

50. Ibid., p. 20.

51. Hobsbawm and Ranger, *The Invention of Tradition*, p. 2. Invented traditions are defined as "a set of practices, normally governed by overtly or tacitly accepted rules and of a ritual or symbolic nature, which seek to inculcate certain values and norms of behaviour by repetition, which automatically implies continuity with the past" (ibid., p. 1).

52. Narita, *"Kokyō" to iu monogatari*, pp. 35–58, 144–45, 151.

Chapter 1

1. Anthony Smith, *National Identity*, p. 9.

2. Letter dated June 18, 1891; quoted in Takitō, *Kunikida Doppo ron*, p. 201.

3. Quoted in ibid., p. 196.

4. Other terms used include "pastoral novels" (*den'en shōsetsu*) and "returning home novels" (*kisei shōsetsu*); see Kitano, *Miyazaki Koshoshi Kunikida Doppo*, p. 5.

5. The term is used in Takitō, *Kunikida Doppo ron*, p. 196.

6. Letter dated Sept. 27, 1894; quoted in ibid., p. 228.

7. From Yanagida Kunio's 1927 "Kunikida Doppo shōden"; quoted in Kitano, *Miyazaki Koshoshi Kunikida Doppo*, p. 122.

8. Vaporis, *Breaking Barriers*, p. 15.

9. See, e.g., Fukuda, *Kunikida Doppo*, pp. 15–21; Sakamoto, *Kunikida Doppo*, pp. 1–12; and Ino, *Meiji no sakka*, pp. 172–75.

10. For Tokutomi Sōhō's review of *Returning Home*, see his "Kisei o yomu." His more general ideas about the furusato are found in "Furusato."

11. For the comment on Napoleon, see "Ware wa ikani shite shōsetsuka to nari ka," *Kunikida Doppo zenshū*, 1: 495–99. Ambition is discussed in "Anbishon (yabōron)," ibid., pp. 169–71.

12. Takitō, "Doppo to shizen," p. 14.

13. The preacher Uemura Kanzō recounts visiting Doppo at his sickbed in 1908 to hear him tearfully confess his inability to pray to Christ; see Yamada, *Kitamura Tōkoku to Kunikida Doppo*, p. 93. Doppo's involvement with Christianity is covered in detail on pp. 85–108.

14. *Kunikida Doppo zenshū*, 9: 134.

15. Ibid., 1: 496.

16. For the comment on Tōkoku, see Yamada, *Kitamura Tōkoku to Kunikida Doppo*, p. 107. Regarding Doppo, see Togawa, "*Dorama,*" "*takai,*" p. 180.

17. See esp. "Fūkei no hakken," in Karatani, *Nihon kindai bungaku*, pp. 5–44.

18. *Kunikida Doppo zenshū*, 2: 115.

19. Ibid., p. 118.

20. Ibid., p. 119.

21. Karatani, *Nihon kindai bungaku*, pp. 26–27.

22. *Kunikida Doppo zenshū*, 2: 120.

23. Karatani, *Nihon kindai bungaku*, p. 23.

24. Ibid., pp. 29–30.

25. *Kunikida Doppo zenshū*, 2: 121.

26. Edward Fowler suggests that the source of Doppo's attraction to western literature was its "personalized narrative voice." He disliked the Ken'yūsha writers for "their lack of emotional involvement with their characters—the inevitable result of their concern for mass appeal at the cost of silencing their own thoughts and yearnings" (Fowler, *The Rhetoric of Confession*, p. 89).

27. Takitō, *Kunikida Doppo ron*, pp. 150–51.

28. *Kunikida Doppo zenshū*, 2: 108, 111.

29. Kitano, *Miyazaki Koshoshi Kunikida Doppo*, p. 134.

30. For details on the publication dates, see Takitō, *Kunikida Doppo ron*, p. 99.

31. *Kunikida Doppo zenshū*, 2: 65.

32. Ibid., p. 69.

33. Ibid., p. 73. In the Japanese, "less than three miles" is 1 *ri*, which is 2.44 miles.

34. Ibid., p. 85.

35. Takitō, *Kunikida Doppo ron*, p. 113.

36. The article was called "Wordsworth" (Kitano, *Miyazaki Koshoshi Kunikida Doppo*, p. 5).

37. *Kunikida Doppo zenshū*, 1: 540.

38. Ibid., pp. 541–42.

39. Ibid., p. 488.

40. Ibid., p. 539.

41. Kitano, *Miyazaki Koshoshi Kunikida Doppo*, p. 125.

42. "Yo to shizenshugi," in *Kunikida Doppo zenshū*, 1: 528–32.

43. Ibid., 1: 542.

44. Ibid., 2: 73.

45. "Kunikida Doppo ron," first published in *Waseda bungaku* in August 1908; see *Tayama Katai zenshū*, 15: 95–104.

46. In the April and May editions of the magazine *Katei zasshi* (nos. 52 and 53), he published "Yo ga tomo no airashiki mōsō," in which he described a fantasy of living the simple life in the "mountains and forests" of Hokkaido with a young and healthy wife.

47. *Kunikida Doppo zenshū*, 2: 75.

48. Ibid., 3: 9.

49. Ibid., p. 10.

50. Takitō, "Doppo to shizen," p. 18.

51. *Kunikida Doppo zenshū*, 3: 10.

52. Schivelbusch, *The Railway Journey*, p. 25.

53. *Kunikida Doppo zenshū*, 3: 12.

54. Ibid., p. 14.

55. *Kunikida Doppo zenshū*, 2: 71.

56. Ibid., 3: 11.

57. Ibid., 2: 183.

58. Ibid., p. 320. As I discuss below, the title is taken from a poem by the Chinese poet Tao Yuanming. *Kōjien* translates the phrase as "to leave the native place in order to return."

59. *Kunikida Doppo zenshū*, 2: 178.

60. Ibid., p. 180.

61. Ibid., p. 181.

62. Ibid., p. 182.

63. Ibid., pp. 176–77.

64. Yamada, "Doppo 'Kawagiri' ron," p. 33.

65. *Kunikida Doppo zenshū*, 2: 185.

66. Ibid., p. 177.

67. Takitō, *Kunikida Doppo ron*, p. 227.

68. *Kunikida Doppo zenshū*, 2: 332. According to Yamada Hiromitsu, Doppo first read Johnson's book in July 1891 during his stay in Yamaguchi; see his "Koshoshi to Doppo," p. 22, where he also gives details about this text's use in Tokyo schools.

69. *Kunikida Doppo zenshū*, 1: 361.

70. Ibid., 2: 329.

71. Ibid., p. 326.

72. Kitano, *Miyazaki Koshoshi Kunikida Doppo*, p. 2.

73. Togawa, "*Dorama*," "*takai*," pp. 177–79.

74. Takitō, *Kunikida Doppo ron*, p. 199.

75. Kitano, *Miyazaki Koshoshi Kunikida Doppo*, pp. 7–8. The advertisement for Koshoshi's book in *Kokumin no tomo* even spoke of an "Eden-like life" (Takitō, *Kunikida Doppo ron*, p. 199).

76. Other Edo writers with similar interests include Shiba Kōkan (1738–1818), Honda Toshiaki (1744–1821), and Furukawa Koshōken (1726–1807) (Sukida, *Tōkagen to yūtopia*, p. 223).

77. *Kunikida Doppo zenshū*, 2: 325.

78. Kwong, *Tao Qian*, p. 51. This work is the source of my information on the Chinese poet.

79. *Kunikida Doppo zenshū*, 2: 322.

80. Ibid., p. 324.

81. Kwong, *Tao Qian*, p. 53.

82. Ibid., p. 29.

83. *Kunikida Doppo zenshū*, 2: 333.

84. Ibid., p. 336.

85. Ibid., p. 334.

86. Karatani, *Nihon kindai bungaku*, esp. "Naimen no hakken," pp. 45–83.

87. *Kunikida Doppo zenshū*, 2: 155.

88. Ibid., p. 186.

89. Karatani, *Nihon kindai bungaku*, pp. 76–77; he is referring to Starobinski, *Jean-Jacques Rousseau*, p. 125.

90. *Kunikida Doppo zenshū*, 2: 341.

91. Hirakawa, "Higashi to nishi," pp. 103–4.

92. Robertson, "It Takes a Village," pp. 124–25.

93. *Kunikida Doppo zenshū*, 2: 322.

94. Maeda, *Tekusuto no yūtopia*, p. 220.

95. Yamada, "Koshoshi to Doppo," pp. 20–21.

96. *Kunikida Doppo zenshū*, 2: 359.

97. For the essay "Conrad: The Presentation of Narrative," see Said, *The World, the Text, and the Critic*, pp. 90–110.

98. *Kunikida Doppo zenshū*, 9: 334.

99. Takitō, *Kunikida Doppo ron*, esp. pp. 134–35, 145. Takitō also discusses wonder in "Doppo to shizen," p. 20.

100. *Kunikida Doppo zenshū*, 2: 119.

101. Ibid., p. 324.

102. Greenfeld, *Nationalism*, pp. 3–6.

Chapter 2

1. [*Shimazaki*] *Tōson zenshū*, 6: 502.

2. Shimazaki, *The Broken Commandment*, p. xvi.

3. Walthall, "Off with Their Heads!," p. 141.

4. [*Shimazaki*] *Tōson zenshū*, 11: 440.

5. Ibid., 12: 264.

6. Okuno, *Bungaku ni okeru genfūkei*, p. 11.

7. [*Shimazaki*] *Tōson zenshū*, 9: 273.

8. Tokutomi Kenjirō, *Roka zenshū*, 6: 347.

9. Shimazaki, *The Family*, p. vii. Tōson and his elder brother Tomoya were taken to Tokyo by their elder brother Hideo and entrusted to the care of their sister, Sonoko, who was married to Takase Kaoru. When the couple returned to Kiso-Fukushima in 1882, Tōson moved to the home of Yoshimura, who was a friend of Kaoru.

10. Ibid., p. vii.

11. It has also been suggested that he was sent away because of declining fortunes and domestic tensions at home; see Shimazaki, *The Broken Commandment*, p. xvii.

12. Gluck, *Japan's Modern Myths*, p. 159.

13. *Tayama Katai zenshū*, 15: 539.

14. Henry Smith, "Tokyo as an Idea," p. 53.

15. Ibid., p. 55.

16. Jinnai, *Tōkyō no kūkan jinruigaku*, p. 99.

17. Ibid., p. 101.

18. [*Nagai*] *Kafū zenshū*, 4: 116.

19. Yamamura, *Mita bungaku*, p. 137.

20. Williams, *The Country and the City*, p. 234.

21. Yamamura, *Mita bungaku*, p. 138.

22. [*Shimazaki*] *Tōson zenshū*, 5: 503.

23. Ibid., p. 504.

24. Ibid., 2: 303.

25. Fowler, *The Rhetoric of Confession*, esp. pp. 3–70.

26. Among other forms, "social novels" (*shakai shōsetsu*), "political novels" (*seiji shōsetsu*), "ideological novels" (*kannen shōsetsu*), "serious novels" (*shinkoku shōsetsu*), and "tragic novels" (*hisan shōsetsu*) (Yoshida, *Shizenshugi no kenkyū*, pp. 19–129).

27. For other useful accounts of the *genbun itchi* movement, see Masao Miyoshi, *Accomplices of Silence*, pp. 3–37; and Kornicki, *The Reform of Fiction*.

28. *Kanbun* was a pseudo-Chinese style in use by Japanese officialdom since the Nara period and a favorite during the Tokugawa period due to a government revival of Confucianism; *sōrōbun* featured the use of *sōrō* as the copula and was the epistolary style for both private and public correspondence, as well as public notices, reports, archives, laws, and ordinances; *wabun* was predominantly Japanese in tone and originated in the Heian period when *kana* were first deployed to reproduced spoken Japanese, but it became separated over centuries from spoken Japanese; *wakankonkōbun*

was a mixture of Chinese and Japanese styles (Twine, "The *Genbunitchi* Movement," pp. 334–36).

29. The title of Yamada's unfinished work was *Ridiculing a Vain Novelist* (*Chōkai shōsetsu tengu*) Apart from its use of *kanbun*, Bakin's work is characterized by complex historical plots and a seven-and-five-syllable meter (*shichi-go-chō*).

30. "Rokotsu naru byōsha" was the title of a highly influential essay published by Katai in February 1904.

31. Inouye, *The Similitude of Blossoms*, p. 40.

32. Yanagida, "Shasei to ronbun."

33. Yanagida, "Genbun no kyori."

34. For a fuller comparison of these two essays by Yanagita, see Ivy, *Discourses of the Vanishing*, pp. 76–78.

35. Karatani, *Nihon kindai bungaku*, pp. 48–49.

36. Fowler, *The Rhetoric of Confession*, p. 77.

37. See Masao Miyoshi, *Off Center*, esp. pp. 9–36.

38. [*Shimazaki*] *Tōson zenshū*, 9: 305.

39. William Naff summarizes Tōson's personal situation around 1899 as follows: "Hideo, Tōson's eldest brother, had sold the family holdings in Magome and gone to Tokyo, where he quickly dissipated what little remained of the Shimazaki family fortune in ill-advised business ventures, two of which netted prison terms for him (naïveté, not evil intent, seems to have been the cause). The second brother was neglecting home and family to engage in a long and ultimately successful political fight for the interests of his former neighbors in the Kiso, while the long-missing third brother soon turned up at Hideo's Tokyo residence, disabled by disease and totally dependent for the rest of his life. Tōson was usually the prime, and not infrequently the sole, support of all" (Shimazaki, *Chikuma River Sketches*, pp. xiv–xv).

40. Yoshida, *Shizenshugi no kenkyū*, p. 338.

41. Shimazaki, *Chikuma River Sketches*, p. xi.

42. For a detailed analysis of *Wakanashū*, see Miyoshi Yukio, *Shimazaki Tōson ron*, esp. pp. 6–70.

43. Yoshida, *Shizenshugi no kenkyū*, p. 339.

44. Ibid., p. 344.

45. Shinbo, *Doppo to Tōson*, pp. 77–78.

46. These two expressions are taken from Matthew Arnold's *Critical Collections* (1865) and F. W. H. Mayers's *Biography of Wordsworth* (1881).

47. Shimazaki, *Chikuma River Sketches*, p. xiii.

48. Among the authors he read were Tolstoy, Turgenev, Dostoevsky, Ibsen, Goethe, Nietzsche, Hauptmann, Stendhal, Flaubert, Maupassant, Balzac, Zola, and Darwin (ibid., p. xvi).

49. Shimoyama, "Shasei," p. 85.

50. Yoshida, *Shizenshugi no kenkyū*, pp. 346–48.

51. Miyoshi Yukio, *Shimazaki Tōson ron*, p. 72.

52. Shimazaki, *Chikuma River Sketches*, p. xxii.

53. Kimura taught English to Tōson at a school in Kanda before he entered Meiji gakuin.

54. [*Shimazaki*] *Tōson zenshū*, 6: 33–34.

55. Ibid., 5: 56.

56. While Tōson was teaching at the Tōhoku gakuin in September 1896–July 1897, translations of two parts of Ruskin's work were published in the December 1896 and May 1897 issues of the literary journal *Tōhoku bungaku* (Shinbo, *Doppo to Tōson*, p. 70).

57. Ibid., p. 71.

58. Marcus, "The Writer Speaks," p. 276n58.

59. Karatani, *Nihon kindai bungaku*, p. 26.

60. Shiki assumed that "writing was something phonetic. In other words, writing was simply a means of transcription, and *kanji* were merely one of those means" (ibid., p. 66).

61. Etō, "Riarizumu no genryū," p. 29. Kyoshi's article is entitled "Shasei shumi to kūsō shumi" (March 1904).

62. [*Natsume*] *Sōseki zenshū*, 11: 21–29.

63. Etō, *Riarizumu no genryū*, p. 28.

64. Ibid., pp. 32–33. My understanding of Etō's article is indebted to Ōkubo, *Shinra-hen'yō*, pp. 65–66.

65. [*Shimazaki*] *Tōson zenshū*, 6: 86.

66. Ibid., 5: 464.

67. Sasabuchi, "Shimazaki Tōson to purotesutantizumu," p. 24.

68. Miyoshi Yukio, *Shimazaki Tōson hikkei*, pp. 34–35.

69. [*Shimazaki*] *Tōson zenshū*, 5: 590.

70. Shimazaki, *Chikuma River Sketches*, p. xvi.

71. Yoshida Seiichi (*Shizenshugi no kenkyū*, pp. 330–33) notes that Tōson was also drawing in the *jōruri* style of Chikamatsu.

72. Takitō, *Kunikida Doppo ron*, p. 392.

73. Miyoshi Yukio, *Shimazaki Tōson ron*, p. 83.

74. Quoted in Itō Kazuo, "Taishō ki ni okeru Shimazaki Tōson," p. 281.

75. [*Shimazaki*] *Tōson zenshū*, 9: 157.

76. Ibid., 13: 20–32.

77. Miyoshi Yukio, *Shimazaki Tōson ron*, p. 332.
78. Sasabuchi, "Shimazaki Tōson to purotesutantizumu," p. 28.
79. Ibid., p. 26.
80. This poem is discussed in detail in Ōkubo, *Shinra-hen'yō*, pp. 27–29.
81. Sibley, "Naturalism in Japanese Literature," p. 159. For a broader discussion of Takayama's work, see Iwasa, "'Shizen' to iu shisō," pp. 164–67.
82. Marcus, "The Writer Speaks," p. 231.
83. Rubin, *Injurious to Public Morals*, p. 60.
84. Sibley makes a similar point in "Naturalism in Japanese Literature," p. 169.
85. Miyoshi Yukio, *Shimazaki Tōson ron*, pp. 107–8.
86. [*Shimazaki*] *Tōson zenshū*, 9: 156.

Chapter 3

1. For the illustration, see *Shashin sakka den*, p. 115.
2. The city of Edo lost half its population of one million in less than seven years following the collapse of the Tokugawa bakufu, but it had recovered by 1890. The transition from Edo to Tokyo is thus characterized by a speedy decline and recovery (Henry Smith, "The Edo–Tokyo Transition," p. 347).
3. Najita and Koschmann, *Conflict in Modern Japanese History*, p. 16.
4. Ericson, *The Sound of the Whistle*, p. 3.
5. Isoda, *Shisō toshite no Tōkyō*, p. 78.
6. Duus, *Cambridge History of Japan*: 6: 395.
7. Noda et al., *Nihon no tetsudō*, p. 49.
8. Ericson, *The Sound of the Whistle*, p. 92.
9. Shinbo, *Doppo to Tōson*, p. 191.
10. *Tayama Katai zenshū*, 5: 650–53.
11. Shinano mainichi shinbunsha, *Shinshū no tetsudō monogatari*, pp. 92–94.
12. Ibid., p. 168. Kiso was favored because of the military's preference for a more direct route, the fact that the Imperial Household Ministry owned valuable forest land in the Kiso region, and the railroad authorities' view that Kiso was easier to handle in terms of engineering technicalities (Ericson, *The Sound of the Whistle*, p. 49).
13. [*Shimazaki*] *Tōson zenshū*, 4: 10.
14. Ibid., p. 7.
15. Ibid., p. 374. An interesting correlation exists between this fictional description and historical facts surrounding the development of the railway. In 1898, the author visited his sister, Sonoko, who was living in Kiso-

Fukushima. The young Tōson lived with Sonoko and her husband, Takase Kaoru, from his arrival in Tokyo until their return to Kiso in 1882. He paid a second visit at the end of autumn 1910, just as the last links in the Central Trunk line were being laid. In the novel, Sankichi is described as making his second visit "at the end of autumn," and during his stay he accompanied a family relative, Toyose, to a station where she was to take a train to Nagoya. This involved a walk along the old Kiso Road until they "arrived at a recently opened station toward evening." This must refer to the new station in Agematsu, opened on October 5, 1910, and about five miles' walk from Kiso-Fukushima. The line connecting Nagoya, Agematsu, and on to Kiso-Fukushima—the obvious station from which to take a Nagoya-bound train for people in Kiso-Fukushima and one that did not require a long tramp through the woods—was completed only on November 25. In other words, Tōson seems to be depicting a scene at his sister's house some time between October 5 and November 25, 1910, and the "half-finished railroad" in the back garden refers to the track being built to connect Agematsu to Kiso-Fukushima. The final link to Kiso-Fukushima from the Tokyo side, which completed the Central Trunk line, was made in May 1911.

16. [*Shimazaki*] *Tōson zenshū*, 4: 375.

17. Ibid., pp. 376–77.

18. Ibid., pp. 376–79.

19. Williams, *The Country and the City*, p. 78.

20. Ericson, *The Sound of the Whistle*, p. 60.

21. [*Shimazaki*] *Tōson zenshū*, 2: 123–24.

22. Kimata, *"Imeeji" no kindai*, p. 96.

23. [*Shimazaki*] *Tōson zenshū*, 2: 105.

24. Ibid., p. 90.   25. Ibid., pp. 105–6.

26. Ibid., p. 51.   27. Ibid., pp. 140–41.

28. Ibid., p. 44.   29. Ibid., 5: 76.

30. Ibid., 2: 44.   31. Kimata, *"Imeeji" no kindai*, p. 90.

32. [*Shimazaki*] *Tōson zenshū*, 4: 68.

33. Kimata, *"Imeeji" no kindai*, p. 91.

34. [*Shimazaki*] *Tōson zenshū*, 2: 47.

35. Ibid., p. 45.

36. Ibid.

37. Ibid., p. 47.

38. Sasabuchi, "Shimazaki Tōson ni okeru 'rōdō to bungaku,'" pp. 31–35. For an English version of the Tolstoy edition, see Cruger, *Labor: The Divine Command*.

39. [*Shimazaki*] *Tōson zenshū*, 2: 304.

40. The letter first appeared in *Kirisutokyō sekai* (Christian world), July 15, 1909; see [*Shimazaki*] *Tōson zenshū*, 6: 525–26.

41. Bermingham, *Landscape and Ideology*, p. 72.

42. Isoda, *Shisō toshite no Tōkyō*, p. 26.

43. Ibid., p. 56.

44. Ibid., p. 32.

45. [*Shimazaki*] *Tōson zenshū*, 5: 8.

46. Ibid., p. 3.   47. Ibid., p. 4.

48. Ibid., p. 8.   49. Ibid., p. 10.

50. Naimushō, Chihōkyoku, *Den'en toshi*, p. 36.

51. Ibid., pp. 25–26.

52. Wigen, "Constructing Shinano," p. 229.

53. [*Shimazaki*] *Tōson zenshū*, 5: 129.

54. Ibid., p. 3.

55. Ibid., 4: 67.

56. Ibid., 9: 204.

57. Shimazaki, *Chikuma River Sketches*, p. xii.

58. [*Shimazaki*] *Tōson zenshū*, 5: 80.

59. Ibid., p. 134. 1 *tsubo* = 3.95 sq. yds., 1 *shō* = 3.18 pints, 1 *tsuka* = measure of tax or rental rice equivalent to 10 *kin* or 13 pounds avoirdupois, 1 *momme* = 58 troy grains.

60. *Tayama Katai zenshū*, 2: 480.   61. [*Shimazaki*] *Tōson zenshū*, 5: 492.

62. Ibid., 12: 477.   63. Ibid., 4: 51.

64. Ibid., 5: 93–94.

Chapter 4

1. Harootunian, *Overcome by Modernity*, pp. 208–9.

2. Keene, *Dawn to the West*, p. 636.

3. *Satō zenshū*, 3: 33–38.

4. Quoted in Napier, *The Fantastic in Modern Japanese Literature*, p. 243.

5. Keene, *Dawn to the West*, p. 634.

6. Jackson, *Fantasy*, pp. 3–4. For another discussion of fantasy in general and its Japanese variants, see Napier, *The Fantastic in Modern Japanese Literature*.

7. Nakagami, *Kishū*, p. 298.

8. Ibid., p. 7.

9. Miyake, *Shugendō shisō no kenkyū*, pp. 313–14.

10. Nakagami, *Fūkei no mukō e*, pp. 95–98. For "A Madman's Death," see *Satō zenshū*, 2: 107–8.

11. *Mushanokōji Saneatsu zenshū*, 9: 309.

12. Togawa, *"Dorama,"* *"takai,"* p. 172.

13. *Satō zenshū*, 3: 211.

14. Ōkubo, *Shinra-hen'yō*, p. 132.

15. See, e.g., Asquith and Kalland, *Japanese Images of Nature*.

16. Hara, "Satō Haruo ni okeru kaiga," pp. 52–53.

17. Keene, *Dawn to the West*, p. 634.

18. Inouye, *The Similitude of Blossoms*, pp. 19–20.

19. Early "modernist period" works include "The Fingerprint" ("Shimon," 1918) and "FOU" (1926). His futuristic novel was *The Nonchalant Records* (*Nonsharan kiroku*, 1929), and he wrote a Freudian psychoanalytical novel, *The Rebirth* (*Kōseiki*, 1929). He also produced a film screenplay as well as plays for the theater. Writings in a traditional style that drew on classical Chinese literature include "The Star" ("Hoshi," 1920), the Chinese-style mystery tale, "A Strange Tale of a Woman's Fan" ("Jokaisen kidan," 1925), and translations of Chinese children's stories such as "The Great Journey of the Locust" ("Inago no dairyokō," 1926). He produced an anthology of Chinese women poets called *The Wagon Dust Collection* (*Shajinshō*, 1929). He also wrote an I-novel, *Unbearably Forlorn* (*Wabishisugiru*, 1922), and an unfinished roman-à-clef about his breakup with Tanizaki over a love triangle involving the latter's wife in *These Three People* (*Kono mittsu no mono*, 1925). See the introduction by Elaine Gerber to Satō, *Beautiful Town*, pp. 3–4.

20. The first five sections of the story were published in the June 1917 edition of the magazine, *Kuroshio*, under the title *The Sick Rose* (*Yameru sōbi*). The final part of *The Sick Rose* was supposed to appear in the same magazine in October, but Satō scrapped it after it was rejected, and the whole work was revised in December of the same year. In September 1918, the story *Rural Melancholy* (*Den'en no yūutsu*), consisting of part of the final version without the first five sections published in *Kuroshio*, appeared in *Chūgai*. The *Kuroshio* and *Chūgai* sections were brought together in November 1918 under the title of *The Sick Rose, or Rural Melancholy* (*Yameru sōbi, aruiwa Den'en no yūutsu*), to appear in a collection of short stories called *The Sick Rose*). In June 1919, thirteen sections of the final version were published in *Yūben*. In the same month, an extra seven sections were added to make up the final revised version of twenty sections, which was published by Shinchōsha. Its full title is *Rural Melancholy, or The Sick Rose* (*Den'en no yūutsu, aruiwa Yameru sōbi*). See Nagata, "Shinteki hen'yō no gūwa," p. 93. The text states that "seventeen" sections were added to complete the final version, but this must be a mistake for "seven" since there are only twenty sections in all.

21. *Satō zenshū*, 3: 202. What I have translated as "sixteen or seventeen miles" is literally six or seven *li* (1 *li* is 2.44 miles). The text uses only the initials T, Y, and H to refer to the cities, but their names are spelled out in full in the story "Okinu and Her Brothers" which is based on similar experiences; see ibid., p. 123.

22. Ibid., p. 213.

23. Stewart, *On Longing*, p. 44.

24. *Satō zenshū*, 3: 209.

25. Bring and Wayembergh, *Japanese Gardens*, p. 203.

26. Ibid., p. 185.

27. *Satō zenshū*, 3: 252–53.

28. Stein, *The World in Miniature*, pp. 52–53.

29. *Satō zenshū*, 3: 248–49. The "fairy tale" he mentions is very likely Swift's *Gulliver's Travels*, parts of which were first translated by Okubo Tsunekichi under the title *Taijin koku ryokō* (Shinkōdō, 1887). Swift's story was discussed by Sōseki in his 1909–10 essay "Bungaku hyōron"; see [*Natsume*] *Sōseki zenshū*, 10: 280–91.

30. Stewart, *On Longing*, p. 71.   31. *Satō zenshū*, 19: 228–29.

32. Ibid., 3: 390.   33. Ibid., p. 391.

34. Quoted in Yamaguchi, *Kōgai jūtakuchi*, pp. 28–29.

35. *Satō zenshū*, 3: 405.

36. Ibid., p. 412.

37. Kawamoto, *Taishō gen'ei*, p. 209. Satō built a second house in Saku, Nagano prefecture, after World War II.

38. *Satō zenshū*, 3: 201.

39. Ibid., p. 237.

40. Ibid., p. 240.

41. Bring and Wayembergh, *Japanese Gardens*, p. 180.

42. *Satō zenshū*, 3: 233.

43. Isoda, *Rokumeikan no keifu*, p. 191.

44. Bring and Wayembergh, *Japanese Gardens*, p. 181.

45. *Satō zenshū*, 3: 236.

46. Schivelbusch, *Disenchanted Night*, pp. 206–7.

47. *Tanizaki Jun'ichirō zenshū*, 12: 124–38.

48. Hashizume, *Meiji no meikyū toshi*, p. 121.

49. Ibid., p. 113.

50. Ibid., pp. 112–14.

51. Takahashi, "'Den'en no yūutsu' ron," p. 137.

52. *Satō zenshū*, 3: 391–92.

53. Takahashi, "'Den'en no yūutsu' ron," p. 139.

54. *Satō zenshū*, 3: 203.
55. Ibid., p. 401.
56. Takahashi, "'Den'en no yūutsu' ron," p. 140.
57. *Satō zenshū*, 3: 264.   58. Ibid., pp. 133–35.
59. Ibid., pp. 242–43.   60. Ibid., p. 202.
61. Ibid.
62. Takahashi, "'Den'en no yūutsu' ron," p. 135.
63. Schivelbusch, *Disenchanted Night*, pp. 158–62.
64. Ibid., p. 162.
65. *Satō zenshū*, 3: 402.
66. Schivelbusch, *Disenchanted Night*, pp. 74–75.
67. *Satō zenshū*, 3: 402.

Chapter 5

1. Cited in Nakamura, *Shiga Naoya ron*, p. 5. Shiga has also been described even more grandly as the "god of literature" (*bungaku no kamisama*); see Orbaugh, "Extending the Limits of Possibility," p. 337. Other terms of praise include "god of prose" (*bunshō no kamisama*) and "god of the novel" (*shōsetsu no kamisama*); see Fowler, *The Rhetoric of Confession*, p. 188.
2. Ivy, *Discourses of the Vanishing*, p. 104.
3. Fowler, *The Rhetoric of Confession*, p. 66.
4. Ibid., p. 194.   5. Ibid., pp. 189–92.
6. Sibley, *The Shiga Hero*.   7. *Shiga Naoya zenshū*, 6: 199–232.
8. See his article "Bungeiteki na, anmari bungeiteki na," in *Akutagawa Ryūnosuke zenshū*, 12: 312–14; as well as his posthumously published story "Cogwheels" ("Haguruma," 1927), in which the main character reads from *A Dark Night's Passing* and bursts into tears when considering his worthlessness in comparison to Shiga (ibid., 9: 123–67).
9. *Dazai Osamu zenshū*, 10: 315.
10. *Kobayashi Hideo zenshū*, 4: 18–19.
11. Ibid., p. 115.
12. Tanikawa, "Watashi no mita Shiga-san," p. 13.
13. Starrs, *An Artless Art*, pp. 23–25.
14. For a recent interesting textual analysis of Shiga's literature, see Orbaugh, "Extending the Limits of Possibility," esp. pp. 350–63.
15. Robertson, "It Takes a Village," p. 117.
16. *Shiga Naoya zenshū*, 4: 253–54.
17. Robertson, "It Takes a Village," p. 117.
18. Goossen, "Connecting Rhythms," p. 22.

19. *Shiga Naoya zenshū*, 3: 79.

20. Keene, *Dawn to the West*, p. 464.

21. Minami, *Taishō bunka*, pp. 128–32.

22. Takada, "Taishō bungaku o dō toraeru ka," pp. 61–62.

23. "Shirakaba" means "white birch"; the title was chosen to recognize the strong influence of Russian literature, since the tree is a common feature of the Russian landscape. I leave the name in Japanese since this is the way it is usually referred to even by non-Japanese scholars.

24. Keene, *Dawn to the West*, pp. 441–42.

25. Honda, *"Shirakaba" ha no bungaku*, p. 34.

26. Ibid., p. 17.

27. *Yasuoka Shōtarō essei zenshū*, 4: 213.

28. *Shiga Naoya zenshū*, 3: 281–390.

29. Ibid., pp. 139–218.

30. Mathy, *Shiga Naoya*, p. 66. Translated by Mathy from the Afterword of the Iwanami edition of the three stories.

31. Harotoonian, "A Sense of Ending," p. 15.

32. For a discussion of Ōgai's story, see Rubin, *Injurious to Public Morals*, pp. 153–54. Edward Seidensticker discusses Kafū's lack of social concern in *Kafu the Scribbler*, esp. p. 46. Rachel Hutchinson ("Occidentalism in Nagai Kafū") has recently argued that Kafū was far more socially concerned than Seidensticker suggests.

33. Waswo, "The Origins of Tenant Unrest," p. 374.

34. See Anderer's *Other Worlds* for an in-depth analysis of Arishima's novel from a spatial perspective.

35. Tansman, "Images of Repose and Violence," p. 110.

36. Kinmonth, *The Self-Made Man*, pp. 206–16.

37. Rimer, *Culture and Identity*, p. 3.

38. Miyoshi Yukio et al., *Taishō no bungaku*, pp. 110–12.

39. Kohl, "Shiga Naoya and the Literature of Experience," p. 212.

40. *Shiga Naoya zenshū*, 4: 127.

41. Ibid., p. 132.   42. Ibid., pp. 132–33.

43. Ibid., p. 135.   44. Ibid., p. 259.

45. Yoshida, "Shirakaba ni okeru Shiga Naoya," p. 20.

46. Keene, *Dawn to the West*, p. 240.

47. Ibid., p. 442.

48. Quoted in Senuma, *Taishō bungakushi*, p. 29.

49. Honda, *"Shirakaba" ha no bungaku*, p. 15; quoting from the September 1911 issue of *Shirakaba*.

50. [*Natsume*] *Sōseki zenshū*, 12: 36.

51. Honda, *"Shirakaba" ha no bungaku*, p. 15.

52. [*Nagai*] *Kafū zenshū*, 3: 556.   53. *Shiga Naoya zenshū*, 4: 142–43.

54. Ibid., p. 142.   55. Ibid., p. 141.

56. See Paul Anderer's analysis in *Other Worlds*.

57. Honda, *"Shirakaba" ha no bungaku*, p. 27. On the Japanese experience of the West mainly through imitation, see also Aeba, *Nihon kindai no seikimatsu*, esp. pp. 7–57.

58. [*Nagai*] *Kafū zenshū*, 18: 559–60. "Pierre Loti" was the pen-name of Louis Marie Julien Viaud, a French naval officer and novelist who visited Japan in 1885 and again in 1901–2.

59. Miyoshi Yukio et al., *Taishō no bungaku*, p. 94.

60. *Kobayashi Hideo zenshū*, 3: 31–32.

61. *Tanizaki Jun'ichirō zenshū*, 17: 73.

62. *Kobayashi Hideo zenshū*, 4: 13.

63. Uno, "Yume miru heya," p. 50.

64. *Kobayashi Hideo zenshū*, 3: 32.

65. Sakaguchi, "Nihon bunka shikan," p. 42.

66. Ibid., p. 70.

67. *Tales of Ise*, pp. 72–73.

68. Sakaguchi, "Bungaku no furusato," p. 29.

69. Ibid., p. 35.

70. *Shiga Naoya zenshū*, 2: 294.

71. Said, *The World, the Text, and the Critic*, p. 90.

72. Sakaguchi, "Nihon bunka shikan," p. 70.

73. *Kobayashi Hideo zenshū*, 4: 18.   74. *Shiga Naoya zenshū*, 2: 297.

75. Ibid., pp. 299–300.   76. *Kobayashi Hideo zenshū*, 3: 30.

77. Uno, "Yume miru heya," p. 44.

78. Sakaguchi, "Nihon bunka shikan," pp. 64–65.

79. *Hagiwara Sakutarō zenshū*, 10: 6.

80. This argument forms the basis of Pollack's *Fracture of Meaning*.

Chapter 6

1. Tansman, "Images of Repose and Violence," pp. 111–12.

2. Keene, *Dawn to the West*, p. 934.

3. Hirotsu, "Shiga Naoya ron," pp. 368–69.

4. Itō Kimio, "The Invention of *Wa*," p. 46.

5. *Shiga Naoya zenshū*, 4: 9.

6. Ibid., p. 15.

7. Bataille, *Death and Sensuality*, p. 16.

8. See, e.g., Fowler, *The Rhetoric of Confession*, p. 243.

9. *Shiga Naoya zenshū*, 2: 247.   10. Ibid., p. 249.

11. Ibid., p. 257.   12. Ibid., 1: 179.

13. Ibid., p. 181.   14. Ibid., 2: 288.

15. Sibley, *The Shiga Hero*, p. 62.   16. *Shiga Naoya zenshū*, 1: 181.

17. Ibid., 4: 128–29.   18. Ibid., 3: 81.

19. Mathy, *Shiga Naoya*, p. 65.   20. *Shiga Naoya zenshū*, 7: 232.

21. Karatani, "Watakushi shōsetsu no ryōgisei," p. 128.

22. *Shiga Naoya zenshū*, 3:. 84.

23. Ibid., pp. 166–67.

24. Ibid., pp. 121–22.

25. Hirakawa, "Mount Daisen Depicted by Two Authors," p. 259.

26. *Shiga Naoya zenshū*, 3: 163.   27. Ibid., 4: 145–46.

28. Ibid., p. 483.   29. Ibid., p. 494.

30. Examples of other flora and fauna-related stories are "Dragonfly" ("Tombo," 1914), "Wall Lizard" ("Yamori," 1914), "Death of a Hermit Crab" ("Yadokari no shi," 1914), "Birds and Insects" ("Mushi to tori," 1940), "Rabbits" (Usagi, 1946), and "Cats" (Neko, 1947).

31. Starrs, *An Artless Art*, pp. 35–61.

32. Nakamura, *Shiga Naoya ron*, pp. 132–33.

33. *Shiga Naoya zenshū*, 4: 144–45.

34. Fowler, *The Rhetoric of Confession*, p. 229.

35. *Shiga Naoya zenshū*, 4: 541–42.

36. Ibid., p. 542.

37. Sudō, "'*An'ya kōro*' no Daisen," pp. 265–66.

38. *Shiga Naoya zenshū*, 4: 542.

39. Sudō, "Shiga bungaku no shizen," p. 99.

40. *Kobayashi Hideo zenshū*, 4: 16.

41. *Shiga Naoya zenshū*, 5: 52.

42. Ibid., pp. 59–60.

43. Hagiwara Takao counts a total of five depictions of airplanes in the novel; see his "Man and Nature," pp. 30–31.

44. *Shiga Naoya zenshū*, 4: 109.

45. Ibid., p. 508.

46. Ibid., p. 500.

47. Tansman, "Images of Repose and Violence," p. 114.

48. Tanaka, *Women Writers of Meiji and Taishō Japan*, pp. 6–7.

49. Ibid., pp. 157–59.

50. Massey, *Space, Place and Gender*, p. 6.

51. Ibid., p. 10.   52. *Shiga Naoya zenshū*, 3: 117.

53. Ibid., 2: 23.   54. Ibid., 4: 11.

55. Ibid., pp. 78–79.

56. This theme is discussed in detail in Ken Ito, *Visions of Desire*, pp. 16–25.

57. *Shiga Naoya zenshū*, 4: 157.

58. *Yasuoka Shōtarō essei zenshū*, 4: 181.

59. Another example of the eroticized blending of memories of deceased mother and newly arrived, beautiful stepmother is to be found in Tanizaki's *Floating Bridge of Dreams*.

60. *Shiga Naoya zenshū*, 4: 60.

61. Ibid., pp. 12–13.

62. Hagiwara, "Man and Nature," pp. 29–30.

63. *Shiga Naoya zenshū*, 4: 320.

64. Ibid., p. 507.

65. Ibid., p. 519.

66. *Kodansha Encyclopedia of Japan*, 7: 182.

67. *Shiga Naoya zenshū*, 4: 487.

68. Ibid., p. 541.

69. Hardacre, "The Cave and the Womb World." For general background on religious practices related to mountain worship, see Hori, *Folk Religion in Japan*, pp. 143–74. On *shugendō* religious practice, see also Miyake, *Shugendō shisō no kenkyū*; and Swanson, "Shugendō and the Yoshino-Kumano Pilgrimage."

70. *Shiga Naoya zenshū*, 3: 416.   71. Ibid., 4: 543–44.

72. Ibid., p. 147.   73. Ibid., p. 148.

74. Ibid., p. 153.   75. Tuan, *Topophilia*, p. 63.

76. *Shiga Naoya zenshū*, 4: 165.

77. Pollack, *Reading Against Culture*, p. 94.

78. *Shiga Naoya zenshū*, 4: 154–55.

79. Rimer in Conant et al., *Nihonga, Transcending the Past*, p. 46.

80. Ibid., p. 49.

81. *Shiga Naoya zenshū*, 4:. 471.

82. Morris, "Cézanne's Mountains," pp. 815–17.

83. Shiga Naoya zenshū, 4: 151–52.

Works Cited

Aeba Takao. *Nihon kindai no seikimatsu*. Tokyo: Bungei shunshū, 1990.

Akutagawa Ryūnosuke. *Akutagawa Ryūnosuke zenshū*. 12 vols. Tokyo: Iwanami shoten, 1977–78.

Anderer, Paul. *Other Worlds: Arishima Takeo and the Bounds of Modern Japanese Fiction*. New York: Columbia University Press, 1984.

Anderson, Benedict. *Imagined Communities: Reflections on the Origin and Spread of Nationalism*. London: Verso, 1990.

Asquith, Pamela J., and Arne Kalland, eds. *Japanese Images of Nature: Cultural Perspectives*. Richmond, Eng.: Curzon Press, 1997.

Bataille, Georges. *Death and Sensuality: A Study of Eroticism and the Taboo*. New York: Arno Press, 1977.

Berger, Peter L., and Thomas Luckmann. *The Social Construction of Reality: A Treatise in the Sociology of Knowledge*. New York: Anchor Books, 1966.

Bermingham, Ann. *Landscape and Ideology: The English Rustic Tradition, 1740–1860*. Berkeley: University of California Press, 1986.

Bring, Mitchell, and Josse Wayembergh. *Japanese Gardens: Design and Meaning*. New York: McGraw-Hill Book Company, 1981.

Carlyle, Thomas. *On Heroes, Hero-Worship, & the Heroic in History*. Berkeley: University of California Press, 1993.

Conant, Ellen P., with Stephen D. Owyang and J. Thomas Rimer. *Nihonga, Transcending the Past: Japanese-Style Painting, 1868–1968*. St. Louis: Saint Louis Art Museum, 1995.

Cranston, Edwin A. *A Waka Anthology*, vol. 1., *The Gem-Glistening Cup*. Stanford: Stanford University Press, 1993.

Cruger, Mary. *Labor: The Divine Command*. New York: Pollard, 1890.

Davis, Fred. *Yearning for Yesterday: A Sociology of Nostalgia*. New York: Free Press, 1979.

Dazai Osamu. *Dazai Osamu zenshū.* 8 vols. Tokyo: Chikuma shobō, 1971–72.

Dodd, Stephen. "Different Feelings: The Intellectual Shift Between Meiji and Taishō." In *Currents in Japanese Culture: Translations and Transformations,* ed. Amy Heinrich, pp. 263–77. New York: Columbia University Press, 1997.

———. "Kunikida Doppo: A Site of No Return." In *Return to Japan: From Pilgrimage to the West,* ed. Yōichi Nagashima, pp. 101–8. Aarhus, Denmark: Aarhus University Press, 2001.

Duus, Peter, ed. *The Cambridge History of Japan.* vol. 6, *the Twentieth Century.* Cambridge, Eng.: Cambridge University Press, 1988.

Ericson, Steven J. *The Sound of the Whistle: Railroads and the State in Meiji Japan.* Cambridge, Mass.: Harvard University, Council on East Asian Studies, 1996.

Etō Jun. "Riarizumu no genryū: shaseibun to tasha no mondai." In idem, *Riarizumu no genryū,* pp. 7–43. Tokyo: Kawade shobō, 1989.

Foucault, Michel. "Of Other Spaces." *diacritics* 16, no. 1 (1986): 22–27.

Fowler, Edward. *The Rhetoric of Confession: Shishosetsu in Early Twentieth-Century Japanese Fiction.* Berkeley: University of California Press, 1988.

Fujii, James A. *Complicit Fictions: The Subject in the Modern Japanese Prose Narrative.* Berkeley: University of California Press, 1993.

Fukuda Kiyohito. *Kunikida Doppo.* Tokyo: Meiji shoin, 1970.

Gavin, Masako. "*Nihon Fūkeiron* (Japanese Landscape): Nationalistic or Imperialistic?" *Japan Forum* 12, no. 2 (2000): 219–31.

Gellner, Ernest. *Nations and Nationalism.* Oxford: Basil Blackwell, 1988.

Gluck, Carol. *Japan's Modern Myths.* Princeton: Princeton University Press, 1985.

Goossen, Ted. "Connecting Rhythms: Nature and Selfhood in Shiga Naoya's *Reconciliation* and *A Dark Night's Passing.*" *Review of Japanese Culture and Society* 5 (Dec. 1993): 20–33.

Gramsci, Antonio. *Selections from the Prison Notebooks.* Ed. and trans. Quintin Hoare and Geoffrey Nowell Smith. New York: International Publishers, 1971.

Greenfeld, Liah. *Nationalism: Five Roads to Modernity.* Cambridge, Mass.: Harvard University Press, 1993.

Grosz, Elizabeth. *Volatile Bodies: Towards a Corporeal Feminism.* Bloomington: Indiana University Press, 1994.

Hagiwara Sakutarō. *Hagiwara Sakutarō zenshū.* Tokyo: Shōgakukan, 1944.

Hagiwara Takao. "Man and Nature in Sinclair Ross' *As For Me and My House* and Naoya Shiga's *A Dark Night's Passing.*" In *Nature and Identity in Canadian and Japanese Literature*, ed. Kin'ya Tsuruta and Ted Goossen, pp. 19–33. Toronto: University of Toronto–York University Joint Centre for Asia Pacific Studies, 1988.

Hara Hitoshi. "Satō Haruo ni okeru kaiga to jiga no mondai." In *Satō Haruo to Murō Saisei: shi to shōsetsu no aida*, ed. Yasuaki Sakuma and Ōhashi Takehiko, pp. 52–68. Tokyo: Yūseidō, 1992.

Hardacre, Helen. "The Cave and the Womb World." *Japanese Journal of Religious Studies* 10, no. 2/3 (1983): 149–76.

Harotoonian, H. D. "A Sense of Ending and the Problem of Taishō." In *Japan in Crisis: Essays in Taishō Democracy*, ed. Bernard S. Silberman and H. D. Harotoonian, pp. 3–28. Princeton: Princeton University Press, 1974.

———. *Overcome by Modernity: History, Culture, and Community in Interwar Japan*. Princeton: Princeton University Press, 2000.

Hashizume Shinya. *Meiji no meikyū toshi*. Tokyo: Heibonsha, 1990.

Hattori Bushō. "The Western Peep Show." In *Modern Japanese Literature: An Anthology*, comp. and trans. Donald Keene, pp. 34–36. New York: Grove Press, 1960.

Hirakawa Sukehiro. "Higashi to nishi no tōgenkyō." In *Bungaku ni okeru "Mukōgawa,"* ed. Kokubungaku kenkyū shiryōkan, pp. 93–133. Tokyo: Meiji shoin, 1985.

———. "Mount Daisen Depicted by Two Authors: Lafcadio Hearn and His Admirer, Shiga Naoya." In *Shiga Naoya's "A Dark Night's Passing": Proceedings of a Workshop at the National University of Singapore*, ed. Kin'ya Tsuruta, pp. 249–84. Singapore: National University of Singapore, 1996.

Hirotsu Kazuo. "Shiga Naoya ron." In *Kindai bungaku hyōron taikei: Taishō ki II*, ed. Endō Yū and Sobue Shōji, pp. 368–76. Tokyo: Kadokawa shoten, 1988.

Hobsbawm, Eric. *Nations and Nationalism Since 1780*. Cambridge, Eng.: Cambridge University Press, 1990.

Hobsbawm, Eric, and Terence Ranger, eds. *The Invention of Tradition*. Cambridge, Eng.: Cambridge University Press, 1993.

Honda Shūgo. *"Shirakaba" ha no bungaku*. Tokyo: Kōdansha, 1954.

Hori, Ichiro. *Folk Religion in Japan: Continuity and Change*. Chicago: University of Chicago Press, 1968.

Hutchinson, Rachel. "Occidentalism in Nagai Kafū: Constructing a Critique of Meiji, 1903–1912." Ph.D. diss., Oxford University, 2000.

Ino Kenji. *Meiji no sakka*. Tokyo: Iwanami shoten, 1966.

Inouye, Charles Shirō. *The Similitude of Blossoms: A Critical Biography of Izumi Kyōka (1873–1939), Japanese Novelist and Playwright*. Cambridge, Mass.: Harvard University Asia Center, 1998.

Isoda Kōichi. *Rokumeikan no keifu*. Tokyo: Bungei shunshū, 1984.

————. *Shisō toshite no Tōkyō*. Tokyo: Kokubunsha, 1979.

Itō Kazuo. "Taishō ki ni okeru Shimazaki Tōson to Bashō." In *Shimazaki Tōson*, ed. Nihon bungaku kenkyū shiryō kankō kai, 1: 278–87. Tokyo: Yūseidō, 1971.

Ito, Ken K. *Visions of Desire: Tanizaki's Fictional Worlds*. Stanford: Stanford University Press, 1991.

Itō Kimio. "The Invention of *Wa* and the Transformation of the Image of Prince Shōtoku in Modern Japan." In *Mirror of Modernity: Invented Traditions of Modern Japan*, ed. Stephen Vlastos, pp. 37–47. Berkeley: University of California Press, 1998.

Ivy, Marilyn. *Discourses of the Vanishing: Modernity, Phantasm, Japan*. Chicago: Chicago University Press, 1995.

Iwasa Sōshirō. "'Shizen' to iu shisō: Meiji 30 nendai o chūshin ni." In *Nihon bungakushi o yomu: Kindai, I*, pp. 146–76. Tokyo: Yūseidō, 1992.

Jackson, Rosemary. *Fantasy: The Literature of Subversion*. London: Routledge, 1995.

Jinnai Hidenobu. *Tōkyō no kūkan jinruigaku*. Tokyo: Chikuma shobō, 1985.

Karatani Kōjin. *Nihon kindai bungaku no kigen*. Tokyo: Kōdansha, 1980.

————. "Watakushi shōsetsu no ryōgisei: Shiga Naoya." *Bungei dokuhon: Shiga Naoya* (1976): 128–36.

Katagiri Yōichi. *Utamakura utakotoba jiten*. Tokyo: Kadokawa shoten, 1983.

Kawamoto Saburō. *Taishō Gen'ei*. Tokyo: Shinchōsha, 1990.

Keene, Donald. *Dawn to the West: Japanese Literature of the Modern Era (Fiction)*. New York: Holt, Rinehart and Winston, 1984.

Keirstead, Thomas. "Gardens and Estates: Medievality and Space." *positions* 1, no. 2 (1993): 289–320.

Kimata Satoshi. *"Imeeji" no kindai Nihon bungakushi*. Tokyo: Taiyōsha, 1988.

Kinmonth, Earl H. *The Self-Made Man in Meiji Japanese Thought: From Samurai to Salary Man*. Berkeley: University of California Press, 1981.

Kitano Akihiko. *Miyazaki Koshoshi Kunikida Doppo no shi to shōsetu*. Osaka: Waizumi, 1993.

Kobayashi Hideo. *Kobayashi Hideo zenshū*. 12 vols. Tokyo: Shinchōsha, 1968.

Kodansha Encyclopedia of Japan. 9 vols. Tokyo: Kodansha International, 1983.

Kohl, Stephen. "Shiga Naoya and the Literature of Experience." *Monumenta Nipponica* 32 (1977): 211–24.

Kornicki, Peter F. *The Reform of Fiction in Meiji Japan*. London: Ithaca Press, 1982.

Kunikida Doppo. *Kunikida Doppo zenshū*. 11 vols. Tokyo: Gakushū kenkyūsha, 1978.

Kwong, Charles Yim-tze. *Tao Qian and the Chinese Poetic Tradition*. Ann Arbor: University of Michigan, Center for Chinese Studies, 1994.

Lefebvre, Henri. *The Production of Space*. Trans. Donald Nicholson Smith. Oxford: Blackwell, 1994.

Maeda Ai. *Tekusuto no yūtopia*. Maeda Ai chosaku shū, vol. 6. Tokyo: Chikuma shobō, 1990.

———. *Toshi kūkan no naka no bungaku*. Tokyo: Chikuma shobō, 1982.

Marcus, Marvin. "The Writer Speaks: Late-Meiji Reflections on Literature and Life." In *The Distant Isle: Studies and Translations of Japanese Literature in Honor of Robert H. Brower*, ed. Thomas Hare, Robert Borgen, and Sharalyn Orbaugh, pp. 231–79. Ann Arbor: University of Michigan, Center for Japanese Studies, 1996.

Massey, Doreen. *Space, Place and Gender*. Cambridge, Eng.: Polity Press, 1994.

Mathy, Francis. *Shiga Naoya*. New York: Twayne, 1974.

Matless, David. *Landscape and Englishness*. London: Reaktion Books, 1998.

Minami Hiroshi. *Taishō bunka*. Tokyo: Keisō shobō, 1965.

Mitchell, W. J. T., ed. *Landscape and Power*. Chicago: University of Chicago Press, 1994.

Miyake Hitoshi. *Shugendō shisō no kenkyū*. Tokyo: Shunshūsha, 1986.

Miyoshi, Masao. *Accomplices of Silence*. Berkeley: University of California Press, 1974.

———. *Off Center: Power and Culture Relations Between Japan and the United States*. Cambridge, Mass.: Harvard University Press, 1991.

Miyoshi Yukio. *Shimazaki Tōson hikkei*. Tokyo: Gakutōsha, 1974.

———. *Shimazaki Tōson ron*. Miyoshi Yukio chosaku shū, vol. 1. Tokyo: Chikuma shobō, 1993.

Miyoshi Yukio et al., eds. *Taishō no bungaku*. Tokyo: Yūhikaku, 1981.

Morris, Robert. "Cézanne's Mountains." *Critical Inquiry* 24, no. 3 (1998): 814–29.

Morris-Suzuki, Tessa. *Re-Inventing Japan: Time, Space, Nation*. New York: M. E. Sharpe, 1998.

Mushanokōji Saneatsu. *Mushanokōji Saneatsu zenshū.* 24 vols. Tokyo: Shinchōsha, 1954–56.

Nagai Kafū. *Kafū zenshū.* 29 vols. Tokyo: Iwanami shoten, 1971–74.

Nagata Mitsunobu. "Shinteki hen'yō no gūwa: 'Den'en no yūutsu' ron." In *Kindai Nihon bungaku ron: Taishō kara Shōwa e*, ed. Chūō daigaku, Jinbun kagaku kenkyūjo, pp. 93–113. Tokyo: Chūō daigaku shuppanbu, 1989.

Naimushō. Chihōkyoku yūshi. *Den'en toshi to Nihonjin.* Tokyo: Kōdansha, 1980.

Najita, Tetsuo, and J. Victor Koschmann, eds. *Conflict in Modern Japanese History: The Neglected Tradition.* Princeton: Princeton University Press, 1982.

Nakagami Kenji. *Fūkei no mukō e.* Tokyo: Tōkisha, 1990.

———. *Kishū: ki no kuni, ne no kuni monogatari.* Tokyo: Asahi shinbunsha, 1994.

Nakamura Mitsuo. *Shiga Naoya ron.* Tokyo: Bungei shunshū, 1954.

Napier, Susan. *The Fantastic in Modern Japanese Literature: The Subversion of Modernity.* London: Routledge, 1996.

Narita Ryūichi. *"Kokyō" to iu monogatari: toshi kūkan no rekishigaku.* Tokyo: Furukawa Hiroshi bunkan, 1998.

Natsume Sōseki. *Sōseki zenshū.* 17 vols. Tokyo: Iwanami shoten, 1965–76.

Noda Masao et al., eds. *Nihon no tetsudō: seiritsu to tenkai.* Tokyo: Nihon keizai hyōronsha, 1986.

Ōkubo Takaki. *Shinra-hen'yō: kindai Nihon bungaku to shizen.* Tokyo: Ozawa shoten, 1996.

Okuno Takeo. *Bungaku ni okeru genfūkei.* Tokyo: Shūeisha, 1972.

Orbaugh, Sharalyn. "Extending the Limits of Possibility: Style and Structure in Modern Japanese Fiction." In *The Distant Isle: Studies and Translations of Japanese Literature in Honor of Robert H. Brower*, ed. Thomas Hare, Robert Borgen, and Sharalyn Orbaugh, pp. 337–70. Ann Arbor: University of Michigan, Center for Japanese Studies, 1996.

Pillow Book of Sei Shōnagon, The. Trans. Ivan Morris. London: Penguin Books, 1984.

Pollack, David. *The Fracture of Meaning.* Princeton: Princeton University Press, 1986.

———. *Reading Against Culture: Ideology and Narrative in the Japanese Novel.* Ithaca: Cornell University Press, 1992.

Pyle, Kenneth B. *The New Generation in Meiji: Problems of Cultural Identity, 1885–1895.* Stanford: Stanford University Press, 1969.

————. "Some Recent Approaches to Japanese Nationalism." *Journal of Asian Studies* 30, no. 1 (Nov. 1971): 5–16.

Rimer, Thomas J., ed. *Culture and Identity: Japanese Intellectuals During the Interwar Years*. Princeton: Princeton University Press, 1990.

Robertson, Jennifer. "It Takes a Village: Internationalization and Nostalgia in Postwar Japan." In *Mirror of Modernity: Invented Traditions of Modern Japan*, ed. Stephen Vlastos, pp. 110–29. Berkeley: University of California Press, 1998.

————. *Native and Newcomer: Making and Remaking a Japanese City*. Berkeley: University of California Press, 1991.

Rubin, Jay. *Injurious to Public Morals: Writers and the Meiji State*. Seattle: University of Washington Press, 1984.

Said, Edward W. *The World, the Text, and the Critic*. London: Faber and Faber, 1984.

Sakaguchi Ango. "Bungaku no furusato." In idem, *Darakuron*, pp. 27–36. Tokyo: Shinchōsha, 2000.

————. "Nihon bunka shikan." In idem, *Darakuron*, pp. 37–72. Tokyo: Shinchōsha, 2000.

Sakamoto Hiroshi. *Kunikida Doppo*. Tokyo: Yūseidō, 1969.

Sasabuchi Tomoichi. "Shimazaki Tōson ni okeru 'rōdō to bungaku.' " In *Shimazaki Tōson*, ed. Nihon bungaku kenkyū shiryō kankō kai, 2: 31–56. Tokyo: Yūseidō, 1971.

————. "Shimazaki Tōson to purotesutantizumu." In *Shimazaki Tōson*, ed. Nihon bungaku kenkyū shiryō kankō kai, 1: 18–32. Tokyo: Yūseidō, 1971.

Satō Haruo. *Beautiful Town: Stories and Essays by Satō Haruo*. Trans. Francis B. Tenny. Honolulu: University of Hawai'i Press, 1996.

————. *Teihon Satō Haruo zenshū*. 36 vols. Tokyo: Ringawa shoten, 1998.

Schama, Simon. *Landscape and Memory*. London: Harper Collins, 1995.

Schivelbusch, Wolfgang. *Disenchanted Night: The Industrialisation of Light in the Nineteenth Century*. Trans. Angela Davies. Oxford: Berg, 1988.

————. *The Railway Journey: Trains and Travel in the 19th Century*. Trans. Anselm Hollo. Oxford: Basil Blackwell, 1980.

Seidensticker, Edward. *Kafu the Scribbler: The Life and Writings of Nagai Kafu, 1879–1959*. Stanford: Stanford University Press, 1965.

Senuma Shigeki. *Taishō bungakushi*. Tokyo: Kōdansha, 1985.

Shashin sakka den: Shimazaki Tōson. Tokyo: Meiji shoin, 1965.

Shiga Naoya. *Shiga Naoya zenshū*. 22 vols. Tokyo: Iwanami shoten, 1999.

Shimazaki Tōson. *The Broken Commandment*. Trans. Kenneth Strong. Tokyo: University of Tokyo Press, 1974.

———. *Chikuma River Sketches.* Trans. William E. Naff. Honolulu: University of Hawaii Press, 1991.

———. *The Family.* Trans. Cecilia Segawa Seigle. Tokyo: Tokyo University Press, 1976.

———. *Tōson zenshū.* 17 vols. Tokyo: Chikuma shobō, 1966–71.

Shimoyama Jōko. "Shasei: Shiki to Tōson." In *Shimazaki Tōson,* ed. Nihon bungaku kenkyū shiryō kankō kai, 2: 80–91. Tokyo: Yūseidō, 1971.

Shinano mainichi Shinbunsha, ed. *Shinshū no tetsudō monogatari.* Tokyo: Shinano mainichi shinbunsha, 1987.

Shinbo Kunihiro. *Doppo to Tōson: Meiji sanjū nendai bungaku no kosumorojii.* Tokyo: Yūseidō, 1996.

Shirane, Haruo. *Traces of Dreams: Landscape, Cultural Memory, and the Poetry of Bashō.* Stanford: Stanford University Press, 1998.

Sibley, William. "Naturalism in Japanese Literature." *Harvard Journal of Asiatic Studies* 28 (1968): 157–69.

———. *The Shiga Hero.* Chicago: University of Chicago Press, 1979.

Smith, Anthony D. *National Identity.* London: Penguin Books, 1991.

Smith, Henry D., II. "The Edo–Tokyo Transition: In Search of Common Ground." In *Japan in Transition: From Tokugawa to Meiji,* ed. Marius B. Jansen and Gilbert Rozman, pp. 347–74. Princeton: Princeton University Press, 1986.

———. "Tokyo and London: Comparative Conceptions of the City." In *Japan: A Comparative View,* ed. Albert Craig, pp. 49–99. Princeton: Princeton University Press, 1979.

———. "Tokyo as an Idea: An Exploration of Japanese Urban Thought Until 1945." *Journal of Japanese Studies* 4, no. 1 (1978): 45–80.

Soja, Edward W. *Postmodern Geographies: The Reassertion of Space in Critical Social Theory.* London: Verso, 1990.

Starobinski, Jean. *Jean-Jacques Rousseau: Transparency and Obstruction.* Trans. Arthur Goldhammer. Chicago: University of Chicago Press, 1988.

Starrs, Roy. *An Artless Art: The Zen Aesthetic of Shiga Naoya.* Richmond, Eng.: Japan Library / Curzon Press, 1998.

Stein, Rolf A. *The World in Miniature: Container Gardens and Dwellings in Far Eastern Religious Thought.* Stanford: Stanford University Press, 1990.

Stewart, Susan. *On Longing: Narratives of the Miniature, the Gigantic, the Souvenir, the Collection.* Durham, N.C.: Duke University Press, 1993.

Sudō Matsuo. "*An'ya kōro* no Daisen to Taishō sannen no Daisen taiken." In *Nihon bungaku kenkyū taisei: Shiga Naoya,* ed. Sakae Machida, pp. 264–74. Tokyo: Kokusho kankō kai, 1992.

————. "Shiga bungaku no shizen: seimeiryoku." In *Bungei dokuhon: Shiga Naoya*, pp. 98–107. Tokyo: Kawade shobō, 1976.

Sukida Hideaki. *Tōkagen to yūtopia*. Tokyo: Heibonsha, 1989.

Swanson, Paul L. "Shugendō and the Yoshino-Kumano Pilgrimage: An Example of Mountain Pilgrimage." *Monumenta Nipponica* 36, no. 1 (1981): 55–79.

Takada Mizuho. "Taishō bungaku o dō toraeru ka." In *Taishō no bungaku*, ed. Nihon bungaku kenkyū shiryō kankō kai, pp. 57–68. Tokyo: Yūseidō, 1988.

Takahashi Seori. "'Den'en no yūutsu' ron." *Nihon kindai bungaku*, Oct. 1982, pp. 134–44.

Takitō Mitsuyoshi. "Doppo to shizen." In *Bungakuteki kindai no seiritsu*, ed. Yukio Miyoshi and Tenyū Takemori, pp. 11–20. Tokyo: Yūhikaku, 1977.

————. *Kunikida Doppo ron*. Tokyo: Hanawa shobō, 1986.

Tales of Ise: Lyrical Episodes from Tenth-Century Japan. Trans. Helen Craig McCullough. Tokyo: University of Tokyo Press, 1968.

Tanaka, Yukiko. *Women Writers of Meiji and Taishō Japan: Their Lives, Works and Critical Reception, 1868–1926*. Jefferson, N.C.: McFarland, 2000.

Tanikawa Tetsuzō. "Watashi no mita Shiga-san." In *Shiga Naoya*, ed. Nihon bungaku kenkyū shiryō kankō kai, pp. 9–15. Tokyo: Yūseidō, 1970.

Tanizaki Jun'ichirō. *Tanizaki Jun'ichirō zenshū*. 28 vols. Tokyo: Chūō kōron, 1966–70.

Tansman, Alan. "Images of Repose and Violence in Three Japanese Writers." *Journal of Japanese Studies* 28 (2002): 109–39.

Tayama Katai. *Literary Life in Tokyo, 1885–1915: Tayama Katai's Memoirs*. Trans. Kenneth G. Henshall. Leiden: Brill, 1987.

————. *Tayama Katai zenshū*. 16 vols. Tokyo: Bunsendō, 1973–74.

Togawa Shinsuke. *"Dorama," "takai": Meiji nijū nendai no bungaku jōkyō*. Tokyo: Chikuma shobō, 1987.

Tokutomi Kenjirō. *Roka zenshū*. 20 vols. Tokyo: Roka zenshū kankō kai, 1929–30.

Tokutomi Sōhō. "Furusato." *Kokumin no tomo* 84 (June 3, 1890).

————. "Kisei o yomu." *Kokumin no tomo* 88 (July 13, 1890).

Tomlinson, John. *Cultural Imperialism*. Baltimore: Johns Hopkins University Press, 1991.

Tuan, Yi-Fu. *Topophilia: A Study of Environmental Perception, Attitudes and Values*. New York: Columbia University Press, 1990.

Twine, Nanette. "The *Genbunitchi* Movement: Its Origin, Development, and Conclusion." *Monumenta Nipponica* 33, no. 3 (1978): 333–356.

Uno Kōji. "Yume miru heya." In *Gendai Nihon bungaku taikei*, 46: 42–63. Tokyo: Chikuma shobō, 1971.

Vaporis, Constantine. *Breaking Barriers: Travel and the State in Early Modern Japan*. Cambridge, Mass.: Harvard University, Council on East Asian Studies, 1994.

Vlastos, Stephen, ed. *Mirror of Modernity: Invented Traditions of Modern Japan*. Berkeley: University of California Press, 1998.

Walthall, Anne. "Off with Their Heads! The Hirata Disciples and the Ashikaga Shoguns." *Monumenta Nipponica* 50, no. 2 (1995): 137–70.

Washburn, Dennis C. *The Dilemma of the Modern in Japanese Fiction*. New Haven: Yale University Press, 1995.

Waswo, Ann. "The Origins of Tenant Unrest." In *Japan in Crisis: Essays in Taishō Democracy*, ed. Bernard Silberman and H. D. Harotoonian, pp. 374–97. Princeton: Princeton University Press, 1974.

Wigen, Kären. "Constructing Shinano: The Invention of a Neo-Traditional Region." In *Mirror of Modernity: Invented Traditions of Modern Japan*, ed. Stephen Vlastos, pp. 229–42. Berkeley: University of California Press, 1998.

Williams, Raymond. *The Country and the City*. London: Hogarth, 1985.

Yamada Hiromitsu. "Doppo 'Kawagiri' ron." In *Shizenshugi bungaku*, ed. Nihon bungaku kenkyū shiryō kankō kai, pp. 30–35. Tokyo: Yūseidō, 1975.

———. *Kitamura Tōkoku to Kunikida Doppo: hikaku bungaku teki kenkyū*. Tokyo: Kindai bungei sha, 1990.

———. "Koshoshi to Doppo: kisei shōsetsu o megutte." *Kokubungaku: gengo to bungei* 63 (1969): 19–26.

Yamaguchi Hiroshi, ed. *Kōgai jūtakuchi no keifu*. Tokyo: Kashima shuppan kai, 1988.

Yamamura Bochō. "Jōkyō-go." In *Mita bungaku*, June 1911. Reprinted in *Mita bungaku*, vol. 2, no.6, pp. 132–50. Kyōto: Rinsen shoten, 1970–71.

Yanagida Kunio. "Genbun no kyori." *Bunshō sekai* 4, no. 14 (1909): 167–72.

———. "Shasei to ronbun." *Bunshō sekai* 2, no. 3 (1907): 30–32.

Yasuoka Shōtarō. *Yasuoka Shōtarō essei zenshū*. Tokyo: Yomiuri shinbunsha, 1976.

Yoshida Seiichi. "Shirakaba ni okeru Shiga Naoya." In *Shiga Naoya*, ed. Nihon bungaku kenkyū shiryō kankō kai, pp. 16–28. Tokyo: Yūseidō, 1970.

———. *Shizenshugi no kenkyū.*, vol. 1. Tokyo: Tōkyōdō shuppan, 1973.

Index

Harvard East Asian Monographs
(* out-of-print)

Harvard East Asian Monographs

Harvard East Asian Monographs

Harvard East Asian Monographs

Harvard East Asian Monographs

Harvard East Asian Monographs

Harvard East Asian Monographs

Harvard East Asian Monographs